PERSPECTIVES ON ANGER AND EMOTION

Advances in Social Cognition, Volume VI

PERSPECTIVES ON ANGER AND EMOTION

Advances in Social Cognition, Volume VI

Edited by
ROBERT S. WYER, Jr.
THOMAS K. SRULL
University of Illinois, Urbana—Champaign

Lead Article by
Leonard Berkowitz

IEA LAWRENCE ERLBAUM ASSOCIATES, PUBLISHERS
1993 Hillsdale, New Jersey   Hove and London

Lawrence Erlbaum Associates, Inc., Publishers
365 Broadway
Hillsdale, New Jersey 07642

Library of Congress Cataloging-in-Publication Data

Perspectives on Anger and Emotion
Advances in Social Cognition, Volume VI

ISSN: 0898-2007
ISBN: 0-8058-1326-8 (cloth)
ISBN: 0-8058-1327-6 (paper)

Printed in the United States of America
10 9 8 7 6 5 4 3 2 1

Contents

Preface

This is the sixth volume of the *Advances in Social Cognition* series. From its inception, the purpose of the series has been to present and evaluate new theoretical advances in all areas of social cognition and information processing. An entire volume is devoted to each theory, allowing the theory to be evaluated from a variety of perspectives and permitting its implications for a wide range of issues to be examined.

The series reflects two major characteristics of social cognition: the high level of activity in the field and the interstitial nature of the work. Each volume contains a target chapter that is timely in its application, novel in its approach, and precise in its explication. The target chapter is then followed by a set of comparison articles that examine the theoretical and empirical issues that the target has raised. These latter chapters are written by authors with diverse theoretical orientations, representing different disciplines within psychology and, in some cases, entirely different disciplines. Target authors are then given the opportunity to respond to the comments and criticisms of their work and to examine the ideas conveyed in the comparison chapters in light of their own. The dialogue created by this format is both unusual and, we believe, extremely beneficial to the field.

The diversity of perspectives represented in the series as a whole is particularly exemplified by this volume. The author of the target article, Leonard Berkowitz, is one of the field's most eminent scholars, having made numerous important contributions to research and theory on the determinants and consequences of anger and aggression. He is not traditionally identified with the field of social cognition. On the other hand, an understanding of the interplay of emotion and cognition is clearly essential to a comprehensive theory of social information processing. The formulation developed in the target article is an important step in attaining this understanding.

Berkowitz develops the argument that experiential and behavioral components of an emotional state are affected by processes some of which are highly cognitive in nature and others of which are automatic and involuntary. Cognitive and associative mechanisms theoretically come into play at different times in the emotion-cognition sequence. The model he proposes, therefore, integrates theoretical positions that have hitherto been artificially segregated in much of the emotion-cognition literature.

The breadth of the implications of Berkowitz's theory is also reflected in the diversity of the companion chapters. These articles, written by researchers whose work focuses on both social cognition and emotion, provide important insights and possible extensions of the "cognitive-neoassociationistic" conceptualization developed in the target article. We believe that the volume, considered as a whole, is a timely and important contribution both to social cognition and to research and theory on emotion per se. Each chapter is a valuable contribution in its own right. The volume, considered as a whole, is a timely and important contribution to research and theory in emotion in particular, and in social cognition more generally.

In addition to the authors themselves, we want to acknowledge the invaluable assistance of Lawrence Erlbaum Associates. Larry's continued support and encouragement of the *Advance* series, and the commitment of his staff to insure the publication of a high quality series of volumes, is deeply gratifying. It is a genuine pleasure to have the opportunity to work with them.

Robert S. Wyer, Jr.
Thomas K. Srull

Towards a General Theory of Anger and Emotional Aggression: Implications of the Cognitive– Neoassociationistic Perspective for the Analysis of Anger and Other Emotions

Leonard Berkowitz
University of Wisconsin-Madison

The remarkable spurt of interest in the psychology of emotion over the past few decades has inevitably generated considerable controversy and theoretical ferment. The mounting research has brought not only new findings but ever more challenges to old ideas. It is now clearer than ever before that the most popular psychological analyses of emotion can readily account for some phenomena but have difficulty explaining other research results. Some examples come quickly to mind: The so-called "peripheral theories" cannot satisfactorily deal with the influence of attributions using only their own terms, whereas the cognitive formulations have problems with the facial feedback effects, and none of the leading analyses can say why the experimental establishment of such negative emotional states as sadness often produces anger as well (Moore & Isen, 1990).

Theorists seeking to resolve these problems might be well advised to broaden their perspective and bring together ideas from widely different research traditions. This chapter suggests one way in which such an integration could be accomplished. Although it appears to be narrow in scope, in that it focuses largely on the anger experience and emotional aggression, its basic formulation, combining both cognitive and associationistic concepts, has significant implications for the analysis of emotions more generally. Thus, although the chapter devotes considerable attention to research on aggression, partly because it is important to understand the origins of this fundamentally antisocial behavior, it also highlights some matters that should be confronted by a truly comprehensive general theory of emotion.

I start by contrasting two different approaches to the study of anger and emotional aggression in order to identify some of the shortcomings in the conventional cognitive formulations of anger. However, it should be clear, this critique is not intended to be a dismissal of the cognitive perspective. Instead, I hope it contributes to the development of a more sophisticated and broader ranging theory of emotion, one that will have major cognitive components, by first, identifying phenomena that have been neglected unduly by most present-day cognitive models, and second, suggesting how these phenomena might be incorporated into such a general theory.

SOME SHORTCOMINGS IN THE RESEARCH ON AGGRESSION

There is a curious division in the psychological research on anger and aggression. Because of differences in interest, theoretical orientation, and methodology, studies of this emotion seem to be proceeding along two independent tracks, with remarkably, and unfortunately, little connection between them. One path is followed by a group of experimental social and personality psychologists who study aggression as a class of behaviors essentially similar to most other antisocial actions. These researchers say little about emotion, and typically are interested in the aggressors' feelings only to validate an experimental manipulation—that is, to determine if an experimentally established provocation was successful. Psychologists concerned with emotions in general seem to be working along very different lines. With the exception of those dealing mainly with the biological aspects of emotional states, their attention is focused largely on people's reports of how their emotional feelings and/or actions came about. Unfortunately for both groups, there isn't very much communication between them, and they do not read and consider as much of each other's research literature as they should.

In my view, most experimental social–personality psychologists, and indeed most social scientists, do not adequately recognize how much of aggression is emotional in nature. With some exceptions (e.g., Berkowitz, 1993; Rule & Nesdale, 1976), their theoretical analyses usually assume violence is just as purposeful and thought out as most other forms of human conduct, and that there are basically few major differences between aggression and other socially disapproved modes of behavior.

This is not to say that social–personality psychologists think all aggression is alike. Although virtually all of them define aggression as the intentional injury of some target, they typically share Feshbach's (1964) distinction between hostile and instrumental aggression, and say it is only in the case of hostile aggression that the victim's injury is the primary aim. Instrumental aggression, on the other hand, attempts to hurt the target but does so largely in pursuit of some other goal such as money or social status. We are here concerned solely with hostile aggression, and more specifically, with those aggressive acts that are part of a strong emotional state. As I indicated before, with some notable exceptions (Rule & Nesdale, 1974), few experimental social psychologists have tried to spell out in any detail the possible relationship between aggression and the fairly specific emotional state commonly termed *anger*.[1] This chapter attempts to do just this.

For their part, emotion theorists have also suffered from their one-sided neglect of the research in the other camp. In particular, I believe their theoretical analyses have been based too exclusively on subjective reports so that they have disregarded pertinent findings obtained from laboratory experiments. People's accounts of why and how they act as they do obviously are susceptible to all too many distortions, some produced by their desire to present themselves in a favorable light and some arising from the intrusion of their theories as to why the given event had occurred (cf. Nisbett & Wilson, 1977). Relatively few emotion researchers have acknowledged these problems or taken steps to deal with them.

Perhaps because of this excessive reliance on self-reports, many of the current analyses of emotional experiences have been, in my estimation, much too cognitive and rationalistic. This is clearly apparent in the typical emotion theorists' discussion of how anger arises. Basing their formulations on what the majority of ordinary persons say about themselves, these investigators usually focus on anger as a reaction to the perception of having been deliberately and improperly mistreated (e.g., Averill, 1982; Frijda, 1986; Smith & Ellsworth, 1985; Weiner, 1982), and disregard the other possible sources of anger mentioned by a minority of the respondents.

There is no doubt that intentional misdeeds can provoke anger, and indeed, a very great proportion of the anger-arousing incidents "in nature" may actually involve the perception of having been deliberately wronged by someone. The question is, however, whether this perception is as necessary as these emotion theorists seem to suggest. A growing body of laboratory experiments and field studies have now demonstrated that unpleasant occurrences can evoke aggressive reactions along with feelings of anger, irritation, and annoyance even though the events are not socially illegitimate and are unintended (Anderson, 1989; Berkowitz, 1982, 1989, 1993). Many persons may not recognize, or care to admit, that they occasionally become angry and aggressive when something bad happens to them even when this event is not controllable, is not aimed at them specifically, and is not even socially improper. But the fact that relatively few people report feeling angry at these times does not mean these anger reactions do not occur at all. And if they do arise, moreover, any truly comprehensive account of anger and emotional aggression must deal with these less common reactions as well as with the more frequent sources of anger and aggression.

This chapter basically assumes the same underlying psychological processes are involved in all of these instances of anger and emotional aggression, whether the precipitating event is a deliberate personal attack or an uncontrollable and not-improper happening, and proposes what some of these processes might be. More than this, however, as I said earlier, the formulation spelled out here is directly relevant to theories of emotion, and thus might also contribute to our understanding of the psychological processes involved in the formation and expression of other emotions as well, especially the negative ones.

The stance taken here is relatively eclectic. I certainly am not arguing that the cognitive theorists are entirely wrong and that cognitive processes have little role in emotional experience and behavior. Rather, my position is that the experiential (such as anger) and behavioral (such as aggression) components of the emotional state are affected by a broad variety of psychological processes, some of which are highly cognitive in nature, but others are governed by more automatic and involuntary systems throughout the body. Associative mechanisms are especially important in this second category. My basic contention is that both the cognitive and associationistic approaches to emotion are right—but at different times in the emotion-generation sequence[2]—and I thus believe it is entirely appropriate to say this formulation adopts a *cognitive-neoassociationistic* perspective.

In order to introduce this attempted integration and emphasize some of the broader issues the present model raises, I return to anger and emotional aggression, concentrating mostly on the effects of situational frustrations. I describe how some of the best known cognitive theories of emotion account for anger and frustration reactions and then try to rebut several of their arguments as a way of identifying problems these conventional formulations leave unresolved. After this, I sketch out briefly my own interpretation of emotional aggression, one that incorporates both associative and cognitive concepts. The remainder of the chapter provides additional evidence consistent with this cognitive–neoassociationistic model and also spells out some of its implications for emotion theorizing generally.

THEORIES OF ANGER/AGGRESSION GENERATION

Cognitions as All-Important

The Conventional Cognitive Analysis

Drawing their ideas largely from everyday beliefs as to how anger arises, psychologists taking a strong cognitive stance generally insist that only arbitrary and unjustified thwartings generate aggressive inclinations. Averill's (1982) statement along these lines is typical:

> Anger ensues primarily when the frustration is occasioned by the actions of another person, actions which are appraised by the angry individual as unjustified or at least avoidable. Experimental research has also demonstrated that it is primarily arbitrary (unwarranted) frustrations that arouse subjects to anger and/or aggression. (p. 128)

This contention is, of course, entirely consistent with the underlying assumptions of conventional cognitive social psychology. With Ross and Nisbett (1991), we can say the dominant theoretical perspective in our field supposes that virtually everything people do and feel in a given situation is determined by their construal of what is happening. More particularly, however, the statement is also in accord with the prevailing social psychological understanding of emotion based on a combination of the Schachter–Singer (1962) two-factor theory of emotion with later attributional formulations.

Schachter's analysis had maintained that the bodily and neural responses to an emotion-precipitating occurrence do not in themselves provide specific stimulation to a given form of behavior or even to the qualitative feelings that are experienced. In the case of a frustration, for example, the failure to reach a desired goal presumably creates only a diffuse and undifferentiated arousal state. What specific feelings are experienced and what actions are undertaken supposedly depend entirely on the afflicted persons' interpretation of their internal sensations. And so, the thwarted people theoretically will not strike out at the perceived obstacle to their goal attainment unless they think of themselves as angry.

Attribution theorizing added to Schachter's argument by proposing that the label the aroused individuals give to their sensations is greatly influenced by their beliefs as to what caused their feelings. They presumably will regard themselves as angry and then attack their frustrater only if they think this person had deliberately and wrongly prevented them from getting what they wanted.

Several aspects of this line of thought are especially important for our present purposes. One, the Schachter–Singer analysis (but not Weiner's, 1982, attributional theory) holds that events are not intrinsically pleasant or unpleasant in themselves; these happenings presumably become positive or negative only as a result of how they are construed by the individual. Second, this conventional formulation suggests that the unhappy occurrence, however it arises, does not in itself produce motor reactions having particular aims. The afflicted individual supposedly behaves in a certain way because of a decision, reached consciously or unconsciously, as to how to act.

Although much of the empirical support for this reasoning rests on people's descriptions of their everyday experiences (e.g., Smith & Ellsworth, 1985; Weiner, 1982), as I mentioned earlier, adherents to this conventional cognitive perspective sometimes also cite a number of laboratory experiments. Zillmann's excitation transfer is especially well-known. In one of his experiments (Zillmann, Katcher, & Milavsky, 1972), as a notable example, the male subjects were first either provoked or not provoked by their partners and then were required to work on either strenuous or easy physical tasks. Shortly afterward, when the men had an opportunity to punish their partners, the men gave these targets the most intense shocks if they had been previously mistreated by them and had then engaged in the effortful activity. According to Zillmann, these subjects (a) had not realized their exercize-induced excitation was produced by the strenuous activity; (b) mistakenly attributed this excitation to the most salient feature of their environment, their partners' earlier provocation; and (c) concluded they were very angry with their partners, and then acted accordingly.

Questions Can Be Raised

I certainly do not intend to dismiss attribution theorizing out of hand. Cognitions about the cause of the emotion arousal can indeed determine what happens next; attributions can influence what is felt and done (cf. Reisenzein, 1983; Rule & Nesdale, 1976). Nevertheless, it should also be recognized, the evidence supporting this view is not as clear and unequivocal as one would like (Maslach, 1979; Reisenzein, 1983). Thus, to mention only one ambiguity, neither the Zillmann, Katcher, and Milavsky (1972) experiment just cited or the conceptually similar one by Konecni (1975) provide any direct evidence that the provoked and then physiologically aroused subjects had actually misattributed their strong arousal to the provocation and therefore felt very angry. And then too, a modified version of Hullian behavior theory gives us a simpler and relatively parsimonious alternative to the attribution explanation of the Zillmann findings. Without going into the details here, this alternative would say that, in the absence of cognitively activated restraints, the arousal produced by the exercize had energized whatever aggressive action tendencies had been generated by the partners' earlier insult.[3]

Frustration-Generated Anger and Aggression

To repeat myself, my point here is not that cognitions and attributions do not contribute to emotional aggression but that they are not all-important. As a matter of fact, a considerable body of experimental research shows that even nonarbitrary frustrations can incite subjects to anger and/or aggression (Berkowitz, 1989). There is no need to review the relevant studies here, but one experiment not mentioned in my survey of the literature (Berkowitz, 1989) is worth summarizing because it raises an important issue.

In the 1960s, Walters and Brown (1963) conducted an experiment with young children based on the Bandura and Walters social learning perspective. Seeking to find if the right kind of rewards for make-believe aggression would heighten the likelihood of later, more realistic fighting, the researchers reinforced the youngsters' hitting of a large plastic doll either continuously or intermittently. More pertinent for us here, after the training sessions were completed, half the children were exposed to a frustration. The experimenters promised to show all of them a highly entertaining movie, but in half the cases the motion picture projector broke down after the film started, supposedly inadvertently, so the subjects in this condition could not see the movies all the way through. When each child interacted with another youngster in a game soon afterward, those subjects whose make-believe aggression had been intermittently reinforced during training were most aggressive in their interactions with their new partner. More importantly, in this learning condition those who had just been thwarted by the accidental breakdown of the movie projector were most assaultive of all.[4] Trained to be aggressive and also frustrated by their inability to enjoy the pleasure they had anticipated, these children were especially nasty—even though they undoubtedly had not believed they had been deliberately mistreated and certainly could not blame their game partner for the frustration.

Does One Have to Learn to Be Aggressive?

Although these results are consistent with the frustration–aggression hypothesis, they can also be interpreted in a different, somewhat less supportive way. In his 1973 discussion of the effects of frustrations, Bandura (1973) emphasized the importance of prior learning. In experiments reporting positive results, he maintained, frustration usually exerts an influence only in conjunction with prior training in aggression or exposure to aggressive modeling influences. It could be argued, then, that the Walters and Brown subjects had become highly aggressive after being thwarted only when they had been adequately trained to hit others.

Learning to be aggressive, and especially learning to respond antagonistically to a frustration, clearly does raise the chances that an unexpected barrier to goal attainment will produce an assaultive reaction (Bandura, 1973; Davitz, 1952; Geen, 1968). Again, however, we can question whether this learning is a necessary precursor to frustration-generated aggression. Infants who have had little if any opportunity to be rewarded for aggression exhibit angerlike facial expressions when they are thwarted by physical restraints. It is as if their inability to move as they want angers them. Citing these observations, Campos, Barrett, and their colleagues (1983) suggested that restraints may well be an inborn elicitor of anger emotion. All in all, considering all of the pertinent research with animals as well as humans, it appears that learning can modify the frustration–aggression relationship but is not a necessary requirement for the establishment of this connection (Berkowitz, 1969).

Theory and Method Biases

These observations, and many others that could also have been mentioned, are neglected, I have suggested, partly because of the emotion theorists' theoretical bent but also because of their excessive reliance on subjective reports. They accept too uncritically what the majority of their respondents tell them about their own reactions. This is not to say that investigators should not employ these reports at all in their research. This methodology can yield data that are valid for some purposes, primarily the study of people's everyday theories about the origin and nature of emotional states. The findings may also be useful in suggesting new hypotheses and pointing the way to further research.

If the researchers are sufficiently alert, they may even obtain suggestive indications challenging their prevailing theoretical orientation. Averill's (1982) own investigation of angering incidents is illustrative. Almost one out of five respondents in his sample said they had been angered by another person's action even when the behavior had not been socially improper (pp. 172–173). Cohen's (1955) replication and extension of Pastore's (1952) better known critique of the frustration–aggression hypothesis shed some additional light on these statistics. When Cohen asked his subjects how they would respond to various arbitrary and nonarbitrary barriers to their goal attainment, relatively few of them said they would be angered by a socially legitimate thwarting. However, over half the participants believed other people could be provoked to aggression by a socially justified frustration. Does this not suggest that the infrequent self-reports of people being angered by nonarbitrary frustrations is partly due to a reluctance to admit such a socially undesirable reaction? Subjects may not care to acknowledge that they themselves might react "unreasonably" to an accidental or nonpersonal failure to satisfy their desires. They are willing to say, however, that other persons could react in this socially disapproved manner. Think back to the frustration Walters and Brown had imposed on their subjects. The youngsters had been looking forward to the movie and then, suddenly and unexpectedly, found that the projector breakdown kept them from seeing how the exciting story worked out. Suppose we had merely described this scenario to the children beforehand and had asked them how they would respond to the frustration. If we can extrapolate from Cohen's results, comparatively few of the subjects would report that they themselves would be annoyed or angry at the projector's breakdown. However, a much higher proportion might well also answer that a good many other children are likely to have this emotional reaction. Maybe their everyday theories of how anger arises do recognize the possibility of frustration-engendered aggressive inclinations—but researchers have to be sufficiently astute in their questioning if these lay theories are to be fully uncovered.[5]

Aversively Generated Aggression

Frustrations as Sources of Displeasure

Of course, I do not want to say that the failure to see that thwartings occasionally generate anger and aggression is due only to a theoretical bias and methodological shortcomings. And I certainly do not claim that every laboratory experiment testing the frustration–aggression relationship has yielded positive results. Indeed, quite a few experiments have not corroborated this thesis (Berkowitz, 1989). It is therefore of considerable theoretical importance to account for these inconsistencies.

There are a number of possibilities besides the deliberate suppression of anger/aggressive tendencies in some of the studies. Acknowledging the variety of processes that could keep frustrations from leading to overt aggression, I have also suggested (Berkowitz, 1982, 1989, 1993) that thwartings give rise to anger and aggression only to the degree that they are aversive. At least some of the investigations obtaining negative results thus may not have exposed their subjects to a sufficiently unpleasant experience. And moreover, we can also say, the factors governing the strength of the aggressive response to a thwarting—such as the intensity of the instigation that is unexpectedly blocked and the degree of interference with the goal attainment (cf. Dollard, Doob et al., 1939)—have this capacity because they determine how unpleasant is the frustration.

This perspective gives us one reason why attributions can be so important: They can have a considerable influence on how much displeasure is felt (Berkowitz, 1989). We are apt to be far more unhappy when we believe that someone had deliberately and unfairly blocked our goal attainment than when we think it was only happenstance that kept us from satisfying our wishes. Yet, there are times when uncontrolled accidents also displease us, and as a consequence, on these occasions we can become angry and display aggression. Should not these seemingly exceptional occurrences also be explained by a comprehensive theory of anger and aggression?

A COGNITIVE–NEOASSOCIATIONISTIC PERSPECTIVE

The Present Theoretical Model

In fundamental accord with other recent formulations (e.g., Barnard & Teasdale, 1991; Bower, 1981; Bower & Cohen, 1982; Lang, 1979, 1984; Leventhal, 1980), the analysis offered here assumes that any given emotional state is best regarded as an associative network in which specific types of feelings, physiological reactions, motor responses, and thoughts and memories are all interconnected. Because these different aspects of the emotional state often operate together, it could be helpful to think of any one emotional network as an *emotional syndrome,* as Averill (1982) recommends.[6] And accordingly, with Averill, I occasionally refer to an "anger/aggression syndrome" when I talk about the set of physiological, motor, and cognitive reactions that often occur when people are emotionally provoked. However, we must recognize that this syndrome is by no means a tightly knit package. The linkages tying the different parts of the emotional network together vary in strength, and the arousal of any one component is not necessarily accompanied by an arousal of the other subsystems to the same degree. As a consequence, measures of any of these components (e.g., self-reported feelings, heart rate, overt actions, etc.) are frequently only weakly correlated with indicators of the other components (see Lang, 1984, p. 193). Nevertheless, to the extent that they are linked together, the activation of any one subsystem in the network (or syndrome) will tend to activate the other components with which it is associated.

Although this network conception of emotion is shared by several contemporary formulations, as was just noted, the present model goes beyond several of the other analyses (e.g., Bower & Cohen, 1982; Lang, 1979, 1984; Leventhal, 1984) in two very important respects. For one, it maintains that in many animal species, including humans, there is a "built-in" association between negative affect and the anger/aggression syndrome so that unpleasant experiences tend, automatically at first, to activate the various components of the anger/aggression network. The negative affect, as I explain shortly, might well at the same time also activate a fear/escape syndrome to some degree. Nevertheless, whatever other emotional states are also evoked at this time, people who are feeling bad, whatever the reason (I suggest somewhat tentatively), are theoretically apt to feel angry, have hostile thoughts, and be disposed to attack a suitable available target. This contention, I should point out here, assumes that feelings of irritation, annoyance, and anger have much in common although they differ in their felt intensity, and can therefore be regarded as initially the same emotional state. That is, at the start of the emotion-generation process the initial, rudimentary experience of irritation or annoyance presumably grows out of the same internal sensations producing the first anger experience. And so, unless they give some thought to their sensations, people who say they feel irritated by, for example, the hot, humid weather, could also describe themselves as experiencing a low level of anger. This assumption; also made by Bower and Cohen (1982), is supported by the consistently high intercorrelations among the measures of these feelings my students and I have obtained in our research.[7]

The present analysis (see Berkowitz, 1982, 1989, 1990, 1993) also holds that the processes influencing the specific nature of the aroused emotional state change with time and thought.[8] Relatively basic and automatic associative processes supposedly are dominant at the outset when the afflicted persons first encounter the aversive event, a situation they ordinarily would prefer to avoid. Complicated thoughts of the kind emphasized by most sociocognitive theories theoretically have little influence at this time, although the affected individuals may have defined the situation as unpleasant in an initial and fairly simple appraisal of what was happening. But then, very soon afterward, cognitive processes become much more important. Figure 1.1 summarizes this postulated sequence.

Let us look at the cognitive–neoassociationistic analysis of anger in somewhat greater detail before we then turn to the empirical research bearing on this formulation.

At the Outset: The Associative Effects of Negative Affect

Initially, the model says, the negative affect generated by the aversive event generates two different sets of reactions: as was just indicated, *a fight tendency* consisting of physiological changes, feelings, ideas, memories, and motor re-

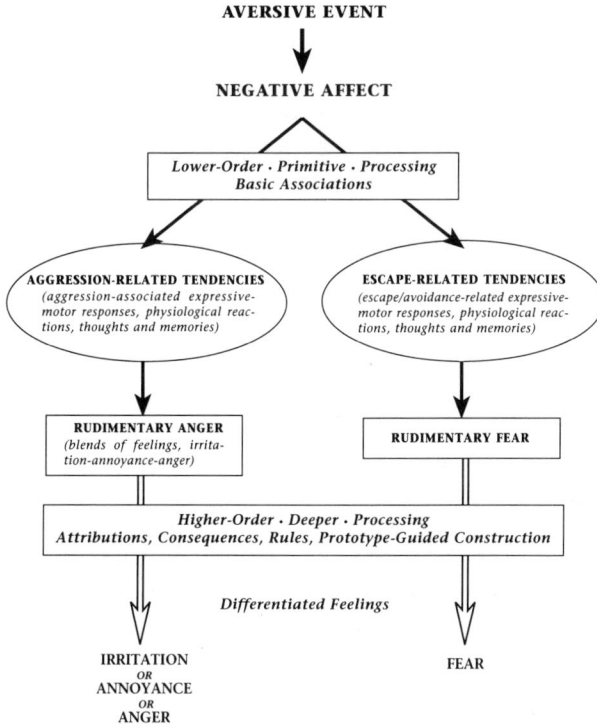

FIG. 1.1.   A cognitive–neoassociationistic conception of anger.

sponses associated with anger and aggression, but also at the same time, *a flight tendency* comprised of physiological reactions, feelings, thoughts, memories, and motor responses linked with escape from the unpleasant stimulation. Thus, from this perspective, noxious incidents give rise to both fight and flight inclinations, not one or the other. Genetic, learning, and situation influences all contribute to determine the relative strengths of these two different tendencies.

The model sees the basic—or rudimentary—anger experience as developing from the conscious and preconscious awareness of the initial anger/aggression reactions, whereas the first, relatively primitive, fear experience supposedly derives from an awareness of the initial escape-associated feelings, thoughts, memories, and expressive-motor responses.

Although I do assume (for the time being, anyway) that virtually any kind of negative affect tends to activate at least parts of the anger/aggression network, it could also be that certain types of unpleasant feelings are particularly likely to set the network components into operation. My guess here is that the more intense and more agitated these negative sensations are, the more likely it is that they will generate recognizable feelings of anger and activate hostile thoughts and aggressive inclinations.[9]

Next: The Fuller Construction of the
Emotional Experience

Obviously, however, people do not always report being angry or afraid when an unpleasant event takes place. They might feel anxious, depressed, envious, guilty, or something else, but experience little if any anger or fright. The present analysis does not claim that the afflicted persons in these cases are only denying their anger. Rather, it suggests, a fraction of time after the initial reactions, as these people think about what has happened, cognitive processes quickly come into play. Complicated appraisals, interpretations, schemas, attributions, and strategies (or whatever other labels are preferred) now rapidly exert a considerable influence, and other emotional states then arise.

Generally speaking, the cognitive–neoassociationistic model sees this influence coming about in two main ways: through a perceptual construction and also through the activation of inhibitions. I discuss these in turn, but give much more attention to the first of these matters.

Somewhat in accord with the formulations offered by Leventhal (1980) and Barnard and Teasdale (1991), the present analysis contends that the later, more highly developed and differentiated emotional experience is essentially constructed as the mind brings together various sensory, ideational, and memorial inputs from all of those available, guided largely by the affected persons' prototypic conception of what emotion they are apt to be experiencing on that particular occasion. In other words, more than only inferring what emotion they are experiencing, these people "build" a perception (i.e., form their conscious emotional feeling), out of the information-"building blocks" that are available to them at that time. Strong, agitated internal sensations probably contribute to this perception of being angry partly because such sensations are part of the anger prototype.[10]

I also suspect that the anger construction at this time is facilitated by the availability of specific targets for aggression. Much as the combined Schachter–attribution theory proposes, the suffering persons are especially apt to think of themselves as angry if some specific targets are present on whom they can focus their activated hostile ideas and thus blame these targets for their affliction.

But whatever information is integrated into the resulting experience, this higher order thinking is presumably responsible for whatever qualitative differences people establish between irritation or annoyance on one hand and anger on the other after the initial rudimentary reactions. Thus, they might perceive themselves as only irritated if their internal sensations are relatively weak and/or they do not have any one to blame for their displeasure but believe they are angry when their feelings are stronger and/or they regard themselves as having been deliberately mistreated.

This elaborate mental construction does not always occur, however, or at least may vary in its degree of complexity. The present formulation maintains that the higher order cognitive processing governing the full development of the emotional experience does not necessarily always go into operation, or may not always proceed to the same extent. The aversively afflicted people presumably have to be motivated to think about the various kinds of information they have received. Once they engage in this higher order processing, however, they consider the nature of their sensations, the perceived causes of their arousal, their conceptions of what emotions they are likely to be experiencing, the social rules regarding the appropriateness of these emotions, and even what ideas and memories have come to mind. To a greater or lesser extent, then, depending on how much thought they give to the process, they theoretically combine this information to form the resulting emotional experience.

Once this emotional perception is constructed it establishes, to a greater or lesser extent, inhibitions against thoughts, action tendencies, and perhaps, even feelings that are semantically incompatible with the perception. Cognitively oriented social psychologists, especially those subscribing to the Schachter-attribution view of emotions, have long assumed that people have a tendency to act in accord with their belief as to what emotion they are experiencing. My guess is that this consistency between belief/perception and subsequent behavior is partly due to the activated inhibitions just mentioned. They serve as filters screening out (not always completely) the incompatible ideas, memories, and feelings, and restraining (to some degree at least) inclinations to act in a perception-discrepant manner.

Evidence Supporting the Theoretical Model

However novel, oversimplified, or even wrongheaded this model might seem to the reader, in my view it is supported by a considerable body of research findings. The next section of this chapter looks at some of this evidence. I begin with a brief review of the research bearing on what is perhaps the most controversial aspect of the present formulation—its assumption that virtually any type of negative affect will tend to activate the various components of the anger/aggression syndrome—and then summarize some initial research bearing on the construction and regulation of the anger experience.

Research on the Aggressive Consequences of Aversive Events

The reader may be surprised at how much evidence there already is indicating that aversive events can produce aggressive reactions—even when these occurrences cannot be viewed as a deliberate, controllable, and wrongful mistreatment of the afflicted parties. I mention only a sample of the relevant investigations that could be cited (cf. Berkowitz, 1982, 1990, 1993, for additional references).

Animal Research

The animal studies carried out by Azrin, Ulrich, Hutchinson, and their associates (e.g., Azrin, Hutchinson, & Hake, 1967; Hutchinson, 1983; Ulrich, 1966; Ulrich & Azrin, 1962) are perhaps the best known investigations along these lines. Employing a variety of species, this research has demonstrated that physical pain can be a fairly potent stimulus to aggression. Some of the exhibited aggression could be a defensive reaction (Blanchard, Blanchard, & Takahashi, 1978),[11] and it is by no means inevitable that the afflicted animal will display any aggression at all; in many species and on many occasions the preferred response to the pain is to flee rather than attack an available target (Potegal, 1979). Nevertheless, when two animals cooped up together in a small chamber are exposed to painful stimulation (such as physical blows, electric shocks, loud noises, or intense heat), they frequently fight. Of course, various conditions such as prior learning, the nature of the available target, and the availability of alternative reactions, including the possibility of escaping from or avoiding the noxious stimulus, can affect the chances that the painful occurrence will lead to aggression.[12] But prior learning to aggress is not necessary for this to happen, and it can also take place even when the aggression clearly will not eliminate or lessen the noxious stimulus (cf. Berkowitz, 1982). In summary, in quite a few animal species, at least, decidedly unpleasant stimulation tends to activate aggressive inclinations apparently without the intervention of attributions or inferences about the pain source's intentions.

Research With Humans

Research with humans indicates that this proposition also applies, to some extent, to our own species and that physical pain is not the only negative stimulus to aggression. And here too, with humans as well as with less highly developed life forms, a broad variety of unpleasant conditions can instigate a disposition to aggression.

Uncomfortable Temperatures.   The best and most systematic evidence comes from investigations of the adverse effects of uncomfortably high temperatures. In some of the more recent studies by Griffitt (e.g., Griffitt, 1970) and Baron (see Baron, 1977) the findings demonstrated that laboratory subjects in unpleasantly hot rooms expressed greater hostility and displayed stronger aggression to a stranger than did their counterparts exposed to normal room temperatures. Goranson and King (cited in Berkowitz, 1982), Baron and Ransberger (cited in Baron, 1977), and Carlsmith and Anderson (1979) extended these observations to more naturalistic settings by showing that the urban riots that racked many U.S. cities in the 1960s were especially likely to arise on unusually hot days and then tended to diminish in intensity when the weather cooled.

Anderson has now pursued this matter further in research combining field and laboratory studies. In a careful and sophisticated review of the relevant findings

(Anderson, 1989), he noted that violent crimes and spouse abuse tend to increase when the temperature is unpleasantly high. This increase in violent offenses cannot be explained away as the result of greater interpersonal contacts on hot days, Anderson maintained, because high temperatures frequently heighten the display of aggression in laboratory experiments as well. Anderson also pointed out that the temperature-increased aggression is not merely an attempt to escape from the unpleasant environmental conditions.

Other Unpleasant Environmental Conditions.   Research by Rotton and his associates has shown that other aversive situations besides high temperature can also generate aggressive inclinations. Making use of archival data, Rotton and Frey (1985) reported that there is a rise in violent crimes when air pollution increases. Similarly, in a laboratory experiment (Rotton, Barry, Frey, & Soler, 1978), subjects exposed to a foul odor rated themselves as feeling more "aggressive" as well as "fatigued," "anxious," and "sad," and also were more hostile in their evaluations of a stranger, than were their controls exposed to normal air. A later experiment (Rotton, Frey, Barry, Milligan, & Fitzpatrick, 1979) confirmed and extended these results, reporting that the foul odor also led to comparatively strong punishment (via electric shocks) of a fellow student.

It is important to note that the participants in these experiments had no reason to believe they were being deliberately mistreated, but they evidently still reacted to the aversive stimulation with what I would term *anger, hostility,* and even *aggression.* Showing these effects of atmospheric pollution even more clearly, when Zillmann, Baron, and Tamborini (1981) attempted to manipulate their subjects' attributions for the irritating cigarette smoke wafting into their cubicles, the researchers found that the noxious stimulation led to greater hostility toward an available target even when the smoke could not be blamed on the target.[13]

Negative Moods.   Much more interesting in my view are the effects of depression and sadness on the anger/aggression syndrome. Mental health specialists from the early psychoanalysts to the present have reported how depression is often accompanied by anger, and these observations have been confirmed by empirical research. Quite a few depressed children and adults are described as being unusually prone to hostile and assaultive displays (see Berkowitz, 1983). This proclivity to anger and aggression is not necessarily revealed in planned or effortful attacks on others but is more likely to be shown in fits of uncontrolled rage. Poznanski and Zrull (1970) have reported just this in their study of highly depressed children. "Frequently," they observed, "the aggression [the children exhibited] was violent and explosive, occurring in short outbursts" (p. 13). In other words, depressives are usually not sufficiently motivated to plan and carry out sustained instrumental aggression, but their aggressive inclinations can still be seen in impulsive outbursts.

But how should this depression–aggression association be understood? Psychodynamic theories generally maintain that the depression is the result of aggressive urges, that depression is aggression toward the self. This could be an over-simplification. Although depressives can indeed be very hostile toward themselves, the present formulation suggests that their depression, as an unpleasant feeling, can also contribute to their aggressive tendencies. Experimental research certainly seems to support this possibility. In a number of laboratory studies designed to test the learned helplessness analysis of depression, as an example, the subjects exposed to the helplessness training became relatively depressed as expected, but they also rated themselves as angry and even displayed some hostility toward others (Miller & Norman, 1979).

More to the point are at least two experiments (Finman & Berkowitz, 1989; Hynan & Grush, 1986) in which the subjects were made temporarily depressed (through the Velten mood-induction procedure) and then were given an opportunity to punish a fellow student. Simplifying the findings somewhat, in both of these studies (which were carried out independently of each other) the strongest aggression was displayed by those persons who (a) were led to be depressed, and (b) gave relatively little thought to what they were doing because of their personalities and also because they had to react fairly quickly (cf. Finman & Berkowitz, 1989). Feeling depressed, they were inclined to be aggressive, but they revealed this aggression openly only impulsively when they did not think much about their actions.

We can also obtain some support for the present analysis in naturalistic studies of the occurrence of emotions in "real-world" situations. Quite a few of the people interviewed in research of this kind report feeling anger along with other negative emotions (e.g., Diener & Iran-Nejad, 1986; Scherer & Tannenbaum, 1986; Wickless & Kirsch, 1988). Ekman (1991) contended that this type of mixture is much more apt to be a shifting from one emotional state to another than a blend of states all occurring at the same time, and so, in some of these mixed instances the other negative feelings might have generated the anger. Wickless and Kirsch (1988) published findings consistent with this possibility. When their respondents said they had felt sad, they were also likely to say they had been angry as well. Going beyond this, moreover, a multivariate analysis showed that the sense of loss, which was the primary determinant of the felt sadness, also contributed to the angry feelings over and above any sense of having been wronged. An unhappy loss evidently could lead to felt anger even when it was not regarded as a transgression.

In perusing these naturalistic investigations, I have been especially impressed by the extent to which sadness is frequently linked with anger and aggression in everyday life (Berkowitz, 1990, 1993). Agreeing with this observation, Termine and Izard (1988) noted that situations or conditions eliciting sadness frequently elicit anger so that, among other things, it is not at all unusual for infants to respond to separation from a loved one by displaying both sadness and anger expressions. Grief can also activate the anger/aggression syndrome. As I have pointed out elsewhere (Berkowitz, 1990),

> The psychological literature on mourning and bereavement also testifies to the connection between sadness and anger. This literature is replete with reports of anger in those grieving over the death of a loved one, and Rosenblatt, Jackson, and Walsh (1972) have commented that 'it is not uncommon for people who are bereaved to be angry and even to engage in violent acts' (p. 271). In many of these instances the mourners could not blame the death on someone's misdeed or even on a human agent, and there also was no possibility that the loved person would be restored to them. Yet they were angry. (p. 496)[14]

I am not saying here that sadness and grief will always be accompanied by displays of anger and aggression. But people who have lost someone or something they loved do exhibit anger and/or aggression at times. The present formulation suggests that this anger/aggression syndrome is most likely to arise when the mourners are exceedingly unhappy, and even agitated, at their loss and do not think much about their feelings and especially about whether the anger they might recognizably experience is proper.[15]

Stimuli Associated With Unpleasantness.   Finally, before concluding this particular section, the reader might be interested in yet another implication of the present argument. Because negative affect tends automatically to activate components of the anger/aggression syndrome, otherwise neutral stimuli that have come to be associated with unpleasant states of affairs could well have a similar effect. Demonstrating this classically conditioned aggressive reaction, Hutchinson, Renfrew, and Young (1971) showed that the mere presentation of a stimulus that previously had been paired with aversive stimulation could start animals fighting (also see Berkowitz, 1982, p. 260).

Fraczek (cited in Leyens & Fraczek, 1983, p. 192) reported conceptually similar findings with humans. The subjects in his experiment were first taught to associate a particular color with either a pleasant or unpleasant event (receiving cigarettes or being given electric shocks). After this conditioning, the men who were most aggressive toward an available target were those who delivered their punishment in the presence of the color that had been paired with the unpleasant state of affairs.

Research results such as these can help us understand some of the ambivalence that is at times shown to ill and handicapped persons. We want to be sympathetic to those who have been afflicted by hardship, or disease, or accidents, and indeed, often do show them care and consideration. But even so, there are occasions when we are not so kind to them and may even treat them with some hostility. Could it not be that these unguarded acts of hostility are partly due to the afflicted individuals' association with aversive situations? They have an unpleasant meaning for normals because of their connection with suffering and unhappiness and, as a consequence, may be all too apt to evoke impulsive aggressive reactions from those they encounter.

Berkowitz and Frodi (1979) published findings consistent with this reasoning. To spell this out, in the second of their two experiments, previously insulted university women were asked to supervise a young boy who they had previously watched on television. Half the women had seen on TV that the child was funny looking rather than normal in appearance, and, crosscutting this variation, half the subjects also found that the boy stuttered when he spoke. The TV was then turned off, each woman was given a task to carry out in order to distract her, and she at the same time was also required to punish the youngster for his mistakes on a learning assignment.

As Fig. 1.2 indicates, the somewhat preoccupied and still-angry women were most punitive in response to the mistakes made by the doubly afflicted child: the boy who was both funny looking and a stutterer. Having both handicaps, and thus having a particularly strong negative meaning for the subjects, this unfortunate youngster readily evoked the aggressive reactions the aroused women were disposed to carry out and did not restrain because their attention was partly elsewhere.

What is the Aim of the Aversively Generated Aggression?   The research summarized up to now demonstrates that negative affect can activate aggressive

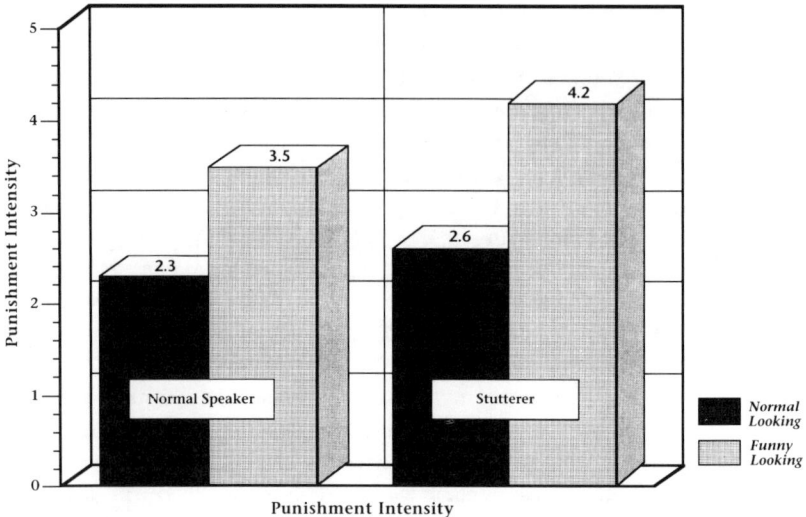

FIG. 1.2.   Mean intensity of punishment to boy as a function of boy's appearance and speech. Data from Berkowitz and Frodi (1979).

inclinations, and I have been arguing that the resulting aggression is aimed at the injury of an available (and suitable) target. I cannot emphasize this last point enough. It is customary for psychologists to interpret aversively generated aggression as being directed toward the lessening or elimination of the source of the noxious stimulation (e.g., Bandura, 1973; Zillmann, 1979), whereas the present model holds that the goal of this reaction is frequently the injury of the attacked target. Most of the findings just reported are consistent with this latter view. The aggression produced by the unpleasant state of affairs (e.g., the high temperature or the foul odor) was frequently directed at people who could not realistically be blamed for the discomfort, and the action certainly could not reduce the unpleasantness.

Two experiments I carried out with Cochran and Embree (1981) have yielded results providing even more direct support for the cognitive–neoassociationistic analysis. In these studies, female university students were asked to evaluate the quality of a peer's solutions to assigned problems while they kept one hand in a tank of water, supposedly because they were participating in an investigation of how "harsh environmental conditions" influenced supervisory performance. One experimental variation had to do with the temperature of this water; it was either a painful 6 C. or a less painful room temperature. And then, within these conditions, half the women were told that any punishment they delivered would help the other person by motivating her to do better, whereas the remaining subjects were informed that punishment would hurt the worker's performance. Each subject was then shown the worker's solutions to a series of business problems and could administer either rewards (one to five nickels) or punishments (one to five blasts of noise) as their judgment of the quality of her ideas.

Figure 1.3 reports the mean number of rewards and punishments the subjects gave to the worker in each of the experimental conditions in the first of the two studies reported by Berkowitz, Cochran, and Embree (1981). As can be seen, the women were clearly reluctant to hurt the other person when they were not exposed to the painfully cold water. In this condition they gave her the most rewards and fewest punishments when they had been told punishment would hurt her. By contrast, those whose hand was immersed in the very cold water tended to administer more punishments and fewer rewards when they thought punishment would hurt than when they believed punishment would help the worker. The pain these subjects were feeling seemed to generate a relatively strong desire to hurt someone, even when the available target was not responsible for their suffering and their punishment could not alleviate their stress.

The Anger/Aggression Syndrome as an Associative Network

As was indicated at the start of this chapter, the cognitive–neoassociationistic model is one of a number of other recent formulations holding that an emotional state is best regarded as an associative network of relatively specific physiologi-

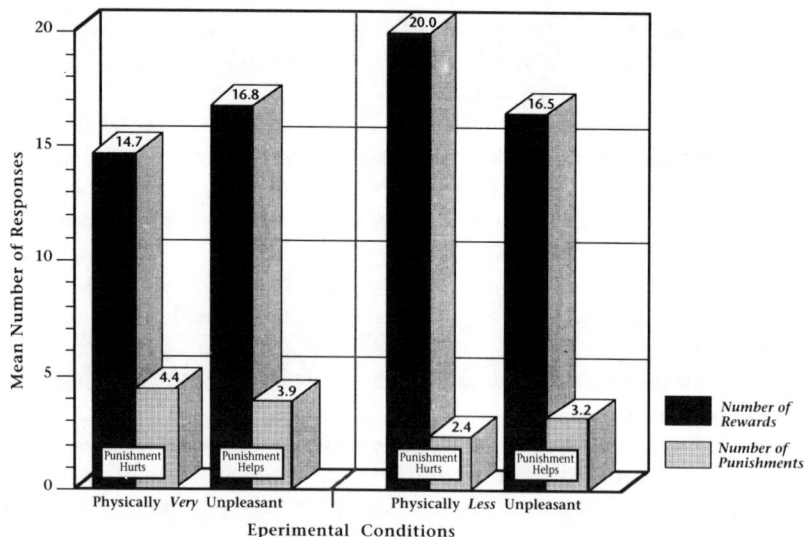

FIG. 1.3. Number of rewards and punishments to "worker" as a function of aversiveness of situation and whether punishment will hurt or help the "worker." Data from Berkowitz, Cochran, and Embree (1981), Experiment 1. (Note: For each condition the maximum total number of responses possible was 50.)

cal reactions, motor tendencies, feelings, thoughts, and memories. Bower's (1981) statement captures the central features of these analyses:

> The semantic-network approach supposes that each distinct emotion . . . has a specific node or unit in memory that collects together many other aspects of the emotion that are connected to it by associative pointers. . . . Each emotion unit is also linked with propositions describing events from one's life during which that emotion was aroused. . . . These emotion nodes can be activated by many stimuli—by physiological or symbolic verbal means. When activated above a threshold, the emotion unit transmits excitation to those nodes that produce the pattern of autonomic arousal and expressive behavior commonly assigned to that emotion. . . . Activation of an emotion node also spreads activation throughout the memory structures to which it is connected, creating subthreshold excitation at those event nodes. (p. 135)

For our purposes, the central idea here is that the activation of any one of these components in a given emotion network/syndrome tends to activate the other parts of the network as well. In the case of the anger/aggression syndrome, then, unless restraining regulatory mechanisms come into play, ideas related to anger/aggression theoretically will tend to activate aggression-associated memories and feelings. A growing body of research has yielded findings consistent with this expectation.

Effects on Memory

Most of the experimental studies testing the network conception, starting with Bower's pioneering research (Bower, 1981; Bower & Cohen, 1982), have investigated the effects of affect on memory. Although there seem to be important exceptions and a number of significant unresolved questions (cf. Blaney, 1986; Parrott & Sabini, 1990), generally speaking, learning and recall tend to be better when the affective tone of the material to be learned or remembered is congruent with one's mood at the time, and also, memory is facilitated when the mood state at learning matches the mood state at recall (see Ucros, 1989). It is as if particular feelings have come to be linked in memory with certain ideas, especially through their semantic relatedness, so that these thoughts are then remembered relatively easily when the associated feelings exist.

The present model goes further than this, as I pointed out earlier, and posits memory-facilitating associative linkages between negative affect on one hand and thoughts and ideas having an anger/aggressive meaning on the other. Just as happy people should tend to remember happy events fairly readily, those who are feeling bad should tend to have memories involving anger and aggression (unless of course, a self-regulatory process has come into operation to block the recall of unhappy occurrences).

There is suggestive evidence of just such a tendency. The female subjects in an experiment by Monteith, Berkowitz, Kruglanski, and Blair (1991) were first led to be either physically very uncomfortable (by having them extend their nondominant arm outward and unsupported for several minutes) or much more comfortable (by having them rest their extended arm on a table for the same period of time). After several minutes had gone by, and with her arm in the specified position, each woman was asked to recall a significant incident involving, on one trial, her mother, on another trial her boyfriend, and yet on another trial a neutral person whom she knew but did not care about one way or another. (The order in which the women were asked to think about these different people was systematically varied.) Assuming that the subject was very apt to feel angry and have hostile ideas when she was in conflict with another person, we were especially interested in the number of spontaneous mentions of conflict in the recollections about each of the target persons.

Table 1.1 summarizes the results obtained with this measure of conflict-related memories. Over all of the target persons combined, those who were physically uncomfortable were significantly more likely to recall conflict incidents than were their more comfortable counterparts. However, as the table also indicates, the uncomfortable women were more likely to talk about conflict than were their less suffering controls when they were thinking about their boyfriend and the neutral person rather than their mother.[16]

TABLE 1.1
Mean Number of References to Conflict in Recalled Incidents Involving Each Target Person

	Subject Discomfort Level	
Incident Involving	Low	High
Mother	.94	1.14
Boyfriend	.69	2.12
Neutral other	.31	1.31

The predicted discomfort level differences in the number of references to conflict were significant only when the subjects were talking about their boyfriend or the neutral person (someone they knew but did not care much about one way of another). Data from Monteith, Berkowitz, Kruglanski, and Blair .

Influencing Evaluations and Actions: Priming Effects

I have also found this general perspective to be exceedingly useful in accounting for the findings obtained in the research on the pro- and antisocial effects of the mass media (Berkowitz, 1984). Largely consistent with the analyses of priming effects advanced by Higgins (e.g., Higgins & King, 1981) and Wyer and Srull (e.g., Wyer & Srull, 1981) and other cognitively oriented social psychologists, I have suggested that the events portrayed or reported on television, radio, or in the press essentially give people in the audience ideas.[17] However, going somewhat further than most of these other priming conceptions, my own formulation—in accord with the associative network model—holds that the media events do more than merely heighten the accessibility of thoughts having a similar meaning; ideas presumably come actively to the viewers' minds, and these persons also have feelings, memories, and even action tendencies that are associated with the depicted occurrences.

We need not review here the media violence investigations I have discussed. A more recent experiment in this latter area is worth mentioning, however. Where a number of investigators have maintained that the priming event only heightens the accessibility of semantically related ideas and does not generate any affect, several studies of media influences indicate that the priming can activate associated feelings as well as thoughts. An experiment by Bushman and Geen (1990) provides one of the best examples of this. Explicitly testing the cognitive–neoassociationistic model, these researchers showed their subjects a videotaped movie that was either highly violent, or only mildly violent, or totally nonviolent in nature. Later, when all of the subjects were asked to list the thoughts that had occurred to them during the movie, those who saw the highly violent videotape produced the greatest number of aggressive ideas. But more important for us here, in this latter condition the greater number of aggressive thoughts was accompanied by the greatest increase in reported hostile (or angry) feelings from before to after the tape was seen.[18] Also relevant to the present analysis, my own research (Berkowitz & Heimer, 1989) suggests that aggression-related thoughts can combine with physically aversive conditions to heighten the felt anger. All in all, then, it is clear that emotion-related thoughts do not stand alone in people's minds. They are often closely linked to feelings, and one can readily activate the other (unless regulatory processes intervene—which they do at times—to minimize the arousal of unpleasant feelings).

Given all of the research results just reviewed, it is reasonable to say that a fairly broad variety of occurrences can "prime" (or activate) components of the anger/aggression syndrome, including decidedly unpleasant events and exposure to ideas and/or activities that have some degree of connection with anger and aggression. One of our Wisconsin experiments provides further evidence of this. The male subjects in this study (cf. Berkowitz, 1982, pp. 281–283) kept their nondominant hand in a tank of water while they wrote a 5-minute-long essay on an assigned topic. For half the men, the water was a very cold 6 C, whereas it was a much more moderate 23 C for the other subjects. Orthogonal to this variation, half the participants were asked to argue in favor of punishment as a disciplinary technique, whereas the remaining subjects had to write about the advantages of life in the cold northern states. When the essay was completed but with their hand still in the water tank, the men were required to deliver rewards and punishments to a fellow student as their evaluations of that person's problems solutions (employing the same research procedure that had been described earlier).

In general, the men who administered the fewest rewards and most punishments were those whose hand was in the painfully cold water and who had written the aggression-related essay. Both the physically aversive environmental condition and the aggression-priming task, arguing in favor of punishment, had activated aggressive tendencies. Other findings suggest that this result was not merely due to some "demand compliance." The subjects in this particular condition also indicated they had the strongest feelings of annoyance. Why should they be so annoyed if they were willingly complying to what they thought the experimenter wanted?[19]

Constructing the Anger Experience

Up to now I have been concentrating on the role of associative processes in the initial, supposedly "primitive," reaction to negative affect, largely because these processes have been unduly neglected in contemporary emotion theories. Cognitions obviously are also important, and the present model maintains they become increasingly influential as the emotionally aroused persons think about their feelings, the arousing incident, and what they might do. Repeating what was said earlier in this chapter, I suggest (along with Leventhal's, 1980, perceptual–motor theory and the Barnard–Teasdale, 1991, ICS model), that the affected individuals form their emotional experience out of the various pieces of information available to them at the time, including their body sensations. This perception construction is presumably guided by the persons' schemas regarding the origin and nature of the emotion they believe they are feeling.

Unfortunately, very few experiments bear directly on this analysis, and all I can do here is summarize some suggestive evidence.

Most people have a fairly clear idea as to just what they feel when they are angry. As Shaver, Schwartz, Kirson, and O'Connor (1987) pointed out, this widely shared conception can be regarded as a prototype consisting of the ideal or best case features of the anger experience, and their research—and other similar studies as well—indicate what are some of the principal characteristics of this prototype: among other things, a relatively intense sense of physiological arousal, muscular tightness throughout much of the body, and tendencies to frown and clench one's fists. The sadness prototype, on the other hand, is very different and encompasses feelings of being tired, low in energy, moving slowly, and having a slumped, drooping posture.[20]

These prototypic conceptions theoretically shape the aroused persons' emotional experience and actions once they start thinking about their feelings and the precipitating occurrence. Feeling bad, they will become more strongly convinced they are angry, and thus will perceive more anger in themselves, if they sense a high level of arousal and feel muscular tightness and clenched fists—but may conclude they are sad, and thus perceive more sadness in themselves, if they feel low and sense their drooping posture.

Eunkyung Jo and I have carried out two experiments following this reasoning in which we sought to determine whether people will combine their hostile thoughts and memories with anger-related body sensations to form a relatively strong anger experience. The first of these studies has been summarized elsewhere (Berkowitz, 1990, pp. 498–499). In brief, we asked our subjects to recall a significant emotional incident in their lives, with some of them being required to think of a happy event, others asked to recall a sad occurrence, and a third group instructed to remember an occasion in which they had been angered. The subjects in a fourth condition were asked to think of an event that had been emotionally neutral for them. Then, as the subjects recalled and talked about this incident, they were also told to squeeze a hand dynamometer at a specified force level, either 1 kg or 7 kg, so that they were clenching their fist either weakly or strongly. After 4 minutes of this combined experience the subjects rated their feelings at that moment. Our prediction, of course, was that the subjects asked to talk about the angering incident would report the most intense anger, but especially if they had been clenching their fist strongly. And furthermore, because a tight fist was inconsistent with the sadness prototype, the strong fist clenching should not intensify (and might even decrease) the feelings of sadness reported by the group recalling the sad incident.

The results were generally in line with this expectation (cf. Table 4, p. 498, Berkowitz, 1990). And moreover, a multiple regression analysis adds to the support given our reasoning by the predicted ordering of the condition means on the emotion measures. In this analysis over all conditions, scores on the anger index were significantly affected by both the number of anger-related ideas the subjects voiced in talking about their emotional incident, and the rated intensity of the muscular tension they felt as they squeezed the hand dynamometer. By contrast, this latter felt tension did not reliably affect the scores on the felt sadness index. The muscular sensation apparently heightened the emotional experience only if it was part of the relevant emotional prototype.

A second experiment (unpublished) explored this phenomenon further by investigating some of the parameters of this effect. As in the former study, subjects were asked to recall an earlier incident, but this time the event was either angering, sad, or neutral in nature. And then too, as they talked about the occurrence, one group of subjects clenched their fists at a relatively mild force level (2 kg), whereas the others did not clench their fist at all and only placed their hand on the dynamometer. Then, as before, the subjects rated their feelings at that time.

As Table 1.2 shows, the condition means on the two principal measures of felt emotion, the anger and sadness indices, are very much in accord with our theoretical expectations. The people reporting the strongest anger, significantly greater than the rated anger in any other group, were those who talked about the angering incident as they clenched their fist. Interestingly, in this study as in its predecessor, the closed fist lowered the ratings of felt sadness; the people who tightened their fist as they described the sad event rated themselves as reliably less sad than their counterparts who talked about the same kind of incident without making a fist.

The results of this research seem promising indeed, but further investigation obviously is required to determine the conditions under which people select and

TABLE 1.2
Effects of Fist Clench and Recalled Incident on Reported Feelings

	Nature of Recalled Incident					
	Angry		Sad		Neutral	
	Hand Position					
Mood Index	Clench	No Fist	Clench	No Fist	Clench	No Fist
Anger	6.3[a]	4.7[b]	2.7[cd]	3.6[bc]	2.0[d]	2.4[d]
Depression /sadness	3.3[ab]	2.3[b]	2.4[b]	4.1[a]	2.1[b]	2.0[b]
Anxiety	2.5[a]	2.2[a]	2.3[a]	3.4[a]	3.0[a]	2.3[a]

The scores reported are the adjusted means on the respective indices holding constant the premanipulation scores. In each row considered separately cells not having a common superscript are significantly different.

combine the information available to them in forming their emotional experience.

The Regulation of Emotional Experience and Action

In the construction of the emotional experience I have just described, cognitive processes presumably intervened to lessen the extent to which the sad memories led to felt anger. As the people recalling these particular unhappy events thought about what had happened and the causes of these occurrences, they might have decided they could not really be very angry; anger, they might have told themselves, just does not arise under these particular circumstances, and as a result, they perceived less anger in themselves.

Cognitive processes can also reduce the degree to which negative events activate the anger/aggression syndrome by weakening the negative affect these occurrences produce. Psychologists, psychiatrists, and other mental health specialists have long observed how normal people tend to defend themselves against their unpleasant feelings by regulating their thoughts. For example, they often adopt an optimistic outlook, anticipating that matters will improve (Taylor, 1983). But however this negative affect-reducing mechanism works, it frequently operates to lessen the adverse consequences of bad feelings and improve one's mood (Isen, 1984).

My guess, as I have proposed in several papers (Berkowitz, 1990; Berkowitz & Troccoli, 1990) is that this negative mood-regulation process does not come about all by itself but has to be activated by at least some degree of thought. Thus, my argument goes, although we are ordinarily inclined to be angry and aggressive when feeling bad, once we become highly aware of our negative feelings we might be more concerned with reducing this unpleasant affect than with lashing out at an available target, and as a consequence, the aggression-generating effects of the aversive incident are weakened.

Bartholomeu Troccoli and I have obtained evidence of just such a process in five separate experiments. In one of these studies, reported elsewhere (Berkowitz, 1990, pp. 499–500; Berkowitz & Troccoli, 1990), as a case in point, we explored the consequences of physical discomfort created by our extended arm procedure. University women individually listened to a job applicant talk about herself while they were either relatively comfortable (their extended arm rested on a table) or much more uncomfortable (because their extended arm was unsupported for several minutes). Equally important, half the subjects in both conditions then rated their feelings so that they were made highly aware of their discomfort, whereas the remaining women were given an equally long extraneous task (thinking of word associates) and presumably were less conscious of their unpleasant feelings.

Immediately afterward, when all of the subjects indicated their impressions of the job applicant's personal qualities, only those who had not been made aware of their feelings displayed the negative affect-hostility relationship; the more uncomfortable they had been, the more bad qualities they attributed to the applicant. This relationship was actually reversed for the subjects who had rated their feelings earlier; the worse they said they felt, the fewer were the negative traits attributed to the target person. It is as if they had "leaned over backward" to avoid letting their bad feelings affect their expressed opinion of the target.

These findings have important methodological as well as theoretical implications, I believe, and it is worth summarizing yet another study, employing a different type of physical discomfort and males instead of females, to demonstrate how reliable these results might be. In a second unpublished experiment by Troccoli and Berkowitz, each man listened to another student's autobiographical statement while they kept one hand in a tank of water that was either very cold (7 C) or at a more comfortable room temperature (23 C), and then rated either their own feelings or other people's personal qualities. After this manipulation, the subjects then indicated their impressions of the target person they had listened to just before.

Despite the differences in procedure and subject gender, we obtained results that were very similar to those in the previously described study. As Table 1.3 indicates, only the men who had thought about other people showed the negative affect-hostility relationship. Being somewhat distracted, the negative affect they were experiencing produced an unfavorable judgment on the target. On the other hand, and as before, those subjects who had been led to be highly aware of their discomfort tended to be more favorable to the target when they were in pain than when they were not so uncomfortable, as if they too were leaning over backward in an attempt to be fair.

It is important for the reader to keep several points in mind in thinking about all this. For one thing, the subjects in these experiments were not committed to a negative judgment of the target person. Not having to justify any earlier hostility to that individual, the self-awareness created by their ratings of their feelings evidently led them to want to do "the right thing" and not let their discomfort

TABLE 1.3
Effects of Different Levels of Aversive Stimulation on Impressions of Target Person as a Function of Attentional Focus

Attention Given to:			
Own Feelings		Others' Qualities	
Water Temperature			
Cold	Warmer	Cold	Warmer
12.8	16.4	15.0	13.0

The scores refer to the mean number of bad traits attributed to the target person. This measure yielded a significant water temperature by attentional focus interaction. Data from Troccoli and Berkowitz.

shape their expressed opinions. They might have felt even worse if they had been "unduly" negative to someone who did not warrant a bad evaluation. And then too, the discomfort the subjects experienced was not chronic. The relatively novel sensations might have prompted increased cognitive activity, leading them to consider not only their feelings but also the rules and regulations governing proper behavior in the situation. And then too, the methodological implication should be clear: Researchers are not carrying out a neutral procedure when they ask their subjects to describe their feelings following a mood/emotion arousal. In complying with this request, the aroused subjects obviously become aware of their feelings and thus may engage in a self-regulation process that otherwise would not have been activated.

The argument offered here is very much in keeping with Brewin's (1989) discussion of how people cope with unpleasant emotions. He suggested that:

> the awareness of unwanted or unpleasant emotions . . . trigger(s) a number of specific subroutines, beginning with a deliberate search of memory and other available sources of information . . . to label or classify the experience, to locate the responsible causal agents, and to assess future severity. . . Where appropriate there will be a further search to generate suitable coping options. (p. 384)

The negative-feelings-awareness created in the Wisconsin experiments just described apparently had generated suitable coping options, inducing the subjects not to let their bad mood lead to openly harsh evaluations of the innocent target.

SOME IMPLICATIONS FOR EMOTION THEORIES

Although the formulation just summarized has grown out of research into emotional aggression, whatever validity it possesses has definite implications for emotion theorizing more generally. It could then be of some interest to spell out what I see as several of these implications. Emotions researchers might want to consider whether the ideas that help us understand affectively generated assaults on some available target are useful in analyzing other emotional states as well. Because of space limitations and the comparative neglect of this class of processes in contemporary theories of emotion, I have more to say about the role played by associative factors than about the important influence exerted by the higher order cognitions such as appraisals and attributions.

Body Reaction Versus Cognitive Approaches to Emotion

As Zajonc and Markus (1984), among others, noted, theories of emotion can be divided into two broad classes, those that emphasize the part played by body reactions (termed *somatic theories* by Zajonc and Markus) and others that give priority to cognitive processes by claiming that certain types of cognitions are necessary if emotions are to arise. The cognitive–neoassociationistic model offered here is a blend of these two approaches, although it is somewhat closer to the former in that more explicit attention is given to involuntary stimulus and body influences. Zajonc's own theorizing is very similar. Thus, although he recognizes how appraisals and interpretations can shape the emotional experience and help determine what actions the emotionally aroused person will deliberately undertake, Zajonc has long contended that emotional/affective reactions such as liking can develop without the complicated cognitions postulated by most cognitive theorists (cf. Zajonc, 1980). This position has been disputed by the latter psychologists, most notably Lazarus (1984), who contend that emotions do not occur unless some incident is appraised as being personally significant.

Setting aside the question of what is an "emotion" (see endnote 7), the present formulation obviously agrees with Zajonc's basic stance, and in at least two important ways: For one, with him it holds that emotional reactions (in the present case, angry feelings and impulsive acts of aggression) can be activated by particular kinds of external stimulation without the intervention of the appraisals, attributions, and interpretations emphasized by the cognitivists. And second, the cognitive–neoassociationistic model also maintains that bodily reactions contribute importantly to both the expression of emotion and the perception of this expression.

Revising the James–Lange Theory of Emotions

In claiming that body reactions contribute to the formation of the emotional experience, the present theoretical model is also consistent with one of the classic theories of emotion and suggests that this hallowed formulation should be looked at afresh, although it probably requires some revision. As the reader might have recognized, the general line of reasoning I've followed has a family resemblance to the James–Lange theory of emotions. William James and, independently, Carl Lange had argued about 100 years ago that people's emotional feelings arise from their somatic reactions to the emotion arousing event. James (1890) summarized his argument this way:

> Common-sense says we lose our fortune, are sorry and weep; we meet a bear, are frightened and run; we are insulted by a rival, are angry and strike. The hypothesis here to be defended says this order of sequence is incorrect . . . and that the more rational statement is that we feel sorry because we cry, angry because we strike, afraid because we tremble. . . Without the bodily states following on the perception, the latter would be purely cognitive in form, pale, colorless, destitute of emotional warmth. We might then see the bear, and judge it best to run, receive the insult and deem it right to strike, but we should not actually *feel* afraid or angry. (pp. 449–450)[21]

James thus proposed that the emotional experience grew out of the aroused persons' awareness of their bodily reactions. In fundamental agreement with James and Lange but adding to their theory, the cognitive–neoassociationistic model holds that the affected people tend to incorporate their emotion-associated ideas and memories as well as their bodily sensations into this experience, and that the feeling construction is guided by their prototypic conception of the emotional state.[22] If some such process contributes to the perception of being angry, it could well also play a part in the formation of other emotional experiences.

Effects of Muscular Feedback

Any revision of the James–Lange theory, and for that matter any truly comprehensive analysis of emotions, must recognize (along with the present associative network formulation) that peripheral body reactions can influence the emotional experience. The model offered here, in essential agreement with other conceptions (e.g., Izard, 1990; Tomkins, 1962), accounts for this affect by proposing that associative linkages connect basic emotional feelings with particular muscle movements.

There is now little doubt that particular facial expressions typically accompany distinctive emotional experiences (Ekman & Friesen, 1978), and we also have evidence that the deliberate movement of certain specific facial muscles can create autonomic changes often characteristic of the theoretically related emotional state (Ekman, Levenson, and Friesen, 1983). (Interestingly, and contrary to Schachter's, 1962, assumption that emotional states are physiologically undifferentiated, in this latter study Ekman and his colleagues found significant autonomic differences between several of the negative emotions.) But more pertinent to the present analysis, there is also increasing reason to believe that, under certain conditions at least, the movement of particular facial muscles can intensify and maybe even evoke the feelings typically associated with these expressions (Adelmann & Zajonc, 1989; Izard, 1990; Leventhal & Tomarken, 1986). As Adelmann and Zajonc (1989) concluded in their review of the research bearing on what they termed *facial efference:*

> To the extent that voluntarily produced efference can be assumed to adequately correspond to spontaneous emotional efference, the experimental evidence suggests that facial efference may play an important causal role in the subjective experience of emotion. In this, other reviewers at least partially agree. Laird (1984) concluded that these experimental studies "have demonstrated effects of varying the magnitude of expressive behavior on both self-reports of emotional experience and on various measures of physiological arousal such as heart rate and skin conductance". (p. 273)

Most of the facial feedback (or body reaction) studies essentially deal with a connection between particular expressive-motor responses and emotional feelings and/or physiological reactions. However, the emotional network conception offered in this paper posits linkages between these emotion-related motor movements and other types of responses as well. In accord with this view, a number of experiments have dealt with the influence of body reactions on learning and memory.

In one of these studies, Ohman and Dimberg (1978) demonstrated that people can learn to associate angry facial expressions with painful stimuli fairly readily so that these particular noxious stimuli-anger expression associations are relatively slow to extinguish. This is the case, they proposed, because humans are genetically "prepared" to connect aversive events with anger-related body reactions.

Other research has shown that facial expressions can influence the degree to which mood-relevant material is easily remembered. In experiments carried out by Laird and his associates (1982), those persons whose mood was affected by their facial expressions readily recalled a passage they had encountered earlier whose content was congruent with their feelings. In their second study, as a case in point, the subjects who reported heightened anger after being induced to frown had the best memory for sentences with an anger-related content. Adding to this evidence, Riskind (1983) showed that facial and postural body movements associated with pleasure can facilitate memories for pleasant events.

Even with these findings, though, the reader should remember that the associative linkages vary in strength. Emotion-related expressive-motor patterns can be linked to particular feelings, ideas, and memories without the connection being a strong one. And so, as a consequence, we often find in the research in this area that (a) emotion-related body reactions are usually at best only weak contributors to the emotion experience; and (b) the performance of emotion-connected facial expressions can more clearly intensify the associated feelings that had been generated by another occurrence than create these feelings de novo (Leventhal & Tomarken, 1986). But even so, as the network approach posits, making particular expressive-motor movements, especially in the face, can activate to some extent the other components in the particular emotional net to which these muscular responses are linked.

Mood and Memory: Is Affect in Itself Linked to Specific Memories?

Perhaps one of the more controversial aspects of the present cognitive–neo-associationistic model has to do with its interpretation of the affective (or mood) congruency effect in memory. As was mentioned before, under some circumstances there is a memorial bias resulting in the relatively better recall of events having the same emotional meaning as one's feelings at the time. I suggested (in accord with the general network approach) that this congruency comes about because of associative links between the particular affective state and semantically related material. Gilligan and Bower (1984) phrased this notion in these terms: "According to the network theory, the induction of the mood activates the corresponding emotion node and (some of) its associates, thereby creating a mental context dominated by mood-related themata" (p. 573).

Of course, there are other possible explanations of the research findings.[23] A number of psychologists contend that the words people apply to their feelings, not the feelings themselves, are what associate the affective state with the prior happening and thus produce the better memory.

We cannot here review the studies bearing on this particular controversy, although it should be acknowledged that the methodological problems in this research are great indeed[24] and there admittedly is evidence in accord with this verbal-mediation view (e.g., Parrott & Sabini, 1990). Nevertheless, several experiments in which the subjects were not explicitly told to adopt a particular mood, so that they did not necessarily think of themselves as being in a given emotional state, suggest that an aroused affect in itself can heighten the accessibility of memories having the same general meaning.

I mentioned one of these studies earlier. In the experiment by Monteith, Berkowitz, Kruglanski, and Blair (unpublished), when the subjects were asked to recall a significant incident involving a particular target person, those who were made to be physically uncomfortable at the time (and who were talking about either their boyfriend or a neutral person) were more likely to think of a prior conflict than were their more comfortable peers (see Table 1.1).

The research conducted by Isen, Shalker, Clark, and Karp (1978) is much better known. In one of the Isen et al. investigations along these lines, the male and female subjects played a computer game that they either "won" or "lost" (the mood manipulation) and then were required to learn a series of words presented to them via an audiotape. This learning period was followed by a second computer game, and again the participants were told either that they had been victorious or were defeated. When the subjects then tried to remember as many of the listed words as they could, their recollections were significantly influenced by their mood at time of recall rather than their feelings at the time of encoding. Moreover, those who had just experienced a positive outcome correctly remembered the greatest number of positive words in the list. The experimental variations did not influence the recollection of either the negative or neutral words. In summary, the aroused good mood had facilitated memory for the words having a good meaning, presumably because the feeling had primed semantically related ideas.

For what it is worth, the reader might also want to consider still another testimony to the way affective experiences can activate associated memories. In his great novel *Remembrance of Things Past,* Marcel Proust told how a taste had brought back recollections of earlier events. Doesn't Garcia's research (e.g., Garcia, McGowan, Ervin, & Koelling, 1968) indicate that tastes can be very strongly associated with prior affective experiences so that these connections are exceedingly difficult to extinguish? Other sensations might also activate memories acquired earlier.

At any rate, even with all this evidence, there clearly are occasions in which the mood congruency effect does not arise (e.g., Parrott & Sabini, 1990; also cf. Blaney, 1986; Fiske & Taylor, 1991), and it is now obvious that other influences such as motivational factors can mask or even counteract this effect. Isen (1984) called our attention to these other influences by emphasizing the frequently observed asymmetry in the way feelings can bias recall; as was found in her experiment with Shalker, Clark, and Karp (1978), under many circumstances still not well understood, negative affects do not activate semantically congruent memories as readily as do more pleasant feelings. She, and other writers (e.g., Parrott & Sabini, 1990), have suggested that this mood asymmetry is probably produced by a self-regulatory mechanism that operates (under some conditions) to lessen the unpleasant mood. Persons motivated to minimize their bad feelings can satisfy this purpose by blocking the recall of aversive events.

But at any rate, whatever factors interfere with the mood congruency effect in memory, they are not anticipated by a purely associative account of the influence of affect on recollections. Any network model of emotions must therefore be prepared to incorporate these additional influences, and I have more to say about this matter shortly.

Activating a Motor Program

Proceeding with the associative network model for the time being, another feature of this conception has to do with the bidirectionality of the postulated influences. Activation presumably can spread in either direction along the network. Particular thoughts can generate semantically related feelings, and the arousal of emotional feelings tends to bring thoughts to mind having much the same emotional meaning. And similarly, according to the present formulation, just as the performance of certain specific facial and body movements tends to increase the associated feelings (assuming there are no interfering thoughts or other counteracting influences), particular feelings can be reflected in specific facial and body movements.

This last point is especially significant for our understanding of emotions because it not only posits a connection between particular emotional states and specific motor programs but also says the arousal of these emotional syndromes tends to generate an impulse to action. Although this may not be true of every emotional state, according to Ekman (1991), people experiencing certain types of feelings presumably have an urge to act in a manner in accord with these states.

This is a relatively novel notion for the social sciences. Most psychologists along with other students of human behavior typically assume aggressors deliberately choose to assault their victims. By contrast, the present account holds that highly enraged persons may well lash out impulsively at their targets, not because they have decided they would benefit from such an attack, but because the anger/aggression network has been so intensely aroused inside them that strong motor impulses to aggression are activated. The cognitive–neoassociationistic perspective holds, furthermore, that other emotional states may operate in a comparable manner.

Other emotion theorists have advanced somewhat similar ideas by proposing that specific motor programs accompany particular emotional states.[25] Zajonc and Markus (1984) made a related observation in proposing how affective states are represented within the central nervous system:

> Feelings, emotions, and moods do result in specific sets of mental representations, but they are most readily identified by responses of the motor and visceral systems such as clenched fists, red faces, bulging veins, slumped postures, silly grins, pounding hearts, and queasy stomachs. The motor system is extensively engaged in affective processes. . . . (p. 74)

Lang (1984) also emphasized the involvement of motor programs in affective states and goes so far as to conceive of emotions as "response dispositions or action sets" (p.). Other writers, however, seem to accept this general line of thought but without explicitly referring to an activated motor program. Frijda (1986; Frijda et al., 1989), for example, maintained that when an emotion is aroused, the individual becomes ready to "engage in interaction with the environment" (p.) in a particular manner. However, it should be clear, for Frijda this tendency is only a *readiness;* the readiness states "*may avail themselves* in their execution, of certain prewired action patterns such as facial expressions and gross behavior modes (flight, attack)" (Frijda et al., 1989, p. 213; italics added), but presumably do not actually involve activated motor responses. The cognitive–neoassociationistic model takes a stronger position and holds that the arousal of the anger/aggression syndrome, and probably some other emotional states as well, produces ongoing impulses to carry out emotion-related actions.

Another difference between these two formulations is also worth mentioning: Frijda believes the action readiness is linked to a certain set of appraisals, whereas the present approach suggests that any component of the anger/aggression network can put the other components into operation. Unpleasant feelings in themselves can produce at least, a weak impetus to anger and aggression.

As I have noted elsewhere (Berkowitz, 1982, pp. 263–264), findings obtained in several animal experiments are in accord with this proposal. To mention only some of these results, in one study by Azrin and his associates, electrically shocked monkeys exerted effort in order to obtain a target they could attack, whereas Weiss and his colleagues found that shocked rats who did not have another rat to strike at were subsequently physiologically more damaged than other pained animals who did have a suitable target for their aggression. The pain evidently created an impulse to aggression spurring work in the interest of obtaining a victim and, in the case of the rats at least, the inability to carry out the instigated aggression was physiologically harmful.

Automatic Versus Controlled Processes in Self-Regulation of Emotion and Priming Effects

Although this chapter has emphasized the role of associative processes in emotion, the present theoretical model, as I have repeatedly stressed, certainly does not intend to slight the importance of cognitions and cognitively controlled mechanisms. Accordingly, I suggested that after the initial, rudimentary emotional reactions to the evocative situation, people construct their emotional experience by combining various kinds of information available to them guided by their prototypic conception of what emotion they think they are feeling. And then too, I also proposed (especially when describing the experiments Troccoli and I carried out but also in the earlier discussion of the mood congruency effect) that cognitive controls can intervene to modulate the emotional experience and regulate what impact affect has on subsequent behavior. Much more should be said about this last mentioned matter.

In several studies (e.g., Berkowitz & Troccoli, 1990), the reader will recall, after subjects were made physically uncomfortable, some of them were induced to focus their attention on their feelings just before they were required to evaluate a target person. This experimental variation led to much the same outcome over the series of investigations I conducted with Troccoli even though the discomfort was generated by different procedures and the evaluations were recorded in different ways. In all of these instances the subjects exposed to the aversive treatment were much harsher to the target person than their counterparts in the more comfortable condition—but only when the participants had not previously attended to their feelings. Those who had become very aware of their negative affect apparently had tended to "lean over backward" to avoid letting their unpleasant feelings influence their judgment of the target.

This reasoning makes several assumptions. First, following my basic argument, it proposes that the experimentally generated negative affect had automatically activated hostile ideas and aggressive inclinations leading to the unfavorable evaluation of the target. But second, it also holds that these ideas and inclinations were substantially inhibited by the cognitive controls set into operation when the afflicted people's attention was focused on themselves. On becoming highly conscious of what they were feeling and what they were tempted to do, these persons presumably engaged in *higher order* thinking so that they considered the possible appropriateness of their emotions and urges in the given circumstances and then decided to restrain themselves. Looked at in another way, this interpretation essentially makes the now familiar distinction between automatic and controlled processes. Automatic processes had led the suffering but distracted subjects to evaluate their peer unfavorably, whereas controlled processes presumably kept this from happening when the participants attended to their feelings.

Recent research into the priming effects discussed earlier in this chapter has also now indicated that attention-activated processing can lead to effects that are very different from those that arise when people are distracted. Martin, Seta, and Crelia (1990) published a noteworthy example. In one of their experiments the subjects were first primed to have either positive or negative ideas by asking them to read and then write about statements that were either positive or negative in content. Immediately after this the participants were given a written description of a target person and were required to form an impression of this individual. What is important here is that half the subjects were distracted as they read the description by also having them listen to a voice read a random string of numbers and letters. When the Martin group then analyzed their subjects' impressions of the target person, they obtained results altogether comparable to the Berkowitz–Troccoli findings. The distracted people displayed the usual priming effect; they assessed the target more positively after the positive as compared to the negative priming experience, probably because the positive material had automatically activated positive thoughts which influenced their view of the target in a positive direction. The nondistracted people did not display this effect, and even exhibited a *contrast* reaction similar to what had happened in the Wisconsin experiments (judging the target more favorably after being primed negatively). Suggesting that this latter failure to show the usual priming effect was probably due to increased thinking by the nondistracted participants, Martin et al. demonstrated that people with a strong "need for cognition" (who tend to think a great deal when given cognitive tasks) were the ones most apt to reveal the contrast effect after the initial priming. As the Martin group speculated (and as my own thesis also proposes), these relatively thoughtful individuals could have considered the possible inappropriateness of their initial inclinations toward the target, and then leaned over backwards in an attempt to be fair and objective.

Again, all of the findings just reported could be different manifestations of a much more general phenomenon—in this case having to do with the attention-spurred activation of higher order control mechanisms in the human brain. Attesting to this generality, in their theoretical account of behavior control Norman and Shallice (1986) postulate an attention-activated supervisory or executive control system that is set into operation by especially demanding or novel situations. Some such mechanism could have been responsible for the Berkowitz–Troccoli and Martin et al. results and also, much more generally, might regulate or even restrain the operation of the motor programs activated by the arousal of an emotional state. Automatic processes have an important part in emotional reactions but these processes can be controlled to a considerable degree by cognitively generated executive systems.

CONCLUSIONS

I close with two general comments, one focused relatively narrowly on the effects of negative affect and the other a more general appeal to emotions researchers.

The first of these remarks is directed toward those who want to believe that good comes out of bad. They try to find recompense for our pain and distress in the virtue and nobility that, they contend, can arise from the bitter ashes. The evidence presented in this chapter takes issue with such a belief, but also holds out some reason for hope. As I put it a few years ago:

> suffering is seldom ennobling. It is the unusual individual whose character is improved as a result of undergoing painful or even merely unpleasant experiences. . . . When people feel bad, they are all too likely to have angry feelings, hostile thoughts and memories, and aggressive inclinations.
>
> But there is also reason for some hope. . . . For one thing, people are often drawn to others who are undergoing the same unpleasant conditions and share their unhappiness. We do not know precisely why this happens, but the tendency for people in misery to love others also in misery seems to limit the ill effects of negative feelings. Perhaps more important, the relatively primitive associative processes producing these ill effects can be countered by higher-level cognitive processes. Afflicted persons can restrain their hostile and aggressive tendencies, perhaps as a result of becoming aware of their feelings and seeing clearly that it is wrong for them to blame or attack others. Here as in so many other ways, it is thought and not suffering that makes us better. (Berkowitz, 1990, p. 500)

For me at least, as I have suggested several times now, there is also a lesson here for those who study the psychology of emotions. Whatever else it attempts to achieve, this chapter seeks to deliver a clear message: Any truly comprehensive analysis of emotions must be far-ranging and broad in scope. Such a general formulation obviously should be compatible with what is known about the neurophysiology of emotions and probably would also do well to make reference to neurophysiological processes. But even purely psychological models of emotion should go beyond the traditional concepts and assumptions in any one of our current theoretical perspectives. We might tell emotion researchers, and especially those of the conventional cognitive persuasion, that there is far more in heaven and earth and even in the psychology of emotions than is dreamt of in their philosophy. They have to know about the operation of cognitions. But they should also recognize that automatic body and associative processes have an important part in this psychology.

ENDNOTES

1. This statement seems to imply that there is no emotional arousal at all in instrumental aggression and no instrumental components whatsoever in emotional aggression. I obviously do not intend to convey this impression and have differentiated between instrumental and emotional aggression as I do here for simplicity and to sharpen the theoretical issues. The definitions of the two types of aggression offered in this article (and in my other writings) are matters of degree. That is, instrumental aggression is prompted largely (but not necessarily only) by the hope of gaining some benefit other

than the victim's injury, although emotional feelings might also be present, whereas emotionally aggressive actions are presumably impelled largely by fairly specific emotional reactions within the body, although the emotionally aroused aggressor might also at times expect to profit from his or her attack. We cannot say, of course, what proportion of all the hostile aggression (where the victim's injury is the primary goal) occurring in society is emotional in nature (as defined here), but I believe that a great deal of the domestic and criminal violence that takes place is of this type (see Berkowitz, 1993).

2. The theoretical model being advanced here is similar in important respects to the Interacting Cognitive Subsystems (ICS) model published by Barnard and Teasdale (1991). Both formulations hold that emotional states are affected by interacting processes and that information from the body is incorporated into the emotional experience. Both also maintain that this interaction among the various subsystems changes with time. The ICS model, however, is more explicitly cognitive and gives less attention to automatic reactions governed by associative processes. To give the reader some of the flavor of the ICS approach, Barnard and Teasdale (1991) observed that the argument as to whether emotion can be independent of cognition or is dependent on cognition is really based on how one defines "cognition." According to Barnard and Teasdale, "ICS avoids this particular difficulty by clearly specifying nine different types of information. Each of these may contribute, either directly or indirectly, to the production or experience of emotion."

3. To elaborate on this possible alternative, evidence summarized later in this paper (also see Berkowitz & Troccoli, 1990) indicates that awareness of one's negative feelings can activate self-controls, presumably especially when these feelings are somewhat unexpected and the person is uncertain as to how appropriate they are. Because there is no evidence the insulted subjects in Zillmann's exercize group actually did think of themselves as very angry, it could be that these people, being not very self-aware, were also relatively unrestrained. As a result, their exercize-heightened arousal state might have readily energized the aggressive tendencies activated by the prior insult (thus leading to the supposed "excitation transfer"). On the other hand, if the subjects had been highly conscious of their feelings, for example because they were extremely strongly aroused and/or because they had been required to rate their feelings, they might have wondered whether this arousal was appropriate, and this questioning could have activated self-controls leading them to hold back in their open display of hostility.

4. This is demonstrated by the significant effect for frustration in the intermittent reinforcement condition that I found when I carried out a post hoc analysis of the published Walters–Brown results. The aggression index was based on the subjects' actual behavior toward their partner, actions that were clearly intended to do harm, and thus that were more than only relatively intense (or "high magnitude") responses or only make-believe actions.

5. Stein and Levine (1989) reported findings also attesting to how many ordinary persons recognize the aggression-generating effects of unpleasant experiences. When the subjects were asked what kinds of emotions are likely to be experienced in various kinds of situations, 60% said the victim of an unpleasant event might well become angry even when the negative occurrence was only accidental or was produced by natural forces rather than some human agent. It should be noted that in this study as in the previously cited study by Cohen, the subjects were asked to say how someone else, not themselves, was apt to react.

6. This notion of an emotional syndrome appears to be somewhat similar to Tomkin's (1981) concept of an *affect program,* an inherited set of mechanisms controlling all of the major components that are usually involved in the basic emotional states (also see Ekman, 1991). In essential agreement with Averill (1982), I believe it is possible to lessen at least some of the many ambiguities and inconsistencies in theoretical discussions of emotion (highlighted so well by Ellen Berscheid, 1990) if we regard any given emotional state as a syndrome of semi-independent components.

7. Many writers prefer to differentiate between moods and emotions, holding (among other things) that there is no perceived source of the arousal state in the case of a mood but that such a perceived source does exist when there is an emotion. From this point of view much of the research

cited in this chapter deals with moods rather than emotions. My contention, however, is that this distinction is arbitrary and is based more on language usage than good evidence. And so, people sometimes report themselves as angry, or are described by others as angry, even when there does not seem to be a clear source for this feeling. More importantly, studies of the effects of aversive environmental conditions—conditions in which there is nothing clearly to blame for the negative affect—indicate that the afflicted persons often describe themselves as feeling angry (or hostile) and also act in an aggressive manner. They seem to be experiencing what I have termed the anger/aggression syndrome.

The reader might find the Gilligan and Bower (1984) discussion of differences in anger intensity of some interest in this connection. Very much in keeping with my general position, they proposed that people learn to label "mild angers as *annoyances,* moderate angers as *angers,* and extreme angers as *rages,*" (p. 577) indicating that these supposedly different states actually have much in common, although they also suggested that because of the different labelings each of these states is represented in a different node in the associative network (p. 577). Although this latter point is certainly reasonable, in my view there are still very strong associative linkages among the somatic and mental representations of irritation, annoyance, anger, and rage, so that for my purposes these states can be thought of as occupying the same emotional node.

8. In accord with the present model, Barnard and Teasdale (1991) said their formulation "envisages a progression from a state in which emotion is an innately prepared response to certain triggering stimulus complexes to a state in which, through repeated experiences within a given familial and cultural context, both the form and elicitation of emotion become modified and elaborated."

9. Yet another, and very intriguing, possibility is suggested by Davidson's emphasis on approach versus withdrawal as a central dimension of emotions (Davidson & Tomarken, 1989). This analysis proposes that all negative emotion states are not alike; in some, such as fear and disgust, withdrawal tendencies predominate, whereas approach tendencies are stronger in other negative states such as anger. It might be, then, that decidedly unpleasant feelings accompanied by relatively strong approach inclinations are especially apt to activate the anger/aggression network.

10. In accord with my own position, Barnard and Teasdale (1991) believe that "peripheral bodily effects may contribute to emotion production" . . . [directly] "not necessarily mediated by propositional-level cognitive appraisals of meaning," although such a propositional mediation may take place at times.

11. There is good reason to say, however, that the pain-elicited aggression is by no means only a defensive response (see Brain, 1981; Hutchinson, 1983). The afflicted animals' aggression may have a defensive component at times, especially when it is clear that the noxious stimulus can be eliminated by attacking its source (Azrin, Hutchinson, & Hake, 1967), but pain can also produce nondefensive animal aggression as well (Berkowitz, 1982).

12. Two studies point to some of the complexities in the effects of prior learning on the pain–aggression relationship. Azrin, Hutchinson, and Hake (1967) reported that the escape tendency acquired prepotency over the tendency to attack, when the animals found they could successfully escape from the shock, whereas Maier, Anderson, and Lieberman (1972) noted that the total inability to escape from the shocks led to a passivity resulting in diminished effortful fighting with another animal. My contention in this connection is that the "learned helplessness" arising from prior exposure to inescapable noxious conditions lessens the motivation to engage in deliberate, planned, and effortful aggression but does not weaken the tendency to display impulsive and relatively automatic outbursts of aggression (cf. Berkowitz, 1983, 1993).

13. Kenrick and Johnson (1979) claimed that the noxious stimulation leads to heightened aggression only when the available target is a hypothetical stranger and is not physically present. Answering this contention, I have pointed out (Berkowitz, 1982) that in several experiments, such as studies by Baron and by Rotton, unpleasant environmental conditions produced increased attacks on a peer the subjects had met previously and believed to be nearby. As I suggested, "it is not the 'real' or

'fictional' nature of the target that seems to be important . . . but whether the other person shares the subject's unpleasant experience" (p. 270). There is the increased liking for the available target that Kenrick and Johnson observed in their experiment "when the participants thought that the other individual was also facing the same aversive occurrence, whereas the heightened hostility to the target came about when the subjects believed that they alone were exposed to the unpleasant event. In sum, we may be dealing here with the effect of a 'common fate:' People who are threatened by the same external stressor often develop a greater liking for each other" (p. 270). The interested reader will find evidence of this "common fate" phenomenon in response to noxious conditions in Dovidio and Morris (1975).

14. Two English writers have recently made this point independently. Timberlake Wertenbaker had a character in her latest London play comment that grief often leads to anger, and similarly, in her latest detective novel, P. D. James observed, through her protagonist, that "You can feel anger and grief together. That's the commonest reaction of bereavement" (p. 381).

15. It is often suggested that the mourners are angry because they blame some particular agency (another person, God, or even fate) for their loss. Although this undoubtedly can happen, it may also be that the mourners' strong negative affect activates hostile thoughts that are then focused on a salient available target so that this particular target is blamed for the tragedy.

16. The subjects also rated their feelings after they had finished talking about each of the target persons. Statistical analyses of these data indicated that the uncomfortable subjects, as expected, rated themselves as significantly higher on an index of irritation, annoyance, and anger (the IAA index) than did their more comfortable counterparts. A multiple regression analysis also showed that this effect of the physical discomfort variation on the IAA index remained significant even when other negative feelings (felt displeasure and felt distress) were controlled. Thus, the subjects were not merely confusing their irritation-annoyance-anger with other negative feelings.

17. In this type of effect, the media-induced priming can be surprisingly broad-ranging at times and exert an influence by evoking thoughts that are only moderately, and not closely, associated with the presented, priming stimulus. Herr (1986) showed that subjects acted in a relatively hostile and competitive fashion toward a partner after being exposed to the names of people whose occupations were associated with aggressive conduct, such as the once well-known prize fighter Joe Frazier, and similarly, Wann and Branscombe (1990) found that giving people the names of aggressive sports, such as boxing, heightened their tendency to attribute hostility to an ambiguous target person.

18. The well-known Velten (1968) mood-induction procedure can also be seen as a priming task that generates semantically related feelings and action tendencies as well as ideas.

19. The demand compliance answer to my rhetorical question, of course, is that the subjects reported feeling annoyed because they realized the experimenter wanted them to be annoyed. To answer this "answer," let me note that our questioning of the subjects at the end of each experimental session indicated that (a) very few of them had caught on to the additive hypothesis we were testing; and (b) they seemed to prefer appearing "cool" and unbothered by the experimental treatment, rather than being upset by it, presumably because of their evaluation apprehension.

20. Rime', Philippot, and Cisamolo (1990) also emphasized the schematic nature of people's conceptions of the peripheral physiological changes that occur within them as they experience an emotion. Contrary to those who maintain these schemata are only socially constructed, as if the physiological basis is unimportant, these researchers demonstrated that the peripheral change schemata are similar across different cultures.

21. Walter Cannon and others criticized James for supposedly focusing exclusively on visceral reactions. However, although James did emphasize these autonomic reactions in his later writings, it is clear from other passages in his 1890 text that he believed visceral changes were not the only determinants of the emotional experience. Changes in breathing, muscles, and even in the skin, he indicated, could also contribute importantly to the emotional feelings.

22. It is also possible to view the Schachter–Singer (1962) two-factory theory as a cousin of the James–Lange theory (although Schachter chose to reject his distant relative). Both essentially con-

tend that the aroused persons' emotional experience is formed on the basis of their awareness—and cognitions about—their bodily reactions.

23. For example, as Bower (1991) pointed out, in some studies the mood congruency results could have been caused by the subjects giving more attention to the mood congruent material (cf. Forgas & Bower, 1987).

24. To mention only one of the methodological ambiguities, Parrott and Sabini (1990) pointed out that in studies employing the Velten mood induction procedure, the subjects typically are asked to place themselves in the mood suggested by the Velten statements, and so these people could have thought of themselves as "depressed" or "elated." This emotion-related thought could have then been responsible for the mood congruency findings obtained in a number of studies.

25. Motor theories of consciousness go even further along these lines. As Cohen (1986) pointed out, these notions generally hold "that no perception, no image, no thought—in fact, no emotional experience—is possible without the occurrence of some unique pattern of activation in the motor system; it is the particular motor activity pattern evoked directly by some external stimulus or associative process that determines which mental experience will occur" (p. 20).

REFERENCES

Adelmann, P., & Zajonc, R. (1989). Facial efference and the experience of emotion. *Annual Review of Psychology, 40,* 249–280.

Anderson, C. A. (1989). Temperature and aggression: Ubiquitous effects of heat on occurrence of human violence. *Psychological Bulletin, 106,* 74–96.

Averill, J. (1982). *Anger and aggression: An essay on emotion.* New York: Springer–Verlag.

Azrin, N. H., Hutchinson, R. R., & Hake, D. F. (1967). Attack, avoidance, and escape reactions to aversive shock. *Journal of the Experimental Analysis of Behavior, 10,* 131–148.

Bandura, A. (1973). *Aggression: A social learning analysis.* New York: Prentice–Hall.

Barnard, P. J., & Teasdale, J. D. (1991). Interacting cognitive subsystems: A systemic approach to cognitive–affective interaction and change. *Cognition and Emotion.*

Baron, R. A. (1977). *Human aggression.* New York: Plenum.

Berkowitz, L. (1969). The frustration-aggression hypothesis revisited. In L. Berkowitz (Ed.), *Roots of aggression* (pp. 1–28). New York: Atherton.

Berkowitz, L. (1982). Aversive conditions as stimuli to aggression. In L. Berkowitz (Ed.), *Advances in experimental social psychology* (Vol. 15, pp. 249–288). Orlando, FL: Academic Press.

Berkowitz, L. (1984). Some effects of thoughts on anti- and prosocial influences of media events: A cognitive–neoassociationistic analysis. *Psychological Bulletin, 95,* 410–427.

Berkowitz, L. (1989). Frustration–aggression hypothesis: Examination and reformulation. *Psychological Bulletin, 106,* 59–73.

Berkowitz, L. (1990). On the formation and regulation of anger and aggression: A cognitive–neoassociationistic analysis. *American Psychologist, 45,* 494–503.

Berkowitz, L. (1993). *Aggression: Its causes, consequences, and control.* New York: McGraw–Hill.

Berkowitz, L., Cochran, S., & Embree, M. (1981). Physical pain and the goal of aversively stimulated aggression. *Journal of Personality and Social Psychology, 40,* 687–700.

Berkowitz, L., & Frodi, A. (1979). Reactions to a child's mistakes as affected by her/his looks and speech. *Social Psychology Quarterly, 42,* 420–425.

Berkowitz, L., & Heimer, K. (1989). On the construction of the anger experience: Aversive events and negative priming in the formulation of feelings. In L. Berkowitz (Ed.), *Advances in experimental social psychology* (Vol. 22, pp. 1–37). New York: Academic Press.

Berkowitz, L., & Troccoli, B. T. (1990). Feelings, direction of attention, and expressed evaluations of others. *Cognition and Emotion, 4,* 305–325.

Berscheid, E. (1990). Contemporary vocabularies of emotion. In B. S. Moore & A. M. Isen (Eds.), *Affect and social behavior* (pp. 22–38). Cambridge/New York: Cambridge University Press.

Blanchard, R. J., Blanchard, D. C., & Takahashi, L. K. (1978). Pain and aggression in the rat. *Behavioral Biology, 23,* 291–305.

Blaney, P. H. (1986). Affect and memory: A review. *Psychological Bulletin, 99,* 229–246.

Bower, G. H. (1981). Mood and memory. *American Psychologist, 36,* 129–148.

Bower, G. H. (1991). How might emotions affect learning? In S. A. Christianson (Ed.), *Handbook of emotion and memory* (pp.). Hillsdale, NJ: Lawrence Erlbaum Associates.

Bower, G. H., & Cohen, P. (1982). Emotional influences in memory and thinking: Data and theory. In M. Clark & S. Fiske (Eds.), *Affect and social cognition* (pp. 291–331). Hillsdale, NJ: Lawrence Erlbaum Associates.

Brain, P. F. (1981). Differentiating types of attack and defense in rodents. In P. F. Brain & D. Benton (Eds.), *Multidisciplinary approaches to aggression research* (pp. 53–78). Amsterdam/New York/Oxford: Elsevier.

Brewin, C. R. (1989). Cognitive change processes in psychotherapy. *Psychological Review, 96,* 379–394.

Bushman, B., & Geen, R. (1990). Role of cognitive–emotional mediators and individual differences in the effects of media violence on aggression. *Journal of Personality and Social Psychology, 58,* 156–163.

Campos, J. J., Barrett, K. C., Lamb, M. E., Goldsmith, H. H., & Stenberg, C. (1983). Socioemotional development. In P. Mussen (Series Ed.) & M. Haith & J. Campos (Vol. Eds.), *Handbook of child psychology: Vol. 2. Infancy and developmental psychobiology* (4th ed.). New York: Wiley.

Carlsmith, J. M. & Anderson, C. A. (1979). Ambient temperature and the occurrence of collective violence: A new analysis. *Journal of Personality and Social Psychology, 37,* 337–344.

Cohen, A. R. (1955). Social norms, arbitrariness of frustration, and status of the agent of frustration in the frustration–aggression hypothesis. *Journal of Abnormal and Social Psychology, 51,* 222–226.

Cohen, B. H. (1986). The motor theory of voluntary thinking. In R. J. Davidson, G. E. Schwartz, & D. Shapiro (Eds.), *Consciousness and self-regulation* (Vol. 4, pp. 19–54). New York: Plenum.

Davidson, R. J., & Tomarken, A. J. (1989). Laterality and emotion: An electrophysiological approach. In F. Boller & J. Grafman (Eds.), *Handbook of neuropsychology* (Vol. 3, pp. 419–441). Amsterdam/New York/Oxford: Elsevier.

Davitz, J. R. (1952). The effects of previous training on postfrustration behavior. *Journal of Abnormal and Social Psychology, 47,* 309–315.

Diener, E., & Iran-Nejad, A. (1986). The relationship in experience between various types of affect. *Journal of Personality and Social Psychology, 50,* 1031–1038.

Dollard, J., Doob, L., Miller, N., Mowrer, O., & Sears, R. (1939). *Frustration and aggression.* New Haven, CN: Yale University Press.

Dovidio, J. F., & Morris, W. N. (1975). Effects of stress and commonality of fate on helping behavior. *Journal of Personality and Social Psychology, 31,* 145–149.

Ekman, P. (1991). A set of basic emotion families. *Psychological Review.*

Ekman, P., & Friesen, W. V. (1978). *The facial action coding system.* Palo Alto, CA: Consulting Psychologists.

Ekman, P., Levenson, R. W., & Friesen, W. V. (1983). Autonomic nervous system activity distinguishes among emotions. *Science, 221,* 1208–1210.

Feshbach, S. (1964). The function of aggression and the regulation of aggressive drive. *Psychological Review, 71,* 257–272.

Finman, R., & Berkowitz, L. (1989). Some factors influencing the effect of depressed mood on anger and overt hostility toward another. *Journal of Research in Personality, 23,* 70–84.

Fiske, S. T., & Taylor, S. E. (1991). *Social cognition.* New York: McGraw–Hill.

Forgas, J. P., & Bower, G. H. (1987). Mood effects on person perception. *Journal of Personality and Social Psychology, 53,* 53–60.

Frijda, N. H. (1986). *The emotions.* Cambridge/New York: Cambridge University Press.

Frijda, N. H., Kuipers, P., & ter Schure, E. (1989). Relations among emotion, appraisal, and emotional action readiness. *Journal of Personality and Social Psychology, 57,* 212–228.

Garcia, J., McGowan, B. K., Ervin, F., & Koelling, R. (1968). Cues: Their relative effectiveness as reinforcers. *Science, 160,* 795–795.

Green, R. G. (1968). Effects of frustration, attack, and prior training in aggressiveness upon aggressive behavior. *Journal of Personality and Social Psychology, 9,* 316–321.

Gilligan, S. G., & Bower, G. H. (1984). Cognitive consequences of emotional arousal. In C. E. Izard, J. Kagan, & R. B. Zajonc (Eds.), *Emotions, cognition, and behavior* (pp. 547–588). Cambridge/New York: Cambridge University Press.

Griffitt, W. (1970). Environmental effects on interpersonal affective behavior: Ambient effective temperature and attraction. *Journal of Personality and Social Psychology, 15,* 240–244.

Herr, P. M. (1986). Consequences of priming: Judgment and behavior. *Journal of Personality and Social Psychology, 51,* 1106–1115.

Higgins, E. T., & King, G. A. (1981). Accessibility of social constructs: Information-processing consequences of individual and contextual variability. In N. Cantor & J. F. Kihlstrom (Eds.), *Personality, cognition, and social interaction* (pp. 69–122). Hillsdale, NJ: Lawrence Erlbaum Associates.

Hutchinson, R. R. (1983) The pain–aggression relationship and its expression in naturalistic settings. *Aggressive Behavior, 9,* 229–242.

Hutchinson, R. R., Renfrew, J. W., & Young, G. A. (1971). Effects of long-term shock and associated stimuli on aggressive and manual responses. *Journal of the Experimental Analysis of Behavior, 15,* 141–166.

Hynan, D. J., & Grush, J. E. (1986). Effects of impulsivity, depression, provocation, and time on aggressive behavior. *Journal of Research in Personality, 20,* 158–171.

Isen, A. M. (1984). Toward understanding the role of affect in cognition. In R. S. Wyer, Jr., & T. K. Srull (Eds.), *Handbook of social cognition* (Vol. 3, pp. 179–236). Hillsdale, NJ: Lawrence Erlbaum Associates.

Isen, A. M., Shalker, T. E., Clark, M., & Karp, L. (1978). Affect, accessibility of material in memory, and behavior: A cognitive loop? *Journal of Personality and Social Psychology, 36,* 1–12.

Izard, C. E. (1990). Facial expressions and the regulation of emotions. *Journal of Personality and Social Psychology, 58,* 487–498.

James. W. (1890). *The principles of psychology.* New York: Holt.

Kenrick, D. T., & Johnson, G. A. (1979). Interpersonal attraction in aversive environments: A problem for the classical conditioning paradigm? *Journal of Personality and Social Psychology, 37,* 572–579.

Konecni, V. J. (1975). The mediation of aggressive behavior: Arousal level versus anger and cognitive labeling. *Journal of Personality and Social Psychology, 32,* 706–712.

Laird, J. D. (1974). Self-attribution of emotion: The effects of expressive behavior on the quality of emotional experience. *Journal of Personality and Social Psychology, 29,* 475–486.

Laird, J. D., Wagener, J. J., Halal, M., & Szegda, M. (1982). Remembering what you feel: Effects of emotion on memory. *Journal of Personality and Social Psychology, 42,* 646–657.

Lang, P. J. (1979). A bio-informational theory of emotional imagery. *Psychophysiology, 16,* 495–512.

Lang, P. J. (1984). Cognition in emotion: Concept and action. In C. E. Izard, J. Kagan, & R. B.

Zajonc (Eds.), *Emotions, cognition and behavior* (pp. 192–226). Cambridge/New York: Cambridge University Press.

Lazarus, R. (1984). On the primacy of cognition. *American Psychologist, 39*, 124–129.

Leventhal, H. (1980). Toward a comprehensive theory of emotion. In L. Berkowitz (Ed.), *Advances in experimental social psychology* (Vol. 13, pp. 139–207). New York: Academic Press.

Leventhal, H., & Tomarken, A. (1986). Emotion: Today's problems. *Annual Review of Psychology, 37*, 565–610.

Leyens, J. P., & Fraczek, A. (1983). Aggression as an interpersonal phenomenon. In H. Tajfel (Ed.), *The social dimension* (Vol. 1). Cambridge, UK: Cambridge University Press.

Maier, S. F., Anderson, C., & Lieberman, D. A. (1972). Influence of control of shock on subsequent shock-elicited aggression. *Journal of Comparative and Physiological Psychology, 81*, 94–100.

Martin, L. L., Seta, J. J., & Crelia, R. A. (1990). Assimilation and contrast as a function of people's willingness and ability to expend effort in forming an impression. *Journal of Personality and Social Psychology, 59*, 27–37.

Maslach, C. (1979). Negative emotional biasing of unexplained arousal. *Journal of Personality and Social Psychology, 37*, 953–969.

Miller, I., & Norman, W. (1979). Learned helplessness in humans: A review and attribution theory model. *Psychological Bulletin, 86*, 93–118.

Monteith, M., Berkowitz, L., Kruglanski, A., & Blair, C. (1991). *The influence of physical discomfort on experienced anger and anger-related ideas, judgments and memories.* Unpublished manuscript, University of Wisconsin, Madison.

Moore, B. S., & Isen, A. M. (1990). Affect and social behavior. In B. S. Moore & A. M. Isen (Eds.), *Affect and social behavior* (pp. 1–21). Cambridge/New York: Cambridge University Press.

Nisbett, R. E., & Wilson, T. D. (1977). Telling more than we can know: Verbal reports on mental processes. *Psychological Review, 84*, 231–259.

Norman, D. A., & Shallice, T. (1986). Attention to action: Willed and automatic control of behavior. In R. J. Davidson, G. E. Schwartz, & D. Shapiro (Eds.), *Conscious and self-regulation* (Vol. 4, pp. 1–18). New York: Plenum.

Ohman, A., & Dimberg, U. (1978). Facial expressions as conditioned stimuli for electrodermal responses: A case of "preparedness"? *Journal of Personality and Social Psychology, 36*, 1251–1258.

Parrott, W. G., & Sabini, J. (1990). Mood and memory under natural conditions: Evidence for mood incongruent recall. *Journal of Personality and Social Psychology, 59*, 321–336.

Pastore, N. (1952). The role of arbitrariness in the frustration–aggression hypothesis. *Journal of Abnormal and Social Psychology, 47*, 728–731.

Potegal, M. (1979). The reinforcing value of several types of aggressive behavior: A review. *Aggressive Behavior, 5*, 353–373.

Poznanski, E., & Zrull, J. P. (1970). Childhood depression: Clinical characteristics of overtly depressed children. *Archives of General Psychiatry, 23*, 8–15.

Reisenzein, R. (1983). The Schachter theory of emotion: Two decades later. *Psychological Bulletin, 94*, 239–264.

Rime', B., Philippot, P., & Cisamolo, D. (1990). Social schemata of peripheral changes in emotion. *Journal of Personality and Social Psychology, 59*, 38–49.

Riskind, J. H. (1983). Nonverbal expressions and the accessibility of life experience memories: A congruence hypothesis. *Social Cognition, 2*, 62–86.

Rosenblatt, P. C., Jackson, D. A., & Walsh, R. P. (1972). Coping with anger and aggression in mourning. *Omega: Journal of Death and Dying, 3*, 271–284.

Ross, L., & Nisbett, R. E. (1991). *The person and the situation: Perspectives of social psychology.* New York: McGraw Hill.

Rotton, J., Barry, T., Frey, J., & Soler, E. (1978). Air pollution and interpersonal attraction. *Journal of Applied Social Psychology, 8,* 57–71.

Rotton, J., & Frey, J. (1985). Air pollution, weather, and violent crime: Concomitant time-series analysis of archival data. *Journal of Personality and Social Psychology, 49,* 1207–1220.

Rotton, J., Frey, J., Barry, T., Milligan, M., & Fitzpatrick, M. (1979). The air pollution experience and physical aggression. *Journal of Applied Social Psychology, 9,* 397–412.

Rule, B. G., & Nesdale, A. (1974). Differing functions of aggression. *Journal of Personality, 42,* 467–481.

Rule, B. G., & Nesdale, A. (1976). Emotional arousal and aggressive behavior. *Psychological Bulletin, 83,* 851–863.

Schachter, S., & Singer, J. (1962). Cognitive, social, and physiological determinants of emotional state. *Psychological Review, 65,* 379–399.

Scherer, K. R., & Tannenbaum, P. H. (1986). Emotional experiences in everyday life: A survey approach. *Motivation and Emotion, 10,* 295–314.

Shaver, P., Schwartz, J., Kirson, D., & O'Connor, C. (1987). Emotion knowledge: Further exploration of a prototype approach. *Journal of Personality and Social Psychology, 52,* 1061–1086.

Smith, C. A., & Ellsworth, P. C. (1985). Patterns of cognitive appraisal in emotion. *Journal of Personality and Social Psychology, 48,* 813–838.

Stein, N. L., & Levine, L. J. (1989). The causal organization of emotional knowledge: A developmental study. *Cognition and Emotion, 3,* 343–378.

Taylor, S. E. (1983). Adjustment to threatening events: A theory of cognitive adaptation. *American Psychologist, 38,* 1161–1173.

Termine, N. T., & Izard, C. E. (1988). Infants' responses to their mothers' expressions of joy and sadness. *Developmental Psychology, 24,* 223–229.

Tomkins, S. S. (1962). *Affect, imagery, and consciousness.* New York: Springer.

Tomkins, S. S. (1981). The quest for primary motives: Biography and autobiography of an idea. *Journal of Personality and Social Psychology, 41,* 306–329.

Ucros, C. G. (1989). Mood state–dependent memory: A meta-analysis. *Cognition and Emotion, 3,* 139–167.

Ulrich, R. E. (1966). Pain as a cause of aggression. *American Zoologist, 6,* 643–662.

Ulrich, R. E., & Azrin, N. H. (1962). Reflexive fighting in response to aversive stimulation. *Journal of the Experimental Analysis of Behavior, 5,* 511–520.

Velten, E. (1968). A laboratory task for the induction of mood states. *Behavior Research and Therapy, 6,* 473–482.

Walters, R. H., & Brown, M. (1963). Studies of reinforcement of aggression. III. Transfer of response to an interpersonal situation. *Child Development, 34,* 563–571.

Wann, D. L., & Branscombe, N. R. (1990). Person perception when aggressive or nonaggressive sports are primed. *Aggressive Behavior, 16,* 27–32.

Weiner, B. (1982). The emotional consequences of causal ascriptions. In M. S. Clark & S. T. Fiske (Eds.), *Affect and cognition* (pp. 185–210). Hillsdale, NJ: Lawrence Erlbaum Associates.

Wickless, C., & Kirsch, I. (1988). Cognitive correlates of anger, anxiety, and sadness. *Cognitive Therapy and Research, 12,* 367–377.

Wyer, R. S., Jr., & Srull, T. K. (1981). Category accessibility: Some theoretical and empirical issues concerning the processing of social stimulus information. In E. T. Higgins, C. P. Herman, & M. P. Zanna (Eds.), *Social cognition: The Ontario Symposium* (Vol. 1, pp. 161–198). Hillsdale, NJ: Lawrence Erlbaum Associates.

Zajonc, R. B. (1980). Feeling and thinking: Preferences need no inferences. *American Psychologist, 35,* 151–175.

Zajonc, R. B., & Markus, H. (1984). Affect and cognition: The hard interface. In C. E. Izard, J.

Kagan, & R. B. Zajonc (Eds.), *Emotions, cognition, and behavior* (pp. 73–102). Cambridge/New York: Cambridge University Press.

Zillmann, D. (1979). *Hostility and aggression.* Hillsdale, NJ: Lawrence Erlbaum Associates.

Zillmann, D., Baron, R., & Tamborini, R. (1981). Social costs of smoking: Effects of tobacco smoke on hostile behavior. *Journal of Applied Social Psychology, 11,* 548–561.

Zillmann, D., Katcher, A., & Milavsky, B. (1972). Excitation transfer from physical exercize to subsequent aggressive behavior. *Journal of Experimental Social Psychology, 8,* 247–259.

2 Putting the Social in Social Cognition, With Special Reference to Emotion

James R. Averill
University of Massachusetts, Amherst

Since the publication of *Aggression: A Social Psychological Analysis* in 1962, few people have contributed more to our understanding of aggression than Leonard Berkowitz, both directly through his own research and indirectly by stimulating the research of others. It is, therefore, a privilege to comment on his latest formulation. In keeping with the spirit of this book, most of my comments are critical, although constructive, I hope.

SIC SEMPER TYRANNIS

It has become hackneyed to speak of the cognitive revolution in psychology, but that does not make the revolution any less real. Unfortunately, like many revolutions, this one has promised more than it can reasonably deliver. Worse, it is in danger of establishing a new orthodoxy, one as tyrannical as the old. Berkowitz does a service in pointing out some of the limitations of a strictly cognitive approach to emotion. In the process, however, he conflates some issues that I believe should be kept separate; more importantly, he does not go far enough in noting the limitations of current cognitive theories, especially with respect to the social bases of emotional behavior.

Berkowitz distinguishes between associationism, on the one hand, and cognition, on the other. He also divides theories of emotion into two broad categories, those that emphasize "automatic body and associative processes" and those that emphasize cognitive processes. He considers his own position to be a blend, but he places it closer to the former.

Rather than neoassociationistic, I believe Berkowitz's approach might better be termed *neobehavioristic,* for associationism is also a feature of many cognitive theories. This can be illustrated with reference to language, which most everyone would consider a paradigm of cognitive activity. Pinker (1991) demonstrated, rather convincingly, I believe, that regular verbs, such as walk–walked, are generated by a suffixation rule for grammatical processing, whereas irregular verbs, such as run–ran are generated by an associative mechanism. Pinker also argued that language is the product of both associative mechanisms and computational modules in which symbols are manipulated according to rules. A similar argument was made by Bechtel (1988) for cognition in general. A more extreme position, known as *connectionism,* assumes that all cognitive activity is ultimately associative.

Berkowitz's brand of associationism has its intellectual roots in Hullian behavior theory (Hull, 1943) and in the frustration–aggression hypothesis of Dollard, Doob, Miller, Nowrer, and Sears (1939). These authors were not, however, much interested in emotions per se, a lack that Berkowitz has done much to correct. With respect to the emotions, Berkowitz places his theory primarily within the James–Lange tradition, which can also be regarded as behavioristic in the broadest sense. To this mix, Berkowitz adds a variety of cognitions (ideas, memories, attributions, prototypic conceptions, and the like). But even these are not beyond the purview of traditional behaviorism. The behavior theory of Tolman (1948), for example, emphasized symbolic representations in rats as well as humans.

If not associationism, what distinguishes a cognitive from a behavioristic theory of emotion? The gist of an answer can be gleaned from Berkowitz's own analysis, with its emphasis on bodily processes. Ultimately, I believe, the distinction can be traced back to Descartes' contrast between the mental (*res cogitans*) and the physical (see Averill, 1974, 1990). Under the mental, Descartes included all conscious thought (images, ideas, judgments, etc.); under the physical, he included all bodily activity. The emotions, he believed, belong to the physical realm. Emotions could impress themselves on the mind, where they would be experienced as feelings; and, conversely, mental activity could influence the form and development of emotional responses—a view not unlike that of Berkowitz.

These observations are not meant as criticism of Berkowitz. Some distinction between cognitive and behavioristic approaches to the study of emotion is necessary and useful. To take a somewhat overworked and oversimplified analogy, the distinction Berkowitz draws is, if I understand him correctly, roughly equivalent to that between the software and hardware of a computer system. I would, in fact, go Berkowitz one step further. Not only must we distinguish between the software and hardware of a system, we much also distinguish between the software and the programmers responsible for its creation. In the case of emotional software, I would argue that the "programmers" are, collectively, society.

As indicated earlier, rules are often invoked by psychologists to explain cognitive processes. Rules in this sense can be likened to steps in a program that instruct a computer to perform certain operations on symbols (represented physically as states of the computer). But let me leave the computer analogy behind. My basic point is that the study of rules per se can be divorced almost completely from any concern with underlying cognitive processes. For example, a logician may be concerned with the rules of inference without regard to the cognitive processes that are involved when people reason logically. Similarly, a grammarian may be concerned with the rules of language without attempting to understand the cognitive processes involved in speech production. And, I would argue, we may profitably enquire about the rules of emotion without taking a stance with regard to underlying processes, whether associationistic or symbolic, behavioral or cognitive. What we cannot ignore is the origin of those rules in social practices.

RULES OF EMOTION

It is becoming increasingly common to treat emotions (anger, fear, love, etc.) as higher order entities created or constructed out of more elementary components. A central problem for any theory of emotion, then, is to clarify the principles according to which emotions are organized. Biological principles (information encoded in the genes) play a role; so, too, do psychological principles (the associative networks and symbolic representations discussed by Berkowitz). But except for very simple reactions such as sudden fright, I would argue that emotional syndromes are constituted according to social rules (see also Hochschild, 1983).

Three types of social rules can be distinguished: constitutive, regulative, and procedural (Averill, 1984, 1991). Strictly speaking, the distinction between these three types of rules does not represent a true trichotomy. Any given rule may have constitutive, regulative, and procedural aspects, albeit to varying degrees. For expository purposes, however, it is convenient to treat these three aspects as though they were separate classes of rules. Again, the domain of language can help illustrate the nature of this distinction. The rules of English grammar help *constitute* the language as English (as opposed to, say, Chinese or Russian). Other rules (e.g., "speak softly in a library") help *regulate* how we speak on any given occasion. Still other rules—*procedural* rules—help determine the quality of speech. Courses in rhetoric and elocution, for example, teach procedures for effective speech.

This is not to say that all aspects of a person's speech are determined by rules. I already noted the example of irregular verbs in English. Going further, it would surely be stretching things to invoke the notion of a rule to explain a person's accent. Similarly, some people habitually speak loudly, others speak softly; some people gesticulate while speaking, others hardly move a muscle. Many such idiosyncracies are undoubtedly acquired by associative learning.

Like languages, emotions are both constituted and regulated by rules, and they require appropriate heuristics for skilled performance. Thus, if a constitutive rule of anger is broken, the response will not be considered real anger, but perhaps some other kind of emotion (envy, for example, or, if the violation is sufficiently extreme, a neurotic syndrome); if a regulative rule is violated, the response may be recognized as anger, but it will be considered inappropriate or illegitimate; and if a procedural rule is broken, the response may be accepted as appropriate, but its expression deemed clumsy or inept.

Also, like languages (or, more accurately, verbal behavior) not all aspects of emotional expression are determined by rules. Emotions, too, have their equivalent of irregular verbs, and they can be expressed with varying accents and idiosyncracies. With the cognitive revolution, these aspects of emotion tended to be ignored. That is undoubtedly a mistake, as Berkowitz has forcefully argued.

In short, I agree with Berkowitz's conclusion that "any comprehensive analysis of emotion must be far-ranging and broad in scope." But whereas he extends the range primarily in the direction of bodily processes and "what is known about the neurophysiology of emotion," I also extend the range to social processes and what is known about the rules of emotion. That, at least, has been the primary focus of my own research. Among the specific emotions examined from this "social–constructionist" perspective are anger (Averill, 1982, 1983), love (Averill, 1985), fear (Averill, 1987), grief (Averill & Nunley, 1988), hope (Averill, Catlin, & Chon, 1990), and generalized stress reactions (Averill, 1989).

A CROSS-CULTURAL COMPARISON

As long as we remain within our own cultural context, it is difficult to appreciate the role that social rules play in the construction of emotional syndromes, especially an emotion so fundamental as anger. To have some basis for comparison, therefore, let us consider briefly an emotionally aggressive syndrome from another culture.

Imagine cutting off the head of another person, a stranger who had done you no wrong. The identity of the victim is of no great importance—a man, woman, child, anyone will do. What emotion would you feel? For a young Ilongot man, a member of a group of headhunters who inhabit a forested area in northern Luzon, the Philippines, the appropriate emotion is *liget*. Rosaldo (1980, 1984) glossed liget as *anger*, but sometimes also as *vital energy*, and *passion*, depending on the context. None of these translations is completely appropriate. Liget is a highly rewarding peak experience. The taking of a head is a way of establishing one's place as an equal member of society; and it is an occasion for celebration, not only for the successful headhunter, but for other members of his group as well.

I cite the example of liget for several reasons. First, it takes little reflection to realize that anger and liget are constituted according to very different rules. Liget can only be understood—and experienced—within its own cultural context. The same is true with respect to anger. Moreover, from Rosaldo's description, it is clear that liget is a highly emotional experience. The taking of heads is not simply an instrumental form of aggression (i.e., to gain recognition). It is that, but it is also an expression of a person's vital energy. And as an emotion, liget is as fundamental to Ilongot society as anger is to our own.

Liget is relevant to several other points that are central to Berkowitz's analysis, namely, the role of anger in the microgenesis of aggressive episodes, and the link between negative affect and aggression.

THE MICROGENESIS OF AGGRESSIVE EPISODES

Implicit in the discussion thus far is the need to distinguish anger as a socially constituted emotional syndrome from aggression as one possible manifestation of anger. By contrast, Berkowitz speaks of the anger/aggression syndrome, as though all emotionally based aggressive responses are a manifestation of anger. Berkowitz recognizes, of course, that not all episodes of anger eventuate in aggression; and conversely, that many emotional syndromes other than anger (envy, jealousy, etc.) can result in aggression.

One way that Berkowitz attempts to circumvent the loose and inconsistent relation between anger and aggression is by dividing the anger/aggression syndrome along a temporal dimension. According to Berkowitz's formulation, the initial response to pain is anger (or fear, depending on the circumstances); the initial anger may, however, be transformed by subsequent cognitive processes into a variety of different emotional and nonemotional responses. (I ignore here Berkowitz's generalization from pain to unpleasant affective experiences of all kinds, although I find the generalization highly questionable.)

The temporal unfolding of a response during the course of a given episode is known as microgenesis. It is tempting to draw analogies among microgenesis (episodic development), phylogenesis (evolutionary development), and ontogenesis (individual development). For example, the doctrine that "ontogeny recapitulates phylogeny" has its psychological counterpart in the common assumption that responses that appear first during individual development are also phylogenetically primitive. The assumption may sometimes be correct, but not always, and seldom without major qualification. Berkowitz, if I read him correctly, implicitly assumes that microgenesis in some fashion also recapitulates phylogenesis and/or ontogenesis. Thus, he speaks of the early stages in the development of an emotional episode as "primitive," and he regards the associative mechanisms that supposedly mediate these earlier stages as more primitive (phylogenetically and ontogenetically) than the cognitive mechanisms that characterize later stages. As far as I can tell, his arguments are largely analogical.

What kinds of evidence might bear on the hypothesis that the initial response to pain is anger, regardless of how that initial response is subsequently transformed? One could, perhaps, measure the immediate (micromomentary) facial expressions to a painful stimulus (Ekman, 1982). At best, the results of such a study would only demonstrate that the initial response to a painful stimulus is (given a suitable target) an aggressive impulse to remove the source of pain—a fact that is not in doubt, as discussed later. But why call the initial impulse *anger*, rather than some other emotion? And what differences does it make?

By calling the initial impulse anger, we impute to it many of the cultural connotations and assumptions that underlie our concept of anger. Even if we wanted to, we could not rid our concepts completely of their everyday meanings when we use them in specialized contexts—and we typically do not want to. There is a strategic value in the use of everyday concepts for theoretical purposes; it allows our theories easy application to problems of everyday concern. But the strategy is not without danger. A dialectical relation is established where the everyday meaning of a concept influences the nature of our theorizing, and the nature of our theorizing feeds back to influence our interpretation of the original concept. Thus, if we accept Berkowitz's microgenetic analysis of the anger/aggression syndrome, both our concepts of anger and of aggression undergo subtle change because of the close linkage forged between them: Anger becomes more aggressive than it often is; and aggression becomes more angry than it often is. Anger is an emotional syndrome in its own right, fashioned according to social rules, and serving a function within the social system; its relation to aggression is to be determined, not presumed (Averill, 1982, 1983).

To gain perspective on the above issue from a somewhat different angle, let us return for a moment to the Ilongot emotion of liget. Within Ilongot society, liget is as fundamental an emotion as anger is within our own; it can be stimulated by unpleasant events; and it provides the strength and courage to overcome obstacles. Hence, it would not be farfetched to postulate liget as the initial or primary response to pain or discomfort. However, liget can be manifested in a wide variety of ways, not all of which are aggressive, and even those that are aggressive (like the taking of heads) are not necessarily motivated by pain or discomfort. Among other things, male liget is implicated in both courtship and mating. Concentrated in the sperm, it helps make babies. It takes little imagination to realize that if we viewed liget as primary, rather than anger, we might develop a far different conception of emotional aggression than the one proposed by Berkowitz; alternatively (or concomitantly), if through our theorizing liget became linked too closely with pain-induced aggression, our everyday attitude toward, and behavior during, courtship and mating might also undergo change, with unforeseen consequences.

In the final analysis, no concept from ordinary language is going to be completely adequate to describe microprocesses that do not come directly to the attention of the verbal community. Thus, rather than describing the initial impulse to pain as anger (or liget, or any other emotion), we should stick with a more neutral description, such as *impulse to aggression,* and then ask: How does this impulse relate to anger? To do otherwise is to prejudge the question.

WHEN BAD COMES OUT OF GOOD

I now turn briefly to the contention that negative affect automatically activates components of the anger/aggression syndrome. There is ample evidence, as reviewed by Berkowitz, that aggression is an automatic response to pain, provided an attackable object is present and escape is not possible. This makes good biological sense. An animal that did not aggress against the source of pain would have little chance of survival. It is important to note, however, that aggression is not a unitary phenomenon, even among infrahuman animals. Moyer (1976), for example, distinguished among six different kinds of animal aggression, only one of which is directly related to pain or discomfort. Because of the intervention of social factors, the variety of aggression among humans is greater by far.

No doubt much human aggression is occasioned by pain and discomfort, and depending on the circumstances, some of that aggression could rightfully be described as angry. But there is also no doubt that much human (emotional) aggression is committed for reasons that have little or nothing to do with prior pain, no less with anger. The emotion of liget, illustrates the point. But we need not go across cultures for examples.

The ancient Romans relished in battle, and during times of peace, they had their circuses where gladiators fought to the death to the delight of the crowds. Elias (1978) noted that in medieval Europe "the pleasure in killing and torturing others was great, and it was a socially permitted pleasure" (p. 194). A martial song attributed to the late 12th-century troubadour, Bertran de Born, and quoted by Elias (1978), goes as follows:

I tell you that neither eating, drinking, nor sleep has as much savor for me as to hear the cry "Forwards!" from both sides, and horses without riders shying and whinnying, and the cry "Help! Help!", and to see the small and the great fall to the grass at the ditches and the dead pierced by the wood of the lances decked with banners. (p. 193)

We have, perhaps, become a little more civilized, or at least, more subtle in our enjoyment of aggression. Nevertheless, violence remains a common form of entertainment—in sports, in movies, and on television. Nor is all the violence vicarious. *Wilding,* in which packs of young men attack innocent bystanders for the fun of it, is but an extreme example of the gratuitous violence that plagues contemporary society.

In the conclusion to his chapter, Berkowitz addresses "those who want to believe that good comes out of bad." "Suffering," he notes, "is seldom ennobling." His warning should be well taken. However, we must also beware of converse belief, namely, that bad never comes out good. The bad in this case is unprovoked aggression, and the good is enjoyable emotional experience.

Morally, we are rightfully repelled by the idea that people might actually hurt one another for no good reason. Hurtful endings should have hurtful beginnings, we like to believe. When we come across examples of behavior that do not seem to fit this paradigm, we search for hidden causes. The aggressor must really have been in a state of pain—or else was suffering from some mental disorder. We thus turn the aggressor into a victim who, if not ennobled, is at least deserving of some compassion. That may be good morals, but I doubt that it is good psychology.

CONCLUDING OBSERVATIONS

Berkowitz presents his analysis of anger/aggression as a potential paradigm for the analysis of emotion in general. However, in spite of the many strengths of his analysis, and it has many, I do not believe it suffices as an adequate analysis of the many emotionally aggressive syndromes within our own culture (e.g., anger, jealousy, hatred, sadism, envy), no less the great variety of syndromes observed across cultures. The major failing is, I believe, one of omission rather than commission. For a social psychological analysis, Berkowitz is almost completely silent on the role of society in the formation of emotional syndromes. So, too, are most other social psychologists.

Berkowitz admonishes emotion researchers, especially those of a cognitive persuasion, "that there is far more in heaven and earth and even in the psychology of emotion than is dreamt of in their philosophy." The admonition applies with equal force, I believe, to Berkowitz's own cognitive–neoassociationistic perspective. Until we give due credit to the role of society in the construction of emotional syndromes, we will continue to view the emotions largely in terms of bodily reactions and lower (automatic) thought processes. But once we recognize that emotions are constituted as well as regulated by rules, we are free to dream of far more than traditional conceptions of emotion allow. Established rules can be broken, and new rules established. And in the process, familiar emotions can be transformed—fundamentally, not just superficially. Creativity applies as much to the emotions as to the intellect (Averill & Thomas-Knowles, 1991; Averill & Nunley, 1992).

ACKNOWLEDGMENT

Thanks are due George Levinger for helpful comments on an earlier version of this chapter.

REFERENCES

Averill, J. R. (1974). An analysis of psychophysiological symbolism and its influence on theories of emotion. *Journal for the Theory of Social Behavior, 4,* 147–190.

Averill, J. R. (1982). *Anger and aggression: An essay on emotion.* New York: Springer-Verlag.

Averill, J. R. (1983). Studies on anger and aggression: Implications for theories of emotion. *American Psychologist, 38,* 1145–1160.

Averill, J. R. (1984). The acquisition of emotions during adulthood. In C. Z. Malatesta & C. Izard (Eds.), *Affective processes in adult development* (pp. 23–43). Beverly Hills: Sage.

Averill, J. R. (1985). The social construction of emotion: With special reference to love. In K. Gergen & K. Davis (Eds.), *The social construction of the person* (pp. 89–109). New York: Springer-Verlag.

Averill, J. R. (1987). The role of emotion and psychological defense in self-protective behavior. In N. Weinstein (Ed.), *Taking care: Why people take precautions* (pp. 54–78). New York: Cambridge University Press.

Averill, J. R. (1989). Stress as fact and artifact: An inquiry into the social origins and functions of some stress reactions. In C. D. Spielberger, I. G. Sarason, & J. Strelau (Eds.), *Stress and anxiety* (Vol. 12, pp. 15–38). Washington, DC: Hemisphere.

Averill, J. R. (1990). Inner feelings, works of the flesh, the beast within, diseases of the mind, driving force, and putting on a show: Six metaphors of emotion and their theoretical extensions. In D. E. Leary (Ed.), *Metaphors in the history of psychology* (pp. 104–132). New York: Cambridge University Press.

Averill, J. R. (1991). Emotions as episodic dispositions, cognitive schemas, and transitory social roles: Steps toward an integrated theory of emotion. In D. Ozer, J. M. Healy, A. J. Stewart (Eds.), *Perspectives in personality* (Vol. 3a, pp. 137–165). London: Jessica Kingsly.

Averill, J. R., Catlin, G., & Chon, K. K. (1990). *Rules of hope.* New York: Springer-Verlag.

Averill, J. R., & Nunley, E. P. (1988). Grief as an emotion and as a disease. *Journal of Social Issues, 44,* 79–95.

Averill, J. R., & Nunley, E. P. (1992). *Voyages of the heart: Living an emotionally creative life.* New York: The Free Press.

Averill, J. R., & Thomas-Knowles, C. (1991). Emotional creativity. In K. T. Strongman (Ed.), *International review of studies on emotion* (Vol. 1, pp. 269–299). London: Wiley.

Bechtel, W. (1988). Connectionism and rules and representation systems: are they compatible? *Philosophical Psychology, 1,* 5–16.

Dollard, J., Doob, L., Miller, N. E., Mowrer, O., & Sears, R. (1939). *Frustration and aggression.* New Haven, CT: Yale University Press.

Ekman, P. (1982). *Emotion in the human face.* Cambridge: Cambridge University Press.

Elias, N. (1978). *The history of manners* (Vol. 1; E. Jephcott, Trans.). New York: Pantheon Books.

Hochschild, A. R. (1983). *The managed heart.* Berkeley: University of California Press.

Hull, C. L. (1943). *Principles of behavior.* New York: Appleton-Century-Crofts.

Moyer, K. E. (1976). *The psychology of aggression.* New York: Harper & Row.

Pinker, S. (1991). Rules of language. *Science, 253,* 530–535.

Rosaldo, M. Z. (1980). *Knowledge and passion: Ilongot notions of self and social life.* Cambridge: Cambridge University Press.

Rosaldo, M. Z. (1984). Toward an anthropology of self and feelings. In R. A. Schweder & R. A. LeVine (Eds.), *Culture theory: Essays on mind, self, and emotion* (pp. 137–157). Cambridge: Cambridge University Press.

Tolman, E. (1948). Cognitive maps in rats and men. *Psychological Review, 55,* 189–209.

3 Where Does Anger Dwell?

Gerald L. Clore
University of Illinois at Urbana-Champaign

Andrew Ortony
Northwestern University

Bruce Dienes
Frank Fujita
University of Illinois at Urbana-Champaign

Unlike detective novels, where the last chapter provides unambiguous evidence about the truth of all hypotheses, scientific mysteries sometimes remain unsolved. The problem often lies not so much in figuring out whether the butler did it as it does in reaching agreement about what a butler is. That is to say, many seemingly empirical issues turn out to be nonempirical matters of definition. The problem cannot be solved simply by insisting on defining one's terms, because explicit definitions presuppose a developed theory. Nevertheless, some sort of implicit definition presumably underlies any claim about a phenomenon. In the study of emotion too, explicit definitions are more likely to be an outcome than a starting point. Our focus, then, is not on defining terms explicitly but on exploring the issues raised by a comparison of the definitions of anger implicit in the model proposed by Berkowitz (this volume) and in an alternative cognitive model we propose.

As an overview, some of the themes that emerge from comparing a cognitive view with Berkowitz's cognitive–neoassociationistic view can be summarized. According to Berkowitz, anger has a special status as a very basic emotion, one that is likely to occur as a reaction to any negative experience. He suggests that "people who are feeling bad, whatever the reason . . . are theoretically apt to feel angry, have hostile thoughts, and be disposed to attack a suitable available target" (p. 10). He suggests that although anger can be mediated by a cognitive analysis, "there is a built-in association between negative affect and the anger/aggression syndrome" (p. 10). Part of our agenda is to explain this association in other than *built-in* terms.

We emphasize the role of cognition in emotional processing, both as an essential input and as a critical output of emotion. In contrast, Berkowitz focuses more on the role of minimally analyzed stimulus input and direct behavioral output. Anger and aggressive tendencies are hypothesized to be directly triggered by any unpleasantness and by certain peripheral cues (e.g., muscle contractions from angry expressions). Berkowitz approaches anger from the standpoint of research on aggression, and he focuses on anger as a primitive reaction that occurs in organisms as low as rats. He believes that cognitive processes play a role but are not essential in the elicitation of emotion. According to Berkowitz, cognition plays a role in the inhibition of emotions that are socially inappropriate, the construction of complex emotions, and the labeling of bodily reactions as emotions. We concur in the view that emotion involves a syndrome of reactions, including cognitive, experiential, and motivational components. But we do not see behavior as a central component of this syndrome. We attempt to distinguish emotion from the symptoms of emotion, reserving the term *emotion* for instances in which these reactions follow an appraisal or evaluation of a situation.

The current chapter is organized into three main parts. In the first part, implicit definitions within the two approaches for such key terms as *cognition, attribution, emotion,* and *anger* are compared. In the second part, a cognitive account of anger is outlined that incorporates work on both the cognitive causes of emotion (Ortony, Clore, & Collins, 1988) and on the cognitive consequences of emotion (Clore, 1992; Schwarz & Clore, 1983, 1988). Finally, in the third part, this cognitive account is applied to some of the interesting phenomena presented by Berkowitz. This chapter is divided, then, into three major parts, including sections on implicit definitions of concepts, theory and research, and applications.

FOUR IMPORTANT CONCEPTS

Where one ends up in the study of emotion depends on where one starts, and where one starts is with implicit definitions of the relevant concepts. In this first section, we discuss some of these, including the concepts of *cognition, attribution, emotion,* and *anger*. In brief the argument is as follows:

1. Some disagreements about the centrality of cognition in emotion can be resolved by adopting a view of cognition, in which cognition encompasses all mental computational activity, not simply conscious, rational, or intentional thought.

2. In a similar vein, we argue that attribution is not restricted to deliberative conclusions. Causal attributions may be utterly implicit in one's perception of an event and need not involve explicit or conscious inferences at all.

3. A common assumption is that the essence of emotion lies in the physiology, phenomenology, or behavior of emotion. We suggest that these are constituents of emotion only when they are tied to (possibly unconscious) cognitive appraisals of situations as personally significant.

4. If one specifies emotions in terms of the cognitive conditions of their occurrence, anger appears distinct from several related states, including frustration, resentment, and reproach (cf. Ortony et al., 1988). The distinction between frustration and anger is particularly important for the current discussion, as described in the section on the cognitive structure of emotions.

Cognition

Berkowitz views emotion in general, and anger in particular, as primitive reactions. The role of cognitive processes is to help us inhibit emotion in the service of civilized behavior, and to help us rationalize emotion so that we can manage our animal instincts in a complex social order. This is compatible with the view of the enlightenment philosophers, of Freud, and contemporary folk psychology. We all find comfortable and familiar the notion that cognition and emotion are at odds, that emotion sometimes overpowers cognition, and that growing up (both developmentally and phylogenetically) consists in part of learning to channel, control, and inhibit primitive impulses.

All of this is partially true, of course, but only partially. We argue that emotion is also a servant of cognition. This is true despite the fact that emotions make our knees knock, put butterflies in our stomach, and produce other bodily manifestations; despite the fact that emotions sometimes make us irrational, that we cannot control them, and that we can be surprised by them. The primary input and some of the primary output of emotional processing is cognitive. At input, what one feels depends on what one perceives the situation to be (cf. Ortony et al., 1988), and at output, emotions affect cognitive processing strategies (e.g., Schwarz, 1990) and judgment (e.g., Schwarz & Clore, 1983). The effects on behavior, we argue, are probably indirect, stemming from changes in goals.

Some investigators reject a cognitive approach to emotion because of an implicit belief that cognition is necessarily conscious, rational, intentional, deliberative, or all of these things. Berkowitz, for example, characterizes cognitive processes as involving "complicated thoughts" (p. 10), and he sees cognition as playing a role late in the emotion process, only after an emotion has been triggered. As he says, "After the initial reactions, as these people think about what has happened, cognitive processes quickly come into play" (p. 12). No doubt this happens sometimes, but this may be too restrictive a view of cognitive processes. In their book on unintended thought, Bargh and Uleman (1989) traced some of the paradoxes inherent in cognitive processes that are forcing theorists to take a more complex view. The act of reading, for example, is intentional, but it relies on the uncontrolled and unconscious activation of word meanings, and the most effective judgment and decision making often involves the use of seemingly irrational heuristics. These and similar observations require a model of cognitive processes that is not limited to conscious, rational, intentional, or deliberative mechanisms.

Particularly problematic in Berkowitz's proposal is that the fact that the model of cognitive processes is drawn from Schachter and Singer (1962). Their work is cited as representative of cognitive approaches to emotion, but, despite its historical importance, few investigators today see Schachter and Singer's view as viable. Indeed, as it is usually understood, their theory relegates the role of cognition to the process of arriving at labels for one's emotional reactions. In contrast, more contemporary cognitive theories assume a wide array of computational and information-processing activities. Although they may be influenced by conscious processing goals or intentions, such cognitive processes are generally unavailable for conscious inspection. It is true that people sometimes experience emotions as being visited upon them, feel seized by their emotions, and even feel puzzled or surprised by them. But none of these observations is incompatible with a cognitive analysis. What Mandler (1984) referred to as the *meaning analysis* involved in appraising events is fully cognitive even when there is no conscious deliberation involved.

Attribution

Berkowitz cites a variety of kinds of data to try to show that emotion in general and anger in particular are not based on attributions. In doing so he is arguing against Schachter and Singer, whose cognitive theory rested on attributions, and he is arguing against social psychologists who focus on the importance of attributions of intention as a variable in anger. With respect to these targets, we suggest simply the acceptance of a cognitive approach to emotion is in no way contingent on the fate of Schachter and Singer's (1962) theory, and that although social psychologists studying anger have often focused on attributions of intent, it is not common to believe perceptions of intent to be a prerequisite for anger.

But, as becomes apparent later, we do see attributional processes as important to this discussion in two ways. First, we argue that perceptions of blameworthiness (attributions of blame) are an important element in an emotion that we call *anger,* but that they are not important in another angerlike emotion that we call *frustration.* From this view, many of the observations Berkowitz makes about anger are better thought of as observations about frustration. Second, attributions are also important in explaining how certain peripheral muscular or sensory cues can cause anger. In these cases, however, the attributions concern subjects' perceptions of the cause of their own affective experience.

Berkowitz's objection to attribution as a factor in emotion is based on a widely shared belief that the attribution process involves deliberation. We should make clear, therefore, that our own view is intended to be compatible with Heider's (1958) original gestalt view of attributions. He believed that causal attributions are an inherent part of our perception of behavior. His point was not that we sit and think, "I wonder what caused my behavior?" Rather, our understanding of what we experience necessarily rests on implicit assumptions about causes. When one billiard ball contacts a second and the second starts rolling immediately, we perceive that the first ball caused the second to move. If we see a group of three sticks on one side of a space and a group of four sticks on the other, we will inevitably see each stick as belonging to one group or the other. Our perception of causation often involves similarly tacit knowledge—a perception of causal belongingness.

Like cognitive processes in general, causal attributions exist on a continuum from those requiring extended deliberation (e.g., an art historian attributing the Mona Lisa to Leonardo) to those that are instantaneous and automatic (e.g., a baseball fan attributing the crack of the bat and the sight of a ball sailing into left field to the action of the batter). Heider was more concerned with the latter than the former. He was interested in the causal assumptions implicit in momentary perception. Thus, causal attributions do not necessarily require time to be made, nor conscious consideration. As a result, experimental observations of the kind cited by Berkowitz about how quickly judgments or responses are made and whether or not subjects report that they have made attributions have no bearing on whether an emotion does or does not involve attributions.

Emotion

Because of their visceral and autonomic components, emotions are often thought of as essentially bodily or biological phenomena. Emotions are bodily or biological, of course, in the sense that everything about living systems is rooted in the biology of those systems. But analyses of the language of emotions show a clear distinction between terms referring to bodily states (e.g., tired, hungry, in pain, aroused) and those referring to emotions (fearful, angry, jealous, happy). The emotions to which these terms refer have important bodily concomitants, of course, but the terms are seen as referring to mental rather than to bodily states (Clore, Ortony, & Foss, 1987; Ortony, Clore, & Foss, 1987). These lexical studies suggest that *good examples of emotion terms refer to internal mental states that are focused on affect.* Affect in this usage refers simply to evaluation; to the perceived goodness or badness of something. Poorer examples may refer to external states (e.g., abandoned), bodily states (e.g., energetic), or nonstates (e.g., moody). Sometimes poor examples do refer to internal mental states but have a primary focus on behaving (e.g., bellicose) or knowing (e.g., confused) rather than on affect. Thus, although recognizing the bodily components of anger, our own approach focuses on anger as a particular kind of mental state.

From this view, mental activity is an essential element in emotions. Emotional experience is a way of communicating this mental state internally, just as emotional expressions communicate it externally. An implication of this general view is that it will be useful to distinguish between emotion and sham emotion. The term *emotion* is reserved for instances in which the characteristic physiology, feelings, and behavior of emotion is a reaction to an appraisal or evaluation rather than arising from other causes. We argue that cognitive appraisals are a necessary condition, because they are basic to what we mean when we refer to emotion.

To such assertions, one might argue that there are other sources of emotion that do not depend on cognitive appraisals—sources such as sweet tastes and physical pain. Surely the avoidance of pain and the approach to pleasure do not require cognitive appraisals? True enough, but none of these—pleasure, pain, approach, or avoidance—are emotions. An emotion in this instance would refer to being pleased or displeased at the experience of physical pleasure or pain, rather than to the pleasure or pain itself.

There are, of course, other possible approaches to defining emotion. One could define emotions in terms of mechanisms in the nervous system as Gray (1971) has done, in terms of distinctive feeling states as Johnson-Laird and Oatley (1989) have done, or in terms of responses as Berkowitz seems to prefer. We argue, however, that emotion does not refer to physiology, feelings, or behaviors per se, but to physiology, feelings, and behaviors that are triggered by appropriate cognitive analyses.

Like diseases, emotions involve particular physical and experiential symptoms. Using the concept of disease to refer to these symptoms, however, is appropriate only if the symptoms are assumed to have a particular kind of cause. In the case of emotions also, the valid use of the concept depends on the physiology, feeling, or behavior having an emotional cause. A patient who complains of a distressing tightening in the chest, for example, is experiencing an emotional panic reaction only if the feeling is caused by fearful preoccupations, not if his or her symptoms are caused by a heart attack.

Although it is popular to take a prototype view of emotion terms (e.g., Russell, 1991), we argue that emotions themselves have necessary components, and that the components that are necessitated are causal in nature (Clore & Ortony, 1991; Ortony & Clore, 1989). Several things follow from this analysis. One of these concerns the status of evidence that peripheral cues can cause emotions, and a second concerns the status of evidence from lower animals in emotion research.

Peripheral Cues.   In support of the view that emotion does not require a cognitive trigger, Berkowitz cites evidence from studies of posed facial expressions and other studies suggesting the possibility of peripheral routes to emotion. Simply contracting the facial muscles involved in a smile, for example, was shown to make cartoons seem funnier (Strack, Martin, & Stepper, 1988).

These are intriguing findings that require explanation. But rather than challenge a cognitive view, they illustrate the circular pattern of the processes involved in emotion.

Ordinarily, emotions are triggered by cognitive appraisals that something is positive or negative for one's concerns. These appraisals activate distinctive physiology, feelings, thoughts, and expressions. Feedback from these cues then provides information and motivation, which direct attention to relevant stimuli, elicit certain goals, and so on. The newly directed attention and the newly activated goals may generate further appraisals that produce further effects on physiology, feelings, and thoughts. These reactions may modulate the same emotion or trigger other emotions. Apparently, one can enter the system at any point, manipulating expression or physiology or feeling directly and thereby cause the rest of the emotional chain to fire. In this way, emotions can be intensified or even initiated by peripheral activity such as posing expressions, engaging in emotional behavior (as an actor might), or conceivably through direct electrical or chemical stimulation of the relevant neurophysiology.

These facts in no way invalidate the proposal that emotions have cognitive causes. Emotion involves a fully integrated system, in which peripheral cues such as feedback from feelings or expressions can become the stimulus for further cognitive appraisal that triggers an emotion. But, in the absence of a relevant cognitive focus, subjects are likely to say, "I feel like I am angry," rather than "I am angry," because anger implies an object. The inadequacy of an analysis of emotion based on symptoms alone can be seen by comparing the feeling of anger with the feeling of a headache (Ortony & Clore, 1989). A headache is nothing more than a feeling. One would never say, "I feel as though I have a headache." If one feels a headache, one has a headache, and that is the end of it. On the other hand, it would be perfectly sensible to say, "I feel *as though* I am angry," because we all understand that anger is more than a feeling, it is a feeling based on a particular kind of cause.

So, can one have an emotion without a cognitive appraisal? We prefer to say that one can have an emotional expression, engage in emotional behavior, feel emotional feelings, or think emotional thoughts, but that these constitute emotions only when they are reactions to the cognitive representation of something as good or bad. Rather than provide evidence that appraisals are unnecessary for emotion, the ability of peripheral cues to trigger emotional appraisals appears to testify to the strength of the usual link between emotional appraisals and peripheral symptoms of such appraisals.

The Status of Data From Rats.   We have argued that whether one accepts Berkowitz's or our own analysis depends in part on whether one shares the implicit definitions of the relevant concepts. Berkowitz approaches the study of emotion from his prior interest in aggressive behavior, and perhaps for this reason, implicitly defines emotion in behavioral rather than information–processing terms. By focusing on behavior, Berkowitz draws inferences about emotion from the behavior of animals as low as rats. Because rats behave aggressively, and because some of the same kinds of physiology are involved when any mammal aggresses, it is assumed that the same principles that govern human aggression can also be found in rat aggression. In addition to studies of animal aggression, Berkowitz also cites instances of aggression triggered by experimental inductions of sadness, instances in which riots are triggered by hot weather, and instances in which depressed mothers beat their children. These are, indeed, all examples of anger according to Berkowitz, because they involve aggressive behavior. From our own view, however, these may or may not involve anger, the key being whether the behavior arises from relevant cognitive eliciting conditions. Pet hamsters, for example, often kill and eat their young, a response that in humans would certainly be classified as aggressive. But does their behavior say anything about anger? We assume not, in part because this behavior presumably has other motivational bases. However extreme, behavior by itself is not an infallible index of emotion.

The series of experiments reported in the 1960s by Bandura and Walters (1963) on aggression illustrates the problems of overreliance on behavior as an index of emotion. The studies generally focused on children hitting large inflated toys called Bobo dolls. The goal of these behavioristic studies was to undermine the idea that explaining aggression required either a special aggressive motivation, as posited by Freud, or a special process like the frustration–aggression hypothesis. Aggression was seen as a class of behavior, and like any other class of behavior its occurrence was governed by its consequences, by rewards and punishments. Experiments in which laughing children hit Bobo dolls for fun were used to make inferences about the problem of aggression and violence in society. However ingenious the experiments, and they were ingenious, and however correct some of the conclusions turned out to be, the fact of the matter is that one simply could not get to where Bandura and Walters wanted to go from the experiments they did. Why?—because aggression cannot be defined as a class of motor behavior. We all understand that hitting behavior is relevant to anger only when it has the right cognitive constituents. Berkowitz implicitly argues that the necessary component of anger is some sort of behavior or inclination to behavior. In the next section we argue, on the contrary, that the necessary components are the causal ones.

Anger

The wide range of events generally lumped together in the *anger* category may be less homogeneous than is implied by this single label. If one differentiates emotions on the basis of their cognitive eliciting conditions, for example, anger appears to be distinct from other emotional states, more aptly referred to by such terms as *frustration, reproach,* and *resentment.* In fact, many of the characteristics ascribed to anger by Berkowitz are, in our view, characteristics of frustration, a simpler state requiring only that some goal be thwarted.

Berkowitz proposes that any negative affect tends to produce anger. The plausibility of this assertion depends in part on how loosely one defines anger. The broader the notion of anger, the more correct the assertion seems. Suppose, for example, that one were to substitute a term that clearly encompasses more than one emotion, a term such as *upset*. The proposal that any negative affect tends to produce upset seem clearly acceptable, because everyone agrees that upset covers a large number of distinct states, including fear, anger, disappointment, frustration, and so on. Similarly, if one substitutes anger back into the assertion but interprets anger in a similarly broad way as a label for a family of more specific emotional states, then the statement is also acceptable. Although the term *anger* is not quite as broad as *upset*, it is, in our view, similarly divisible into specific states with different causes and effects. Moreover, the more facets of emotion one considers, we suggest, the more different the various anger-like states may become. If one calls such states as frustration, being indignant, feeling resentful, and other similarly diverse states, all anger, then the hypothesis appears more correct. But if we distinguish among kinds of anger, the proposal loses power. The degree to which Berkowitz's proposal is seen as radical and controversial may depend, therefore, on whether one takes the term *anger* in a more or a less restrictive sense.

Berkowitz also suggests that what is activated by negative affect may not be anger and aggression per se, but elements of anger and aggression. As it happens, our own view makes the same claim, although for different reasons, as described in the next section. The next section has two parts. First, we summarize a theory that focuses on the cognitive conditions for specific emotions. In this view, emotions have a predominantly hierarchical structure, which means that the elicitation conditions for some emotions include some of the eliciting information for other emotions. Hence, the activation of an emotion located on one branch of the hierarchy increases the likelihood of other emotions along the same branch being triggered. Second, when characterized in terms of these conditions, anger turns out to be different from some other emotional states that Berkowitz's analysis lumps together. These include frustration, resentment, reproach, and anger.

THE COGNITIVE STRUCTURE OF EMOTIONS: THEORY AND RESEARCH

Ortony, Clore, and Collins (1988) proposed an account of the cognitive structure of emotion that takes a very different starting point than the work of Berkowitz. This theory (hereinafter referred to as the OCC account) is congenial to, but different from, that of a number of other cognitively oriented emotion theories (e.g., Abelson, 1983; Mandler, 1984; Roseman, 1984; Scherer, 1984; Smith & Ellsworth, 1985; Weiner, 1985). The goal of the work has been to investigate the cognitive causes of emotions and the relationships among different emotions in terms of those causes.

The theory proposes three broad classes of emotions. Each class is distinguished in terms of the focus that it involves. According to the theory, one can focus either on events, actions, or objects. All emotions involve some kind of affective (i.e., positive or negative) reaction, and the nature of these reactions differs depending on one's cognitive focus.

A major aim of the theory is to use a consistent set of terms in a clear and precise way. To do this, some terms take on specialized meanings. For example, *being pleased/displeased, approving/disapproving,* and *liking/disliking,* are used to refer to three kinds of affective reactions. And *desirable/undesirable outcomes, praiseworthy/blameworthy actions,* and *appealing/unappealing attributes,* are used to refer to the three kinds of appraisals. Thus, there are several possible paths to an emotion. One can have the affective reaction of being pleased when outcomes are appraised as desirable, or one can have the affective reaction of approving of actions one has appraised as praiseworthy, or one can have the affective reaction of liking (the attributes of) objects that one finds appealing.

These three kinds of appraisals—desirability, praise/blameworthiness, and appealingness—are in turn made with respect to three different kinds of cognitive structures—*goals, standards,* and *attitudes (or tastes).* Thus, according to the OCC account (Ortony et al., 1988) all emotions are differentiated forms of one of three affective reactions—*being pleased at the outcome of events appraised as desirable with respect to one's goals, approving of the action of agents appraised as praiseworthy with respect to one's standards,* and *liking the attributes of objects appraised as appealing with respect to one's tastes or attitudes.*

To communicate the dependence of specific emotions on one's cognitive focus, Fig. 3.1 distinguishes between event-based emotions (involving reactions of being pleased at the desirability of events or displeased at their undesirability), agent-based emotions (reactions of approval toward the praiseworthy actions of agents or disapproval of blameworthy actions), and object-based emotions (reactions of liking appealing objects or disliking unappealing ones). In this context, "liking" and "disliking" are used in the momentary sense of experiencing a feeling of liking or disliking rather than in the dispositional sense of having an attitude toward something. We should emphasize that Fig. 3.1 is intended to emphasize a logical and not a temporal structure.

Specific emotions are differentiated forms of these affective reactions. For example, fear is a differentiated form of being displeased. The formal specification of fear in this system is "being displeased at the prospect of an undesirable event". To see what this means in the context of Fig. 3.1, follow the event-based

ORTONY, CLORE, AND COLLINS' TYPOLOGY OF EMOTIONS

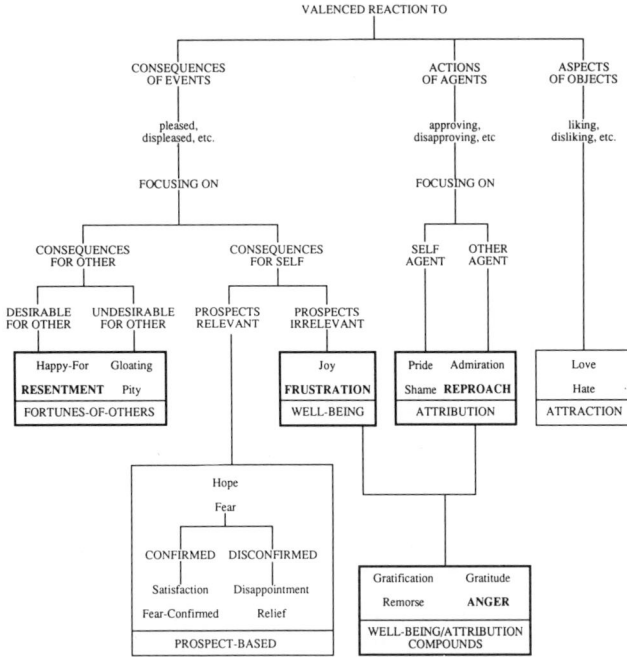

FIG. 3.1.   The OCC Account: Twenty-two emotion types arranged in six groups on the basis of their cognitive eliciting conditions. The three major arms of the structure correspond to a focus of attention on events, actions, or objects. From Ortony et al. (1988).

branch. Assume one is focusing on the consequences for self (rather than for another), on the prospect of an event happening (rather than on an event that has definitely occurred), and on the possible outcomes that are undesirable (rather than desirable). When these cognitive conditions exist, then the resulting affective reaction is a kind of fear emotion.

Figure 3.1 gives the eliciting conditions for 22 such emotion types. The emotions that share common eliciting conditions form groups (fortunes-of-others emotions, well-being emotions, prospect emotions, attribution emotions, attraction emotions, well-being–attribution compounds). It is not assumed that there are only 22 emotions. Presumably the number of emotions that can be distinguished on some basis is large. Indeed, even these 22 emotion types encompass many, emotion tokens—terms denoting specific states within the same type. The states denoted by these tokens may differ in any number of ways from others in the same type, but they all share the same general eliciting conditions.

Consider the well-being emotions in this regard. This is a particularly large category, because it includes all states in which one focuses on events and is displeased at the undesirable outcomes for oneself. One might well find meaningful subtypes within this category, but many of them differ from each other mainly in the specific goal that is involved. For example, one can grieve (be distressed at the loss of a loved one), be lonesome (distressed at being alone), be homesick (distressed at not being home), or be lovesick (distressed at not being with a lover). Some may involve seemingly irrevocable losses, as in sadness, some may involve the interruption of subgoals on the way toward a larger goal, as in frustration. These different emotions may have different implications, but all share the same kind of eliciting conditions and hence are all considered for the present purposes as examples of one emotion type. In Fig. 3.1, we have labeled this emotion *frustration*.

Frustration, Resentment, Reproach, Anger

There are at least two distinct accounts that can be given of anger emotions. One, the prototype view, argues that all anger emotions are related by family resemblance and involve greater or lesser approximations to *prototypical* anger. The other view, the *distinct emotion* view, argues that the word anger is used to refer to more than one distinct emotion. The OCC theory (Ortony et al., 1988) maintains that there are four different angerlike emotions. These include frustration emotions (involving undesirable outcomes), resentment emotions (involving the outcomes received by others), reproach emotions (involving the attribution of blame), and anger emotions (involving both undesirable outcomes and blame).

Berkowitz would classify all of these simply as anger. But as shown in Fig. 3.1, these can be differentiated in terms of their eliciting conditions. Frustration and resentment are ways of being *displeased at outcomes* deemed undesirable. In Fig. 3.1, frustration is located within the well-being group. The formal specification of frustration is *being displeased at an undesirable event*. Resentment falls within the fortunes-of-others emotions. The formal specification of resentment is, *being displeased at an event presumed to be desirable for another*. Other emotion types within the fortunes-of-others groups include gloating and pity. These are emotions triggered by focusing on the outcomes for others, and the nature of the reaction depends on one's orientation toward the other (e.g., disliking them or seeing them as undeserving). If one sees another person's good fortune as undeserved, for example, the negative reaction to their good fortune might be termed *resentment*.

Reproach and anger differ from frustration and resentment because they include a different kind of affective reaction—disapproval of an action. The center branch of the structure shown in Fig. 3.1 represents emotions based on the affective reaction of approving or disapproving of the praiseworthy or blameworthy actions of an agent. The formal specification of reproach is, *disapproving of someone else's blameworthy action.* Other emotions in the attribution group depend on one's focus. If one focuses on one's own actions, emotions within the pride and shame types are likely; if one focuses on the actions of others, emotions within the admiration and reproach types are likely. Collectively, these are called the attribution emotions. Thus, when one disapproves of the actions of another on the basis of a perception that their behavior falls short of applicable standards, one may feel indignant, outraged, incensed, or experience reproach toward the agent.

But, if the emotional person is focusing not only on the blameworthiness of the actions of another person, but also on the undesirability of outcomes, then their emotion falls into the anger type, within what we have referred to as the well-being–attribution compounds. The formal specification of anger is, *disapproving of someone else's blameworthy action and being displeased about the related undesirable event.* A focus on blameworthy actions and undesirable outcomes differentiates anger both from frustration (a focus on undesirable outcomes) and from reproach (a focus on blameworthy action). One implication of the hierarchical nature of the emotions is that the intensity of anger should be influenced by whatever influences the intensity of frustration and of reproach. Thus, one gets more angry the more undesirable the outcome and more blameworthy the action. But when focusing merely on the undesirability of outcomes for one's goals, without agency being an issue, one is likely to say "I am frustrated," but not necessarily "I am angry." Conversely, if outcomes are not an issue, but someone did something they shouldn't have done, one feels reproach toward them, but not frustrated or angry (unless having them refrain from blameworthy behavior is a goal, as it might be for the person's parent for example).

Other emotion types in the well-being–attribution compounds include emotions such as gratification, gratitude, remorse, as well as anger. All arise from simultaneously focusing on both the action of an agent and the resulting event and its consequences. We call them compounds because they involve more than the mere co-occurrence of their corresponding constituent emotions. Anger, for example, is not simply the co-occurrence of reproach toward the action of an agent and frustration at a resulting undesirable outcome. It is a unified emotion in which the constituents need not necessarily be independently experienced.

Figure 3.1 captures only one of the several possible facets of the structure of emotions, albeit one of the most important. Structures could also be sought in terms of how emotions feel, what social implications they involve, the order of their developmental or phylogenetic emergence, or in terms of their neurochemistry, their neuroanatomy, and so on. Whether these maps would look similar to the one based on cognitive eliciting conditions is unclear. Russell's (1980) work on the structure of emotional feelings, for example, gives a different picture of the relations among emotions, drawn on a dimensional rather than a categorical basis. Thus, it is probably not reasonable to imagine a number of different maps fitting together in some elegant polyhedron that captures all facets of emotion in one representation.

Research

One of our current research projects involves exploring several angerlike emotions that are distinguishable from each other in terms of their eliciting conditions and the conditions that make them intense or mild. These emotions include frustration, resentment, reproach, and anger, all of which can have angerlike qualities, but which our analysis suggests belong to different families of emotions. Such emotions are of interest in their own right, but they are particularly interesting in the context of the theory because they constitute powerful test cases of its scope and limits. The formal specifications, eliciting conditions, intensity variables, and examples of each are summarized in Table 3.1.

Native speakers of English might use anger or upset to encompass all of these, but we argue that it is useful to distinguish among them. Just as the term *upset* covers many emotions that are intuitively discriminable (grieving, ashamed, anger, etc.), so the term *anger* is used to refer to a number of discriminable states—discriminable in terms of their eliciting conditions and perhaps other aspects as well. In an attempt to be systematic about our terminology, we have reserved the term *anger* for one of these emotions and have tried to distinguish between this sense of anger and other angerlike states.

We are exploring the differences among these emotions in terms of three aspects—input (eliciting conditions), throughput (phenomenal quality, including awareness of bodily reactions, thoughts, feelings), and output (desires and actions). On the input side, the question is whether these states share sufficiently common eliciting conditions to warrant their coclassification, or whether distinct groups of eliciting conditions are associated with each. Similar questions will be asked for the throughput side (feelings, thoughts, and bodily reactions) and the output side (desire and behavior). It is possible that separable clusters of anger emotions will be found in none, some, or all of these facets.

This research is in progress. A sample of university students has been asked to report instances of one of the four angerlike states—frustration, reproach, resentment, and anger. They were assigned specific emotions and carried forms with them during the day so they could fill them out during or as soon as possible after experiencing the relevant emotion. Since many of the items involve reporting momentary experiential symptoms, it is desirable to have subjects respond while the emotion is still "hot." Subjects responded to an extended series of items concerning the situation, how they felt, including thoughts and bodily reactions, what desires they experienced, and what behaviors they engaged in. In addition, subjects gave open-ended descriptions of their experiences, examples of which follow.

TABLE 3.1
Four Different Kinds of Anger-Like Emotions According to the OCC Theory

Emotion	Tokens	Specification	Focus	Example
Frustration	angry distressed displeased dissatisfied distraught feeling bad frustration grief homesick lonely sad unhappy upset	Being displeased about something undesirable that happened	On the negtive outcome for oneself	The organizer of the picnic was frustrated when it rained
Reproach	angry apalled contempt disdain indignation	Disapproving of someone else's blameworthy action	On the blameworthiness of another person's action (not negative outcomes if any)	Many people despised the spy for having betrayed his country
Anger	angry annoyed exasperated incensed indignation irritation offended outraged fury livid etc.	Both disapproving of someone's else's blameworthy action and being displeased about undesirable outcomes	On both the blameworthy action and the undesirable outcome	The woman was angry at her husband for forgetting to buy the groceries
Resentment	angry envy jealousy resentment	Being displeased about an event presumed to be desirable for someone else	On positive outcomes for someone else that one feels to be undeserved or otherwise undesirable	The executive resented the large pay raise awarded to a colleague whom he considered incompenent

From Otony et al. (1988).

Four Examples

Resentment is illustrated by a subject who focused on the fact that someone he knew who regularly cheated on homework and tests had received an award for being a model student. The subject commented that, "He didn't deserve this award or the grades he received . . . I was mad when I learned that he received the award." This negative reaction was occasioned by the positive outcome for another person that was seen as undeserved. Although the reference to cheating might have suggested reproach as the correct category, the focus was mainly on the injustice of the person having received the award.

Reproach is illustrated by a subject's report of being upset that a friend of a friend had stolen $300 in new textbooks from a bookstore where she worked and had then sold them to another bookstore. The subject commented that, "I can honestly say that I feel only contempt for her. It angered me so badly because it violates all my principles. I don't know how to tolerate people who have no care or respect for anyone but themselves." Clearly, the central issue here is the disapproval resulting from the violation of standards with less focus on specific negative outcomes.

Frustration is illustrated by a student who could not find the key to her dorm room after she finished cleaning her room. "I looked everywhere and I still can't find my key." Hers appears to be an example of pure goal thwarting. The student might have berated herself for misplacing the key (which would have been an instance of self-anger), but her extended remarks focused solely on the negative outcomes of having lost it.

Anger is illustrated by a player in an important intramural softball game who believed he was wrongfully called out at first base. "Because he called me out and our man did not score, we lost and they won. I was furious at him for cheating and started a big fight." The key in this example is the joint focus on what was perceived as a blameworthy action on the part of another person and on the goal thwarting represented by losing the game.

Results

Thus far, data have been analyzed from an initial sample only of frustration and anger experiences. A stepwise multiple regression analysis was conducted to discriminate anger from frustration on the basis of responses to individual items, and then a multiple discriminant function analysis was applied to look at effect sizes. Because we were interested in qualitative differences between these states rather than differences in intensity, ratings of the intensity of their feelings were entered first in the regression equations. Looking at intensity alone, one can correctly classify 65% of the frustration and anger episodes (50% being chance). Reactions that subjects label as *anger* tend to be more intense experiences than those they label as *frustration*. Sets of items from different facets of the emotions were then compared to this baseline.

For example, taking account of differences in bodily symptoms allowed a 70% correct classification ($R = .45$). In addition to intensity differences, there was a greater tendency for angry subjects to endorse such items as "having clenched fists," "being paralyzed," "having focused attention," "blushing and flushing," "feeling hot," and "crying."

Taking account of thoughts allowed one to classify 73% of the events correctly ($R = .54$). In addition to intensity differences, angry subjects were more likely to endorse thoughts of the following kinds: "I couldn't believe what was happening," "how unfair it was," "how another person was to blame," "how thoughtless someone else was." Frustrated subjects were more likely to endorse such items as, "I couldn't get it out of my mind."

Looking at the feelings allowed 69% of the states to be correctly classified (R = .42). Angry subjects were more likely to endorse such items as "feeling aroused," "excited," and "victimized," whereas frustrated subjects were more likely to endorse such items as "feeling inferior."

Information was also collected on what subjects wanted to do in these states. These desires allowed 69% of the states to be correctly classified (R = .46). Angry subjects were more likely to endorse items indicating that they wanted to "see justice done," wanted to "compete," wanted to "tell the person what I thought," wanted to "raise my voice," and wanted to "psychologically hurt or insult someone."

Looking at what subjects actually did allowed 66% of the events to be correctly classified (R = .41). Angry persons more often said they "saw justice done," "told the person what I thought," "kept him or her at a distance," and "displayed exaggerated reactions."

Finally, consistent with our emphasis on the cognitive antecedents of emotions, causes were among the best ways to distinguish the two states, with 74% correct classification (R = .54). Situations that caused anger were more likely to be situations that were unexpected and situations in which another person was blameworthy. Situations that caused frustration were more likely to be ones that were confusing and that decreased self esteem (perhaps because without some external cause to blame, subjects who were frustrated felt incompetent).

These items were all significantly more likely to be endorsed by subjects reporting one rather than the other of the two emotions. But if all of these significant items are included together in one stepwise multiple regression analysis, it is clear that there is a great deal of redundancy in the item-by-item discriminations. Altogether, they allow 72% correct classification of anger and frustration episodes at the .05 level (Canonical R = .55). The largest beta weights in the regression equation were for causes (another person doing something blameworthy, B = .53), intensity (B = .48), bodily symptoms (clenched fists, B = .40), and thoughts (how thoughtless someone else was, B = .33). So, the most salient characteristics of anger relative to frustration are that anger is more likely to involve blame, to be intense, to involve clenched fists, and to involve preoccupations about the thoughtlessness of others.

Many of these results may seem intuitively obvious, but what they show is precisely the point that we are making, that many aspects of emotion follow from the conditions that elicit the emotion. Thus, for example, it is not surprising that angry subjects but not frustrated subjects report being preoccupied with seeing justice done because the elicitation of anger but not frustration often involves a perception of some sort of injustice, which is a particular sort of standards violation. Similarly, it should be the case that anger would involve perceptions of blame and thoughts about others' thoughtlessness, and that anger would be more intense than frustration (because anger has more sources of intensity than frustration; i.e., anger includes those associated with blame as well as those that arise from sources of frustration).

Distinguishing Agent-Focused and Event-Focused Emotions

Perhaps the most important distinction made in the OCC theory (Ortony et al., 1988) for the current discussion is the distinction between agent-focused and event-focused emotions. The idea is that some emotions are primarily reactions to the outcome of events for one's goals, as in the case of frustration, some involve reactions to the actions of agents on the basis of one's standards, as in the case of reproach, and some involve both, as in anger. In agreement with most theorists, Berkowitz refers to all of these as anger, but we propose that there is utility in making a distinction among them.

The utility of distinguishing state-focused and agent-focused emotions can be seen in a recent study (Clore, Ortony, Brand, & Levine, in prep; Ortony, 1990). The study concerned the reactions of basketball fans to the wins and losses of their college team. The results showed that fans' reports of *disappointment,* one of the emotions under study, took two different forms. It became clear that when fans said they were disappointed, some were disappointed about the outcome of the game, and some were disappointed in the team. In this distinction between disappointed about and disappointed in, one can see the essential differences between event-focused emotions like frustration, sadness, and disappointment and agent-focused emotions like shame or reproach. In our system, the determinants of being frustrated, or being disappointed about the failure to obtain some desired outcome, are different from the determinants of reproach, or being disappointed in someone for failing to meet some standard.

The distinction between these two states was apparent in the fact that some instances of disappointment clustered together with agent-based emotions like ashamed and embarrassed and some with event-based emotions like sad and frustrated. A second form of evidence concerned the variables that governed the intensity of emotion. Those that clustered with agent-based emotions were made more intense by perceptions that the team had "not played well," that they had "not hustled," and that they did "not deserve to win"—all concerned with standards of play. In contrast, those instances of disappointment that looked more like event-based emotions were made more intense by perceptions that the game was an important one and that the fan had expected the outcome to be different— factors concerned with goals and outcomes.

One kind of disappointment reflected disapproval of the team for not trying hard enough, whereas the other kind of disappointment reflected dashed hopes about an important goal. The meaning of any concept ultimately depends on the nature of its relationships to the network of other variables and concepts within which it resides. Some fans perceived the behavior of the team as blameworthy and felt an agent-focused emotion, and some attended to the outcome alone and felt an event-focused emotion. But both used the same label—disappointed. We think the label *anger* is also used to refer both to agent-focused and event-focused emotions.

FIVE QUESTIONS ABOUT ANGER

How Can Sadness Make You Angry?

Berkowitz indicates that the most controversial aspect of his formulation is "its assumption that virtually any type of negative affect will tend to activate the various components of the anger/aggression syndrome." If one takes this statement to mean that people *get angry* at some level whenever they experience negative affect of any kind, we believe it to be false. It is not plausible, for example, that anger is felt in cases of apathetic depression or when encountering the proverbial bear in the woods. But if one takes the statement to mean that any negative affect activates *some components that play a role in anger as well as in other emotions,* then it is quite compatible with the hierarchical organization of emotions proposed in the OCC account (Ortony, et al., 1988).

As can be seen in Fig. 3.1, being displeased, is part of anger and other negative emotions in the well-being–attribution compound group. But being displeased is also part of the eliciting conditions for all other negative emotions in the event-based emotion branch (including such emotions as resentment, sadness, frustration, and fear). We therefore agree that many (although we might not go so far as to say "virtually any") kinds of negative affect will activate some components of anger. These components of anger, however, are also components of fear, sadness, frustration, resentment, and so on. Which of these is actually elicited depends further on whether the undesirable event at which one is being displeased is an actual event (sadness, frustration) or a potential event (fear, anxiety). Beyond that, it also matters whether the undesirable event has happened to oneself or someone else (sympathy, pity), and so on. The specific emotion that is elicited depends on the focus of the perceiver, but all negative event-based emotions involve the component we refer to as "being displeased at an undesirable event." In that sense, it is surely true, as Berkowitz maintains, that many negative emotions involve components that are components of anger and that make anger more likely. But we would not predict anger to be involved in all negative affect.

Reviewing findings from a study of grief by Wickless and Kirsch (1988), Berkowitz says that "a multivariate analysis showed that the sense of loss, which was the primary determinant of the felt sadness, also contributed to the angry

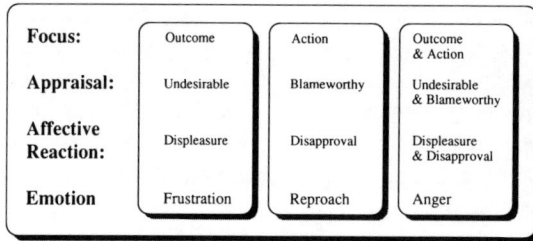

Focus:	Outcome	Action	Outcome & Action
Appraisal:	Undesirable	Blameworthy	Undesirable & Blameworthy
Affective Reaction:	Displeasure	Disapproval	Displeasure & Disapproval
Emotion	Frustration	Reproach	Anger

FIG. 3.2. *Frustration:* Being displeased about an undesirable event. *Reproach:* disapproving of someone else's blameworthy action. *Anger:* Disapproving of someone else's blameworthy action and being displeased about the related undesirable event. From Ortony et al. (1988).

feelings over and above any sense of having been wronged" (p. 16). This kind of observation is to be expected if one assumes as we do that anger involves a focus on both loss (or some other goal thwarting) and blame (see Fig. 3.2). According to the OCC account (Ortony, et al., 1988), the intensity of anger is affected both by the intensity variables for attribution emotions, as well as by the intensity variables for well-being emotions.

What Do Emotions Do?

We propose that the experience of emotion functions as feedback about the state of one's personal concerns (Carver & Scheier, 1990; Clore, 1992). The thoughts and feelings that constitute emotional experience reflect the particular ways in which a situation is positive or negative for those concerns. If one situation is different in important ways from another situation, one might expect such differences to be reflected in the emotional feedback provided. A system in which anger was elicited indiscriminately in any and all negative situations would seem nonoptimal. Distressing situations in which someone is to blame, for example, would seem importantly different from distressing situations in which no one is to blame. A view that emphasizes emotion as information, therefore, hypothesizes that discriminably different emotional states should exist to reflect that difference. The OCC account (Ortony, et al., 1988) proposes that one emotion (that could be labeled *anger*) is triggered when a person's distress includes a perception of agency or blame, and that another (that could be labeled *frustration*) is triggered when a perception of agency is not part of the distress.

Although the eliciting conditions for anger and frustration differ, frustrating situations might often lead to anger, very much as Berkowitz proposes. Being in a negative affective state appears to trigger a natural human tendency to find a cause. To the extent that one's explanation includes the possibility that someone is responsible, then anger may occur. Frustration is presumably a powerful impulse to such explanation seeking. Indeed, the power of this impulse is such that without an animate cause, people sometimes resort to treating inanimate causes as animate. Anger appears to arise in otherwise unlikely situations, therefore, as a result of an inclination to find something responsible.

According to the OCC account, anger occurs when the cognitive/perceptual conditions underlying frustration and reproach are both satisfied. But because reproach depends on the perception that some standard has been violated, reactions of disapproval are subject to variation in social and cultural sophistication in terms of what is seen as blameworthy. Thus, for the rat who experiences shock and attacks a cage mate, association is apparently sufficient (Azrin, Hutchinson, & Hake, 1967). Simply focusing attention on another animal during unpleasant stimulation may create the same sort of link that in humans might be characterized as a perception of agency or blame. For humans, we suggest that the requisite link is the perception of blame, but the criteria for that perception vary with the experiencer.

In support of this logic, note that anger is especially unlikely to arise in cases that do not involve the urge to find someone or something responsible. If one fears that one is about to be struck by lightning in an open field, anger would not be a likely emotion. Similarly, if one met a bear in the woods, anger seems unlikely to arise. One would not become angry in such situations, even though they involve no social context within which anger would be inappropriate. Hence, it could not be said that the failure of anger to arise in these situations was due to an effort to suppress anger in the service of being socially appropriate, as Berkowitz suggests for other examples.

Does Cognition Cause Anger or Inhibit Anger?

Cognition as Inhibition.   Berkowitz frequently refers to situations in which "people do not think much about their feelings and whether their anger is proper." The model is that the natural course of events is for distress to elicit anger and aggression, and when this does not occur, it is because people exercise control over their emotions. Cognitive activity is relegated to the role of keeping incipient anger from developing fully or from being displayed when it is socially inappropriate. Hence, the best evidence about anger, according to this view, comes from animals, children, or drunks in whom such civilized impulses are absent, undeveloped, or dulled. It is true that such specimens are more likely to show unbridled emotion, but it is not clear that this is evidence in favor of the claim that the main role of cognition is to inhibit inappropriate anger.

We have reservations about this view to the extent that the role left for cognition is as an epiphenomenon. In this regard, the model implied by much of Berkowitz's analysis is reminiscent of that invoked by Freud. For Freud, the ego monitors reality through perception and cognition, and one of its chief roles is to restrain the primitive aggressive impulses of the id. The later ego psychologists had to revise Freud's theory precisely because they realized that it lacked a generative role for cognition. Similarly, one of the attributes that separates cognitive from neobehaviorist and liberalized behaviorist views is whether or not cognitive processes are seen as a source rather than merely as a constraint on behavior.

In contrast to this theme of cognition-as-inhibition, however, Berkowitz also includes a brief but fascinating discussion of the role of cognitive processes in the construction and elaboration of emotion. The notion is that some elements of anger are included in the reaction of frustration when goals are thwarted, and that one role of cognition is to construct this reaction as full blown anger or to keep it from developing. We are much more attracted to this line of thought, and it seems close to our own view in which cognition is seen as a cause and not merely as a constraint on anger.

Cognition as Cause.   In our usage, one must attribute one's distress to another person or thing (or at least associate it with them) in order to be angry at them. However, the criteria for making these attributions may vary across persons, situations, and roles. Drunks, children, and certain grieving people may have a relaxed set of criteria for seeing someone, or perhaps everyone, as blameworthy. It is not that sober, rational, adults are like drunks except that they restrain themselves, rather, they have more stringent criteria for assigning blame in the first place. Although it is true that people differ in self-control once they are angry, they may also differ in the assiduousness with which they apply the criteria for assigning blame and perceiving agency. However much one may be frustrated and upset, and however much one may be motivated to find someone else at fault, anger at someone or something (as opposed to a more general state of frustration or distress) may not be triggered without casting someone in the role of agent or in some way seeing them as responsible.

For a rat or a child, it may be enough that an animate object is nearby when distress strikes. But for most of us, some principle or set of expectations must be seen to have been violated. Indeed, the intuitive knowledge of these eliciting conditions lead policemen, for example, to be courteous and to enact a fairly rigid script when issuing a ticket for a traffic violation in order not to draw the motorist's anger. The policeman's role enactment can be seen as giving the citizen little opportunity to see the policeman as blameworthy, and to ensure that the motorist's desire to find someone else to blame is not satisfied. In short, the policeman's behavior is aimed at maintaining the motorist's emotion as frustration or self-anger and not letting it develop into anger at others.

How Distraction Causes Inappropriate Anger?

In commenting on the angry and occasionally violent acts of grieving persons, Berkowitz focuses on the idea that people are most likely to do such things when they "do not think much about . . . whether the anger they might recognizably experience is proper" (p. 17). Again, this assumes a model of the frustration–anger–aggression linkage that is hard-wired, and that cognition serves primarily to inhibit what would otherwise run off as an automatic process. The idea is that we see people's true stripes when they are distracted, tired, or otherwise less likely to hold themselves to high standards of behavior. This is, historically speaking, a philosophical position reminiscent of Thomas Hobbes, whose view of the relation of humans to society was predicated on the idea that society served as a brake on people's animal instincts. There is surely much that is valid in this view, but it is only part of the picture.

The role of distraction and tiredness in excessive or inappropriate anger has another possible explanation. Schwarz and Clore (1983, 1988) examined the conditions under which irrelevant affective states influence people's judgments. This research showed that for moods and emotions to influence judgment, a person must experience the affective cues as part of his or her reaction to the stimulus being judged. Ordinarily, such perceptions are accurate. But the experiential cues from preexisting moods can also bias judgment, because there is only one window to our affective experience, and it is not generally possible to say which part of one's experienced affect is due to prior mood and which part is a reaction to a current stimulus. Thus, for mood to influence judgment requires one to misattribute those feelings as a reaction to the object of judgment.

The biasing effects of mood on evaluative judgment is one of the most reliable phenomena in the cognition–emotion domain. The rose-colored glasses effect and its reverse can be readily observed in everyday life as well as in the laboratory. Forgas and Moylan (1987), for example, interviewed nearly 1,000 people as they left movie theaters, and found that, after seeing happy, sad, or aggressive films, the moods of viewers influenced their judgments about political figures, future events, crime, and life satisfaction. There are now a number of demonstrations that moods affect judgment in this way (see Forgas & Bower, 1988). The key to these studies, however (and also for studies of nonemotional priming), is that subjects often fail to distinguish between their prior mood and their reaction to the object of judgment (Clore, 1992, Schwarz & Clore, 1988). If one makes a plausible external cause for their feelings salient to subjects, the effect disappears. When subjects are children or adults who are tired and distracted, mood is more likely to affect judgment than otherwise. The reason is not simply that subjects who are distracted and tired are not on their best behavior, but simply that such distractions decrease the likelihood that they will make the correct attribution for their feelings.

Presumably, when one runs out of energy to cope with the demands of civilized social interaction, even the smallest obstacle can cause a sizable frustration reaction. When the tired and hungry father screams at his child for spilling her milk, his appraisal of blame is not based on feelings of tiredness or hunger directly, but on feelings of frustration caused by a momentary inability to muster the resources to handle the situation. Unlike feelings of hunger, feelings of frustration are an appropriate component of anger. The father is not likely to confuse his hunger and tiredness with his frustration at the child's accident, but he is quite likely to confuse his frustration at things in general with frustration at her accident. Because emotion serves as informative feedback, the mood-intensified frustration reaction experienced by the father will make the child's infraction seem more blameworthy or the spilt milk a more serious outcome or both. In either case, an increment in the level of punitiveness could be expected.

Berkowitz cites an experiment (Berkowitz & Frodi, 1979, pp. 30–31) on female subjects' reactions to children who were working on a learning task. The results showed that, when distracted, the women were more punitive toward a child who was odd looking and who stuttered than toward a normal child. Berkowitz would assume that the child's condition evoked a reaction of displeasure which elicited anger and aggression directly. In the case of the women who were not distracted, Berkowitz presumably assumes that the women still had angry and aggressive impulses toward the child but suppressed them or inhibited their development because they saw their reactions as inappropriate. We assume, on the contrary, that the women who were not distracted were less punitive because, in the absence of distraction, it was easier for them to correctly attribute their negative reactions to the child's appearance and stuttering. But when they were distracted, they were less able to separate their reaction to the child's performance from their reaction to the child's appearance and speech. Failure to make the correct attributions resulted in contamination of their evaluations of the child's performance on the learning task. In fact, such contamination and decontamination effects have now been studied extensively (e.g., Clore, 1992; Clore & Parrott, 1991; Schwarz & Clore, 1983, 1988). Again, the issue is not one of cognitive processes failing to restrain basic aggressive impulses, but one in which negative affect is misattributed as a reaction to the child's task performance because of distraction.

Berkowitz also cites studies that show increased punitiveness after minor stress such as that provided by a cold stressor task. These experiments are subject to this same alternative explanation. According to the affect-as-information view (Schwarz & Clore, 1983, 1988), the negative affect from cold water on other sources is misattributed to the target and leads to biased negative judgments that contribute to punitive behavior. Distraction is often important in the process, but, we suggest, its role is to allow the necessary misattribution to occur. Thus, any negative experience can easily increase any negative emotion, not because of an inborn link between aversiveness and aggressiveness, but because evaluations of other people and objects are easily influenced by misattributed affect. Any manipulation (e.g., cold water, electric shocks, writing aggressive essays) that elicits a negative or aggressive experience can bias judgment and behavior in this way.

Motor Versus Cognitive Processing Output of Emotions

Progress has been made in the past decade toward specifying the input of the emotion system—the cognitive eliciting conditions for particular emotions (e.g., Ortony et al., 1988; Roseman, 1984; Smith & Ellsworth, 1985). Attention is now turning toward specifying the nature of the output of particular emotions. Recent attempts by Frijda (Frijda, Kuipers, & ter Schure, 1989) to characterize emotions in terms of particular patterns of *action readiness* appear only partially successful. Except in the most primitive and limited sense, we question whether behavior is a direct output of the emotion system.

It is true that certain facial expressions appear very closely linked to emotions (Ekman, 1984), but any attempt to specify close links of emotion to behavior quickly run into more exceptions than regularities. Indeed, one supposes that the whole advantage of having emotions is to go beyond the limitations of reflexes and fixed action patterns (see Scherer, 1984, for an excellent discussion of this point). The point is not that emotions have no behavioral implications; surely they do. But those implications are not direct or hard-wired. Rather, we see the output of emotion as input to cognitive processes—attention, motivation, memory, judgment, decision making, and problem solving. As opposed to action readiness, perhaps emotions should be thought of as affecting what might be called *processing readiness*. Indeed, some of Frijda's action readinesses turn out, upon reflection, to be processing styles (e.g., paying attention).

A position that sees emotion as relevant to behavior but that avoids assuming a direct link to behavior is one proposed by Carver and Scheier (1990). They suggest that behavior is guided by a hierarchy of control mechanisms in which the output of one often serves as the input to another at a higher level. Emotion, then, is a signal to pursue a particular superordinate goal. A person who is about to touch a snake as part of a treatment for snake phobia, for example, is likely to experience fear. The function of the fear is to inform the system that a superordinate goal is being thwarted, in this case, the goal of safety. The person is motivated to achieve safety, and it may take considerable resolve on the part of the phobic to ignore those signals and proceed to approach the snake.

Behavior Readiness.   Emotional states may involve a number of processes that facilitate action in a general way without priming any particular behavior. It is easy to imagine that emotion involves changes in arousal, in blood distribution, in muscle tension, and so on. To the extent that these or related changes occur, the organism might be prepared to engage in any action more quickly or forcefully. It seems less implausible, however, that emotions in humans involve activation of motor programs for particular actions.

It is, nevertheless, common to assume that fear involves behavioral tendencies to escape, that anger involves activation of aggressive responses, that shame involves tendencies to hide, and so on. But on closer inspection such assumptions seem questionable. Such words as *behavior, response,* and *action,* even when qualified by such words as *tendencies, readiness,* or *inclinations* can only mean that specific muscle groups and motor circuits are activated when angry, fearful, or ashamed. Such claims imply, for example, that one's legs are programmed to run when afraid, one's arm is programmed to hit when one is angry, or one's hands programmed to cover one's face when ashamed. It is presumably true that an emotion such as fear involves a redistribution of blood from the viscera to the large muscles, and such effects would presumably enable one to engage in rapid action or extreme exertion. But such general activation is not at all the same thing as a specific action tendency or a motor program.

Fewer problems arise if one assumes that the direct effects of emotions are motivational rather than behavioral. One can achieve more agreement about the likely goals of angry, fearful, or ashamed persons than about their likely behavior. It seems clear enough, for example, that fear involves a heightened desire to avoid harm or loss, but not at all clear whether achievement of this goal would necessitate selling one's stocks, listening to the weather report, or running like hell. Thus, the immediate effects of emotion may be mental rather than behavioral.

Information for Judgment and Decision Making. Although emotion may bias behavior indirectly, the advantage of emotional over reflexive processes is precisely that emotions do not commit the organism to one and only one course of action. Rather, emotion, especially the experiential aspects of emotion, appear to serve as input to judgment and decision-making processes, which then may or may not lead to behavior. This view is based on research suggesting that affective feelings provide information that is routinely used to answer affective and evaluative questions (e.g., Schwarz & Clore, 1983, 1988). The general idea is that emotions are functional in that they provide information to the organism about the personal relevance of situations. These informational properties appear to be responsible for many of the consequences of emotions.

We are inclined, then, to view emotional experience rather than behavioral tendencies as the business end of emotion. It is via emotional experience that one is informed of the nature and importance of personally significant situations. It is also the urgency of emotional experience that is responsible for the motivational and attentional properties of emotion. One seeks pleasurable experience and avoids unpleasant experiences, and it is clear that the pleasurable and unpleasant experiences of emotion have motivational properties. As discussed by Simon (1967), it is through emotional experience that attention is commandeered so that information about the emotional situation can be processed with an urgency appropriate to its importance. This claim carries with it the assumption that there is some relationship between the perceived importance of a situation and the intensity of one's emotional response.

EMOTIONS AS BIOLOGICAL AND AS COGNITIVE

As Berkowitz suggests, there is a difference in orientation evident between investigators who begin with a cognitive view and those who begin with a behavioral or biological view. Everyone agrees, of course, that emotions involve biology, behavior, and cognition, but many emotion theorists believe that because emotions are felt, because they lead to extreme actions, because they have bodily concomitants, and because lower creatures sometimes display analogous reactions, emotions are therefore really biological processes that must be understood with that as a starting point (e.g., Panksepp, 1992). What can be said about this assumption? First, of course, emotions are biological processes. Cognition is also biological in the sense that it requires a living brain. But it will never be possible to understand cognitive processes from within, say, biochemistry. One need not retrace the entire histories of the idea of emergence, of arguments against reductionism, and of cognitive psychology against behaviorism to see that this is so.

Emotion is, perhaps, the most truly psychological of phenomena. It is the marriage of mind and body, the intersection of motivation, behavior, cognition, physiology, phenomenology, and on and on. In many ways Berkowitz says this eloquently, and he gives a provocative account of how emotional experience is constructed. But this flowering of cognitive theory seems grafted onto an older stalk where the roots of his proposals go. This view is built on the conviction that cognition is an outcome, not a starting point, an interesting display, but not a cause. It assumes that emotion is really a biological occurrence that seizes us unawares and with which we must then cope with our civilized ideas and understandings. We agree with many aspects of this analysis but we see cognitive processes as fundamental to emotion. We focus on emotion as a phenomenon for which cognition is both the source (the appraisal that something is positive or negative for one's desires, goals, and concerns) and also the primary output (the informational and motivational feedback that affects attention, cognitive processing, judgment, and memory).

SUMMARY

We have made several points in response to Berkowitz's interesting and far-reaching proposals. In brief these are as follows:

1. The implicit definitions of four relevant concepts—cognition, attribution, emotion, and anger—were discussed. We argued that cognition need not be conscious, rational, or deliberative, and that attributions are an integral part of everyday perception. Although emotions may involve distinctive physiology, feelings, and behavior, we argued that these elements signal an emotion only when they are caused by relevant cognitive appraisals. Finally, a distinction was made between various angerlike states, including frustration (a reaction to undesirable outcomes), reproach (a reaction of disapproval of actions seen as blameworthy), anger (a joint focus on undesirable outcomes and blameworthy

action), and resentment (a negative reaction to the positive outcomes of another person).

2. The basis of the distinctions among various angerlike states is the cognitive account of the emotions proposed by Ortony et al. (1988) [referred to as the OCC account]. This theory, summarized earlier, gives an account of 22 emotion types grouped according to similarities and differences in their cognitive eliciting conditions. Each emotion is a cognitive differentiation of one or more of three kinds of affective reactions—being pleased or displeased at the desirable or undesirable outcomes of events, approving or disapproving of the praiseworthy or blameworthy actions of agents, and liking or disliking the appealing or unappealing attributes of objects. The three reactions correspond to three aspects of situations (events, actions, or objects) and to three bases for the appraisals (goals, standards, and attitudes or tastes). In this system the four angerlike emotions occur in four different emotion groups. Ongoing research was discussed that is aimed at exploring similarities and differences among the four states.

3. Five questions about anger and emotion that arise from Berkowitz's proposals were addressed. Proposed answers were drawn from work on the cognitive causes of emotion (Ortony et al., 1988) and the cognitive consequences of emotion (Schwarz & Clore, 1988).

The observation that sadness can make one angry was explained as evidence for the hierarchical structure of emotion rather than as evidence for the primary of anger. It is not the case that people have angry and aggressive impulses activated automatically by any negative affect, rather these states share some of the same components with any negative affect (Ortony et al., 1988). Putting one's hands in cold water, holding one's arm out in an uncomfortable position, and similar manipulations are ways of inducing negative experiences that influence judgment. Making subjects aware of their feelings and making salient a possible external source of their feelings eliminates the effects of these states (Schwarz & Clore, 1983). This is true not because people want to do the right thing, but because once the feelings are experienced as irrelevant to the target, the target is simply no longer experienced as blameworthy.

Evidence was cited that people who do not think about the social appropriateness of their anger, such as children or people in a state of grief, tend to show anger even when there is no one to blame. These observations were interpreted as indicating that anger is elicited in any negative affective situation but is often suppressed by the operation of higher cognitive processes when socially appropriate reasons are not evident. An alternative view is that anger (as we have characterized it) always involves attributions of blame. The fact of socially inappropriate anger among those who are unsophisticated or distraught may reflect lax standards for blaming others for their distress. Hence, variation in the appropriateness of anger may reflect variation in willingness to assign blame as well as variations in self-control.

The view was taken that emotional experience serves as information about one's affective appraisals. This feedback also motivates changes in the priority with which one processes information. Within this functional view it was seen as unlikely that the system would have evolved so that anger cues toward others would be elicited independently of causal attributions that they are responsible for one's distress.

Berkowitz cites data showing that in negative affective situations distraction increases angry behavior because the distracted person is less able to inhibit the inappropriate anger. We are inclined to say that the role of distraction is to make one less able to be discriminating about assigning blame, so that frustration is more likely to become inappropriate anger. Distraction can keep people from making the proper attributions for their experience, and as a consequence negative affect from irrelevant sources can contribute to the perceptions and judgments that make anger and aggression more likely and more extreme.

Perhaps because behavior under emotion is sometimes intense, irrational, and uncontrollable, the idea that emotions are directly linked to behavior has often been proposed. This idea is bolstered by observations that some emotional behavior in humans seems analogous to fight or flight reactions in lower animals. Although some emotions do involve a general preparation for muscular exertion, evidence for a direct link between emotion and any specific behavior seems lacking. In addition, from a design point of view, many of the advantages of the emotion system would seem to be vitiated if emotions committed a person to particular actions.

Emotional activation of facial and expressive muscles has been documented, of course, and appears functional for communicative purposes. But the preparation of specific large muscle groups or the activation of motor programs for specific overt action seems to us less likely. It seems more plausible that emotions direct motivational outcomes. Emotions arise in the first place because one sees a situation as relevant to one's goals and concerns. And as a consequence, new goals and a reordering of existing goals take place.

REFERENCES

Abelson, R. P. (1983). Whatever became of consistency theory? *Personality and Social Psychology Bulletin, 9*, 37–54.

Azrin, N. H., Hutchinson, R. R., & Hake, D. F. (1967). Attack, avoidance, and escape reactions to aversive shock. *Journal of the Experimental Analysis of Behavior, 10*, 131–148.

Bandura, A., & Walters, R. H. (1963). *Social learning and personality development*. New York: Holt, Rinehart & Winston.

Bargh, J. A., & Uleman, J. A. (1989). Introduction. In J. S. Uleman & J. A. Bargh (Eds.), *Unintended thought.* (pp. xiii–xxvi). New York: Guilford.

Berkowitz, L., & Frodi, A. (1979). Reactions to a child's mistakes as affected by her/his looks and speech. *Social Psychology Quarterly, 42,* 420–425.

Carver, C. S., & Scheier, M. F. (1990). Origins and functions of positive and negative affect: A control-process view. *Psychology Review, 97,* 19–35.

Clore, G. L. (1992). Cognitive phenomenology: Feelings and the construction of judgment. In L. L. Martin & A. Tesser (Eds.), *The construction of social judgments* (pp. 133–163). Hillsdale, NJ: Lawrence Erlbaum Associates.

Clore, G. L., & Ortony, A. (1991). What more is there to emotion concepts than prototypes? *Journal of Personality and Social Psychology, 60,* 48–50.

Clore, G. L., Ortony, A., Brand, S., & Levine, S. (in prep.) *The joy of victory and the agony of defeat: Emotions and the sports fan.*

Clore, G. L., Ortony, A., & Foss, M. A. (1987). The psychological foundations of the affective lexicon. *Journal of Personality and Social Psychology, 53,* 751–766.

Clore, G. L., & Parrott, W. G. (1991). Moods and their vicissitudes: Thoughts and feelings as information. In J. Forgas (Ed.), *Emotion and social judgment* (pp. 107–123). Oxford: Pergamon Press.

Ekman, P. (1984). Expression and the nature of emotion. In K. Scherer & P. Ekman (Eds), *Approaches to emotion* (pp. 319–344). Hillsdale, NJ: Lawrence Erlbaum Associates.

Forgas, J. P., & Bower, G. (1988). Affect in social and personal judgments. In K. Fiedler & J. Forgas (Eds.), *Affect, cognition, and social behavior* (pp. 183–208). Toronto: C. J. Hogrefe.

Forgas, J. P., & Moylan, S. (1987). After the movies: The effects of mood on social judgments. *Personality and Social Psychology Bulletin, 13,* 465–477.

Frijda, N. H., Kuipers, P., & ter Schure, E. (1989). The relationships between emotion, appraisal, and emotional action readiness. *Journal of Personality and Social Psychology, 57,* 212–228.

Gray, J. (1971). *The psychology of fear and stress.* Weidenfeld & Nicolson: London.

Heider, F. (1958). *The psychology of interpersonal relations.* Hillsdale, NJ: Lawrence Erlbaum Associates.

Johnson-Laird, P., & Oatley, K. (1989). The language of emotions: An analysis of the semantic field. *Cognition and Emotion, 3,* 81–123.

Mandler, G. (1984). *Mind and body: The psychology of emotion and stress.* New York: Norton.

Ortony, A. (1990, August). *The cognition-emotion connection.* Paper presented at the American Psychological Association, Boston.

Ortony, A., & Clore, G. L. (1989). Emotion, mood, and conscious awareness. *Cognition and Emotion, 3,* 125–137.

Ortony, A., Clore, G., L., & Collins, A. (1988). *The cognitive structure of emotions.* New York: Cambridge University Press.

Ortony, A., Clore, G. L., & Foss, M. A. (1987). The referential structure of the affective lexicon. *Cognitive Science, 11,* 341–364.

Panksepp, J. (1992). Comment on Ortony and Turner's "What basic about basic emotions." *Psychological Review, 99,* 566–571.

Roseman, I. (1984). Cognitive determinants of emotion: A structural theory. In P. Shaver (Ed.), *Review of personality and social psychology* (Vol. 5, pp. 11–36). Beverly Hills: Sage.

Russell, J. A. (1980). A circumplex model of affect. *Journal of Personality and Social Psychology, 39,* 1161–1178.

Russell, J. A. (1991). In defense of a prototype approach to emotion concepts. *Journal of Personality and Social Psychology, 60,* 37–47.

Schachter, S., & Singer, J. E. (1962). Cognitive, social, and physiological determinants of emotional state. *Psychological Review, 69,* 379–399.

Scherer, K. R. (1984). Emotion as a multicomponent process: A model and some cross-cultural data. In P. Shaver (Ed.), *Review of personality and social psychology* (Vol. 5, pp. 37–63). Beverly-Hills: Sage.

Schwarz, N. (1990). Feelings as information: Informational and motivational functions of affective states. In E. T. Higgins & R. M. Sorrentino (Eds.), *Handbook of motivation and cognition.* (Vol. 2, pp. 527–561). New York: Guilford.

Schwarz N., & Clore, G. L. (1983). Mood, misattribution, and judgments of well-being: Informative and directive functions of affective states. *Journal of Personality and Social Psychology, 45,* 513–523.

Schwarz, N., & Clore, G. L. (1988). How do I feel about it? The informative function of affective states. In K. Fiedler & J. Forgas (Eds.), *Affect, cognition, and social behavior* (pp. 44–62). Toronto: C. J. Hogrefe.

Simon, H. (1967). Motivational and emotional controls of cognition. *Psychological Review, 74,* 29–39.

Smith, C. A., & Ellsworth, P. C. (1985). Patterns of cognitive appraisal in emotion. *Journal of Personality and Social Psychology, 48,* 813–838.

Strack, F., & Martin, L. L., & Stepper, S. (1988). Inhibiting and facilitating conditions of the human smile: unobtrusive test of the facial feedback hypothesis. *Journal of Personality and Social Psychology, 54,* 768–777.

Weiner, B. (1985). An attributional theory of achievement motivation and emotion. *Psychological Review, 92,* 548–573.

Wickless, C., & Kirsch, I. (1988). Cognitive correlates of anger, anxiety, and sadness. *Cognitive Therapy and Research, 12,* 367–377.

4 Affect, Appraisal, and Action: Towards a Multiprocess Framework

Joseph P. Forgas
University of New South Wales

Why do people tend to display more noninstrumental aggression when experiencing negative affective states? Or to use a more prosaic and accessible metaphor, why are we more likely to kick our cat after we had a particularly bad day at the office? Surprisingly, psychologists appear to be still some way from being able to provide a convincing account of the chain of events that link noxious stimuli to negative affective states, and eventually, aggressive responses. Perhaps the difficulty of suitably dealing with this problem has something to do with the fact that it touches on some of the most fundamental issues in all of psychology: the relationship between affect, cognition, and behavior (Hilgard, 1980).

In the target chapter, Berkowitz presents what will undoubtedly be regarded as a classic contribution to the literature of emotional experience and behavior. Its global aim is to address the current fragmentation of the literature, by proposing a comprehensive multistage model linking emotional states and social behavior within a single integrated framework. Specifically, Berkowitz deals with the links between the emotional experience of anger, and the behavioral response of aggression, although the kind of analysis he proposes can also be applied to other negative emotions, or indeed, all emotional experiences in general. He proposes that "highly enraged persons may well lash out impulsively at their targets, not because they have decided they would benefit from such an attack, but because the anger/aggression network has been so intensely aroused inside them that strong motor impulses to aggression are activated. The cognitive–neoassociationistic perspective holds, furthermore, that other emotional states operate in a comparable manner" (p. 33). By suggesting that emotional states directly cue appropriate action tendencies, without the need for elaborate cognitive appraisal and goal setting, Berkowitz reaches back to an earlier tradition in trying to

89

redress what he sees as the current preponderance of cognitively based theorizing in the literature.

Berkowitz's chosen vehicle to accomplish such a comprehensive reinterpretation of the affect–cognition–behavior triad is his cognitive–neoassociationist (CNA) model. This is essentially a two-stage model of emotional responses, where aversive events first elicit direct action tendencies as well as various other networked associations, followed by a second stage of higher order processing when cognitive principles are used to construct an integrated affective experience. The critical point is that according to the model cognitive appraisal and elaboration is not an essential prerequisite for action, a view that seems consistent with classical theoretical positions taken by James (1890) and more recently by Zajonc (1980), Laird and Bresler (1991), and others, but represents a challenge to the currently dominant cognitivist approach to emotion (cf. Averill, 1982; Lazarus, 1984; Schachter & Singer, 1962). There is a wealth of material considered here, and in his illuminating discussion Berkowitz makes many insightful points of relevance to several active areas of contemporary social cognition theorizing, not least to my own area of interest, the study of affective influences on social judgments.

In discussing this stimulating chapter, I try to make three major points: the first one is by way of a comment, the second one is a query, and the third one is a suggestion. The first comment has to do with what might be termed the *heroic* nature of the integrative task Berkowitz seeks to accomplish. I suggest that the relationship between affect, cognition, and behavior is, indeed, historically one of the central issues in psychology, and that Berkowitz's integrative work deserves to be seen as a model worthy of emulation in other domains if the current trend towards fragmentation in our discipline is to be arrested. My second point (or rather, a series of points) related to Berkowitz's conception of cognition, and his use of associative network concepts in particular, issues that are critical for the success of the CNA framework. I think that just as in the earlier debate between Zajonc (1980) and Lazarus (1984), the way one defines cognitive and cognition has a major bearing on the how one interprets this model, and there are several instances where Berkowitz's use of these terms may benefit from additional sharpening. Finally, I discuss the role of cognitive appraisal mechanisms in the elaboration of emotional experiences that occurs at the stage of higher order processing in Berkowitz's model. In particular, I suggest that recent affect–cognition theories, and current multiprocess conceptualizations of appraisal processes especially (cf. Forgas, 1992a, 1992b) may have much to offer in complementing the theoretical framework proposed by Berkowitz.

AFFECT, COGNITION, AND BEHAVIOR: A GRAND INTEGRATION

In the first part of the chapter Berkowitz correctly points out that there exists a "curious division in the psychological research on anger and emotion." Contemporary theories of emotion suffer from a lack of integration, with a number of conceptual formulations existing side by side, each capable of accounting for some, but not all, of the available empirical data. In fact, the fragmentation of the emotion literature is probably even more serious than that, because it is not only the lack of integration that we have to contend with, but also the compart-mentalized existence of models, which on closer inspection, turn out to be conceptually and methodologically incompatible.

Emotions: Visceral or Cerebral?

The CNA model outlined by Berkowitz is presented as an attempt to integrate the two major alternative approaches to conceptualizing emotions: models that em-phasize invariable bodily reactions, and theories emphasizing cognitive in-terpretations. We may term these the *visceral* and the *cerebral* approaches to affect, respectively. However, the CNA is clearly somewhat closer to the former view, in that "more explicit attention is given to involuntary stimulus and body influences" (p. 29), a view that Berkowitz takes to be similar to Zajonc's (1980) well-known position. It is suggested that this account is in fact quite similar to the classic James–Lange theory of emotion, where bodily states and motor reactions are seen to give rise to the affective experience, rather than the other way around.

The critical empirical question here is whether one sees different emotional states as incorporating essentially indistinguishable physiological responses, as Schachter and Singer (1962) believed, or assume that there are demonstrable differences at the physiological, neural and even muscular level between qualitatively different emotions, as some theorists now believe (cf. Ekman, Levenson, & Friesen, 1983). Berkowitz relies on the notion of emotion networks to explain how internal states, muscular configurations or other proprioceptive cues can directly give rise to an affective experience, only to be followed later by cognitive elaboration. As is suggested later, there is a profound difference be-tween associative networks as used in cognitive psychology to deal with adaptive learning and memory processes, and Berkowitz's use of this term to refer to essentially invariant linkages in the emotion network. Nevertheless, the integra-tion of visceral and cerebral conceptualizations of affect in the CNA framework is a major achievement, that lays the foundations of an even grander integrative scheme between affect, action, and appraisal.

Affect and Action

Anger is often part of hostile aggression, and aggression is frequently the conse-quence of anger. Yet these phenomena, as Berkowitz points out, have been traditionally studied by psychologists as if they were totally unrelated to each other. Research on anger, an emotion, is predominantly based on self-report data and a conceptual framework that emphasizes the cognitive, interpretational aspects of the anger experience. Research on aggression, in contrast, is mainly carried out by experimental social psychologists, often using manipulated laboratory methods, designed to discover the antecedents and consequences of this important class of antisocial behaviors. The first group has little interest in aggressive behavior, the second cares little for anger as an emotion, even though the two phenomena, as Berkowitz persuasively argues, are closely related and indeed, are often in a sense two sides of the same coin. The two traditions thus differ along a variety of dimensions: the definition of their subject matter (an emotion vs. a behavior), their conceptual orientation (cognitive–interpretational vs. causal–predictive), and their preferred research strategy (analysis of verbal reports, vs. manipulative experimentation).

Although this state of affairs is clearly undesirable, on closer inspection the kind of fragmentation of psychology's subject matter Berkowitz documents appears to be endemic to our discipline. The way to such divisions was already paved by some of the earliest categorizations of mind into cognitive, affective, and conative faculties. As Hilgard (1980) persuasively argued, the notion of distinct mental faculties can be traced at least to the German psychology faculty of the 18th century, and, probably, to much earlier than that.

What then is the nature of the links between the experience of a negative affective state, such as anger, the behavioral intentions, conations, it generates, and the cognitive processes involved? This is precisely the core issue Berkowitz is concerned with here, although he does not put it into quite this kind of historical perspective. Considered in this light, this challenging chapter indeed touches on some of the oldest and most focal issues of psychological theorizing. In attempting to reintegrate anger and aggression, Berkowitz seeks nothing less than to once again put together constructs—or if you like, "mental faculties"— that have been separated for a very long time. This is, indeed, an heroic enterprise. Seen from this perspective, the problem of fragmentation and the two cultures of research on emotion are not only merely an interesting and topical theoretical problem, but also a quest that goes to the roots of psychology as currently understood. Anyone concerned with the seemingly irresistible fragmentation of psychology's subject matter, driven by powerful centrifugal forces, must applaud the constructive, integrative force of Berkowitz's arguments.

The path chosen by Berkowitz to accomplish the kind of major reintegration he considers necessary is basically eclectic: He suggests that "the experiential (such as anger) and behavioral (such as aggression) components of the emotional state are affected by a broad variety of psychological processes, some of which are highly cognitive in nature, while others are governed by more automatic and involuntary systems such as associative mechanisms" (p. 4). I think Berkowitz is fundamentally correct in taking such an eclectic approach. The process of integrating previously separate research domains necessarily implies the need to deal with phenomena at a higher order of complexity, and to take into account a broad variety of relevant variables. The ability to focus on a highly selected set of variables is a luxury that often accompanies theoretical fragmentation. Integration requires eclecticism, and nowhere is this more so than in the difficult domain of emotion research (Forgas, 1992b). It seems that the Achilles heel of such an elaborate conceptual scheme is how effectively it can deal with the role of cognitive appraisal in affective experience and action. We consider some of these issues in the next section.

THE STATUS OF COGNITION IN THE CNA MODEL

Terms such as *cognition, appraisal, interpretation,* and *elaboration* are frequently used in Berkowitz's discussion, often to refer to a variety of quite different ways of knowing, highlighting one of the perennial epistemological questions in psychology: What is the status of cognition in psychological functioning? On occasion, cognitive is simply used to refer to introspective, self-report or paper-and-pencil approaches to the study of emotional experiences. At other times, cognitive approaches are depicted as fundamentally different from associationistic approaches, a distinction that may at first seem surprising. After all, associationist principles remain one of the mainstays of contemporary cognitive theorizing, including such dominant affect–cognition models as Bower's (1981, 1991) semantic network theory. I suspect that in proposing the cognitive–neoassociationist perspective (p. 4), Berkowitz may be using this terminology in a way that is, perhaps, unconventional, particularly to those more accustomed to the contemporary information-processing terminology in social cognition.

The Role of Appraisal

In describing what he considers the "conventional cognitive analysis" of anger as an emotion (p. 4), Berkowitz identifies the process of appraisal and construal as at the heart of these models (Averill, 1982). The implication of such models is that (a) negative events do not produce specific affective reactions directly, but only after the cognitive processes of appraisal and attribution; and (b) negative events also do not in themselves produce goal-oriented behavioral reactions: "The afflicted individual supposedly behaves in a certain way because of a decision, reached consciously or unconsciously, as to how to act" (p. 5). Evidence for such a view comes from self-report analysis of emotional experiences, as well as experimental research such as Zillmann's (1978) transfer of arousal studies. Berkowitz suggests that the evidence for the role of cognition (in the sense of appraisal and attribution) in affective reactions is less clearcut than commonly assumed, and that more parsimonious alternative explanations, for example, based on Hullian behavior theory, have been given insufficient attention. As he points out, alternative behavioral theories and research suggest that neither prior learning of aggressive responses, nor appropriate attributions are a necessary requirement for the anger/aggression syndrome. Why then have these findings been relatively neglected in the recent literature? It is suggested that a theoretical bias toward cognitive accounts and an excessive methodological reliance on self-report techniques may be at the heart of the problem. Even though people do sometimes react to negative events with unthinking aggression, these tendencies will be underrepresented in self-report data because of their lack of social desirability.

Even though such unappraised aggressive responses do occur, anger is clearly neither a sufficient nor a necessary condition for aggression. Paradoxically, Berkowitz is forced to invoke the concept of appraisal to explain such inconsistencies in the literature, by suggesting that "thwartings give rise to anger and aggression only to the degree that they are aversive." The extent to which the blocking of goal-oriented behavior is experienced as aversive, however, is clearly dependent on the appraisals and attributions of the actor. If aversiveness is a matter of appraisal, it is unclear how such an account can be reconciled with the view that affective reactions are, in essential respects, precognitive.

The Network Principle

One way out of the appraisal dilemma is to suggest that emotional states may be understood as a complex associative network of feelings, thoughts, motor responses and physiological reactions, in effect, all part of a diffuse *emotional syndrome*. However, it is important to understand that such associative links between various components of the emotional syndrome are fundamentally different from associative network principles as commonly used in cognitive models (cf. Bower, 1991). Berkowitz believes that "there is a *built-in* association between negative affect and the anger/aggression syndrome so that unpleasant experiences tend, automatically at first, to activate the various components of the anger/aggression network" (p. 10). Thus, people feeling bad are also apt to feel angry, have hostile thoughts, and be disposed to aggression, at least initially. These strong associative reactions to aversive events should be strongest at the outset. The CNA model as depicted in Berkowitz's Fig. 1.1 suggests that negative affect brought on by an aversive event strongly and simultaneously cues behavioral, cognitive and physiological tendencies associated with fight or flight, anger or fear.

Because aggression is thus part of a wired-in emotion syndrome, it is performed without the benefit of cognitive appraisal, and is, therefore, not necessarily directed at the elimination of the source of the noxious stimulus; in other words, it need not be instrumental aggression. Some of the reviewed research seems consistent with this view, as are several relevant experiments by Berkowitz, showing that subjects exposed to aversive situations are more likely to cause pain to others, and do so more when they believe pain would be hurtful rather than helpful to their victims. These are interesting and in some ways counterintuitive findings, although the role of high-level cognitive appraisal mechanisms in these results again cannot be excluded.

The use of network principles to account for the close and, perhaps, invariant links between the experience of anger and aggression in the immediate aftermath of an aversive event is a potentially problematic aspect of the CNA model. One would expect associative network principles, if anything, to be more characteristic of the second, elaborative stage of cognitive interpretations, as I argue later. It is important then to spell out at least two of the differences between associative network models as used in cognitive research (cf. Bower, 1981, 1991), and the associative principles implied by the cognitive–neoassociationist model. The first crucial difference is that cognitive network systems are essentially plastic, molded by past experiences and learning. In contrast, the CNA predicts fairly rigid, invariant associations. To illustrate, according to cognitive network models, aversive events may instantly remind one person of past defeats, losses, and misery, yet, the same event might evoke associations of victory, pride, and success in someone else. In contrast, the CNA model suggests an invariant anger/aggression syndrome, with little allowance for malleable associations. A second difference is that Berkowitz draws on associative network models mainly to account for the initial, primitive reactions to negative affect. It seems to me that network models could far more suitably be employed to deal with the later, elaborate construction of affective experience rather than invariant early reactions. In several recent studies we have found that extensive, elaborate thinking of the kind Berkowitz identified as characteristic of the second stage of his model has considerably enhanced emotional priming effects, consistent with the operation of associative network principles at that stage (Forgas, 1992c; in press-a, in press-b; Forgas & Moylan, 1991). In general, the role of different processing strategies at Stage 2 of the CNA deserves careful attention, a point we return to shortly.

The concept of networked associations is used in yet another sense in the chapter: to refer to the direct priming of affective reactions, for example, following exposure to aggression-related information in the media. Such stimuli not only have a cognitive priming effect on the thoughts and ideas of observers according to Berkowitz, but also the CNA goes further by suggesting that in addition to cold priming, exposure to violence also directly primes related feelings. When subjects see highly violent films, they not only report more aggressive thoughts, but also indicate more hostile feelings, according to some of the supporting research reviewed. There may be some problems with the suggested notion of directly primed affective reactions. It is not at all certain that associative network models of cognition can be so simply applied to affective states. There is also the troubling methodological question that what subjects report here, and what is taken as prima facia evidence for primed feelings are in fact thoughts about feelings rather than feelings per se. In other words, it is not really possible in self-report experiments of this kind to distinguish between the semantic priming of thoughts as distinct from the suggested direct priming of affective states. To do that, direct evidence about affective states, perhaps in the form of psychophysiological data, may be necessary. In conclusion, it may be desirable to further clarify the different ways associative network principles are invoked in the chapter in order to avoid some of these potentially ambiguous sections.

Are All Negative Emotions Linked to Aggression?

As Berkowitz recognizes, "perhaps the most controversial aspect of the present formulation is its assumption that virtually any type of negative affect will tend to activate the anger/aggression syndrome" (p. 13), a prediction again based on network principles. The evidence cited to support this claim include animal and human studies showing that aversive stimuli such as pain, high temperature, or stressful environments may (but need not) enhance aggression and hostile re-sponses. But would sadness and depression also generate aggression? Such a link seems at least possible according to psychodynamic theories that often see de-pression as aggression toward the self. Berkowitz claims that there is also a strong empirical association. Depressed or sad adults and children are sometimes more prone to hostility and aggression, and experimentally induced learned helplessness may also lead not only to depression, but also to anger and hostility. Other studies found that depression induced through the Velten procedure can also increase aggressive inclinations, but only when subjects have little oppor-tunity to reflect on their actions.

Against this evidence, we must consider the overwhelming weight of clinical studies suggesting that depression is essentially a passive, low-arousal, and self-centered affective state that is largely incompatible with aggression. Many theo-ries of emotion also make a clear distinction between different classes of negative feelings that are characterized by high activation levels (e.g., anger), and low activation (e.g., sadness). Indeed, in several places in this paper Berkowitz also recognizes that anger and sadness are very different and even incompatible affective states, characterized by mutually exclusive bodily reactions and pro-prioceptive cues (p. 24). One of the studies by Berkowitz clearly bears on this point: Subjects asked to engage in anger-related behaviors "rated themselves as reliably less sad" (p. 25) (see also data in Berkowitz's Table 1.2), suggesting the incompatibility of these experiences. On balance, I think that the hypothesis that both sadness and anger should lead to aggression with the kind of invariability predicted here requires a lot more supporting evidence than is so far available. Although Berkowitz has convincingly shown that sadness may also involve hostility and aggression, there is less clearcut evidence for the kind of regular, deep-seated link between depression and aggression as has been claimed for anger and aggression. Attempting to extend the anger–aggression link to all negative affective states may thus ultimately be counterproductive, and weakens rather than strengthens the basic predictions of the model.

It is also somewhat surprising that although the model assigns equal importance to fight and flight as predominant affective reactions to aversive stimuli, aggression (fight) is emphasized here almost to the total exclusion of flight (escape and withdrawal). Assuming that fight and flight are fundamentally incompatible reactions under the model, is it suggested that depression is in fact more likely to lead to fight rather than flight? An exploration of the selective links between depression and flight, and anger and fight would have been of considerable interest, as a more plausible response system than the proposed depression–aggression syndrome.

The Cognitive Regulation of Affect

The CNA model also suggests that soon after the initial affective experience and its "networked" consequences, cognitive processes, involving thoughts, interpretations and attributions are superimposed on these basic affective reactions. At this stage, the model sees cognitive processes as having two kinds of influences; (a) the perceptual construction and interpretation of the situation; and (b) the activation of inhibitions. Such higher order thinking is then responsible for the construction of a more differentiated affective experience, that may lead to the qualitative distinction between states we may label *anger, annoyance, irritation,* or *displeasure* depending on various contextual associations.

One interesting suggestion of the CNA model is that once such an elaborated emotional experience is constructed (and according to Berkowitz, this is by no means always the case), it will act as a filter to inhibit or block conflicting, incompatible interpretations. In practice, this provision may significantly detract from the empirical falsifiability of the model. Thus, it is suggested that the model predicts "memory-facilitating associative linkages between negative affect on the one hand, and thoughts and ideas having an anger/aggressive meaning on the other . . . unless, of course, a self-regulatory process has come into operation to block the recall of unhappy occurrences" (p. 21). In other words, mood-congruent and mood-incongruent experiences may be equally compatible with the model. The precise prediction of the conditions likely to lead to either reaction may require the incorporation of the principle of multiple processing strategies in the CNA framework, a topic we return to shortly (cf. Fiedler, 1991; Forgas, 1992a, 1992b; Martin, 1986).

The model also suggests that at this stage of higher order processing, *affect-regulation mechanisms* may interfere with negative reactions, and in particular, that "cognitive processes can also reduce the degree to which negative events activate the anger/aggression syndrome" (p. 26). Berkowitz suggests that such affect-regulation comes about largely as a result of conscious thought processes, oriented toward reducing unpleasant affective states. He also describes several experiments where the tendency for subjects experiencing pain to be hostile to uninvolved others is reduced when they are made highly aware of the origins of their discomfort.

Does increased awareness indeed trigger affect-regulation and thereby reduce hostility as Berkowitz suggests? There may be a more parsimonious explanation for these results. In terms of contemporary multiprocess theories of affect and social judgments (Forgas, 1992a, 1992b), negative mood may inform reactions to a target but only if certain processing requirements are satisfied. In the experiments described by Berkowitz "unaware" subjects may have relied on the "how do I feel about it?" heuristic, misattributing their negative affective state as informative about their reactions to a target (Clore & Parrott, 1991; Schwarz & Bless, 1991). When subjects are made aware of their feelings, they can no longer rely on this judgmental shortcut, and their judgments become less hostile. Several experiments supporting such an interpretation are reported by Schwarz and Bless (1991). In other words, the data Berkowitz presents in support of the affect–regulation hypothesis may be more parsimoniously explained as a judgmental effect. Perhaps direct psychophysical evidence for reduced negative affect after extended processing would offer more persuasive evidence for Berkowitz's affect–regulation hypothesis.

Affect–regulation as understood by Berkowitz is not unlike Clark and Isen's (1982) distinction between the role of "automatic" and "controlled" processing in various moods. However, there is now considerable evidence that the kind of motivated mood-repair strategies considered by Clark and Isen (1982) need not be controlled, but can be invoked quite automatically. One of our recent experiments illustrates this point nicely (Forgas, 1991a). We gave happy and sad subjects an opportunity to choose a partner either for themselves or for somebody else. We then carefully monitored and analyzed the kind of information search and decision strategies they used to select a partner, and the kind of choices they made. We found clear evidence for motivated mood-repair strategies, in that sad subjects selectively looked for and found partners for themselves with potentially rewarding qualities. However, they did this in a manner that appeared more automatic than controlled: They were faster, more directed and ultimately more efficient in making their choice than others with no need for mood-repair (Forgas, 1991a).

Such data suggest that affect–regulation need not involve extended processing and highly conscious cognitive appraisal. Indeed, it seems more likely that affect–regulation, and the control of negative affect in particular, is one of the more routinized and automatic skills required for effective social living. Throughout childhood, we are taught how to cope with and control our negative feelings, and success at this task is an essential prerequisite for social adjustment. In the light of this, Berkowitz's suggestion that the control of negative affect is based on the rather slow and unreliable process of consciously invoked thought strategies seems somewhat implausible.

AFFECT APPRAISAL WITHIN A MULTIPROCESS FRAMEWORK

The CNA framework outlined by Berkowitz is a two-stage model, where noxious events first trigger negative affect and basic action tendencies and associations, followed by higher order cognitive constructions and elaboration. In this second stage construction of an affective experience, people are in fact engaged in a standard judgmental task that may perhaps be best understood in terms of contemporary multiprocess affect–cognition formulations (Fielder, 1991; Forgas, 1992a, 1992b). Berkowitz repeatedly stresses the importance of cognitive mechanisms in the way people construct and elaborate their emotional experiences after their initial, rudimentary reactions. However, as suggested, the model does not fully specify the precise processing principles involved at this stage of affect appraisal. In this section, I suggest that some of the recent multiprocess models in the affect–cognition literature may help to complete the picture (Forgas, 1992a, 1992b).

Assumptions of Multiprocess Approach

Such a multiprocess framework makes several assumptions about the nature of social appraisal processes. The first assumption is that people can in fact choose between several alternative processing strategies when performing an appraisal. This is in stark contrast to the single process assumptions traditionally implied by most existing cognitive models (Forgas, 1981, 1983), purporting to deal with relatively robust, universal, and context insensitive cognitive processes. Berkowitz touches on the issue of automatic versus controlled processing, leading to mood-congruent versus mood-incongruent judgmental effects. In reality, the picture seems far more complex than that. Fielder (1991) suggested recently that for affect–congruence to occur it is also necessary that people should engage in open-ended, constructive processing. Several recent dual-process models in the social cognition literature make somewhat similar distinctions between processing dychotomies (Brewer, 1988; Kruglanski, 1989; Martin, 1986; Petty, Gleicher, & Baker, 1991; Schwarz & Bless, 1991). Add to this recent evidence for the role of motivated reasoning in social cognition (Kunda, 1990), and the notion of automatic versus controlled processing becomes woefully inadequate to deal with the variety of thinking styles characteristic of affect-laden cognition (Forgas, 1992a, 1992b).

A second assumption of the multiprocess model is that the outcome of affect appraisal should largely depend on what kind of processing strategy is used. Thus, the model should be able to accommodate a range of complex and apparently inconsistent findings, including evidence for affect-congruent as well as affect-contrast effects (Martin, 1986), and symmetrical as well as asymmetrical effects (Peeters & Czapinski, 1990).

A third assumption of the multiprocess framework is that affect itself plays a dual role in cognitive appraisals. Affective states can influence both how people think (the kind of *processing* strategies they use), and what they think (the kind of *information* they consider in forming an appraisal), through mechanisms such as affect-priming (Bower, 1991), and affect-as-information (Clore & Parrott, 1991; Schwarz & Bless, 1991). Finally, the multiprocess model also assumes that people are principally lazy, effort minimizing information processors—cognitive misers—using the simplest and least effortful appraisal strategy consistent with the requirements of the situation. What are the principal processing strategies, and the variables that influence processing choices? We look at this issue next.

Alternative Appraisal Strategies

To deal with the problem of multiple processing strategies, in our recent integrative theory of affect and social judgments, we proposed a distinction between four basic processing styles, and also specified the conditions likely to lead to their adoption (Forgas, 1992a, 1992b). The same processes should also be applicable to strategies of affect appraisal. Thus, the outcome of the affect appraisal should depend on which of the following four processing strategies is adopted; (a) the *direct-access* strategy, involving the simple retrieval of preexisting, crystallized appraisals and reactions; (b) the *motivated* processing strategy, designed to achieve a specific, potentially rewarding or self-serving interpretation; (c) the *heuristic* processing strategy, when subjects seek to simplify and short-circuit the substantive processing of relevant information and try to construct an appraisal by the least effortful means; and (d) the *substantive* processing strategy, involving the detailed on-line processing and interpretation of the available information.

Direct-access appraisal should be used when the situation is familiar, preexisting interpretations are already available, and the person is relatively uninvolved, with no strong motivational forces mandating a particular appraisal outcome. The direct retrieval of preformed appraisals is probably the way most everyday affective situations are interpreted. Motivated processing occurs when an appraisal is driven by a specific preexisting goal, leading to selective, guided information search and integration strategies in support of an often self-serving objective. In this case, preferences do indeed come to guide inferences (Zajonc, 1980). Motivated processing may support mood maintenance as well as mood repair as we found in some recent studies of affiliative judgments (Forgas, 1989, 1991a). Heuristic processing is likely to be used when the situation is simple or typical, the person in uninvolved, has little motivation to be accurate, and there are no demands for detailed processing. Judgments will then be computed with the least effort, using whatever shortcuts are available to achieve an appraisal. Finally, substantive processing is likely when the situation is unusual, the person is motivated to be accurate, and engages in open, constructive processing to make sense of the experience. Substantive processing is the typical strategy used by the dutiful information processor, the kind of processing that is implicitly assumed by most information processing theories (Forgas, 1981, 1983). Such substantive processing is largely automatic and uncontrolled, when affect itself can inform an appraisal through the indirect priming and activation of cognitive categories (Bower, 1981; Forgas, 1992c; in press-a, in press-b; Forgas & Moylan, 1991).

Implications of the Multiprocess Framework

Distinguishing between these processing strategies has considerable benefits for a comprehensive theory of affect appraisal. This classification suggests that substantive processing, implicitly assumed to be the standard mental procedure by most theories including the CNA model, is more often merely a default option, used only when no other strategy is appropriate. The model also highlights that affect appraisal often involves various shortcuts typical of the direct-access, motivated, or heuristic processing styles. A critical aspect of the model is its focus on the variables predicting the use of particular processing strategies, a topic we turn to next.

Factors Determining Processing Choices

Figure 4.1 presents a comprehensive summary of the four processing strategies, and the conditions most likely to lead to their adoption. Which processing strategy is used when elaborating an emotional state depends on a combination of variables associated with the *situation* and the *judge* (cf. Fielder, 1991). Situational features include *familiarity,* as well as *typicality, ambiguity,* or *complexity.* Familiar affective situations may best be processed using a direct access strategy, by retrieving past evaluations. Atypical complex situations or judgmental targets in turn are more likely to receive substantive processing (Forgas 1992c; in press-a, in press-b; Forgas & Moylan, 1991).

Person features include the personal *importance* of the appraisal, the available *cognitive* capacity, and the *affective* state of the person. Judges may also rely on a *specific motivational goal* in their appraisal (e.g., mood-repair; Clark & Isen, 1982; Forgas, 1991a), or a general *motivation* to be accurate and careful (Martin, 1986; Schwarz & Bless, 1991). *Affect* itself may reduce processing capacity (Ellis & Ashbrook, 1988; Isen, 1984), induce motivated processing (Forgas, 1991a), or influence motivation for accuracy (Schwarz & Bless, 1991). Of

JUDGMENTAL TARGET

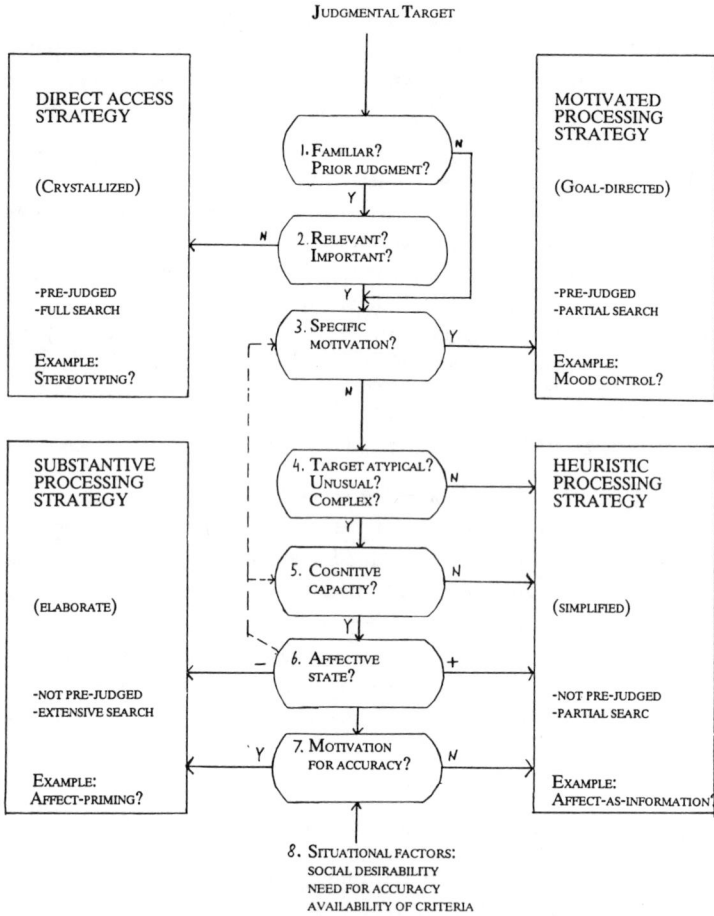

FIG. 4.1. A multiprocess model of affective influences on social appraisals and judgments, showing four processing strategies, and the conditions likely to lead to their adoption (after Forgas, 1992a).

course, not every factor influences every appraisal, nor is the decision sequence depicted in Fig. 4.1 necessarily invariant. However, the pattern of processing choices depicted in Fig. 4.1 is likely to apply to a broad range of appraisal judgments, as we see in Fig. 4.1.

The familiarity of the situation should have a major influence on processing choices. Affective situations present us with many strong recognition cues, priming the retrieval of stored appraisals from memory. This direct access strategy should be adopted only if the appraisal is of low personal relevance. Despite the obvious appeal of personal relevance as a mediating factor in appraisal strategies, it has received relatively little attention in the past (cf. Brewer, 1988; Forgas, 1991a). In affect appraisal, we often know the kind of interpretation we are looking for, and specific motivations such as ego-enhancement, mood-repair, or mood-maintenance may come to guide our information search strategies (Forgas, 1989, 1991a). The typicality or complexity of the situation may influence whether simplified, heuristic, or elaborate, substantive processing is used. Re-' cently we found clear evidence for the more elaborate processing, and attendant greater mood-congruent effects when people deal with unusual, atypical information (Forgas 1992c; in press-a, in press-b; Forgas & Moylan, 1991), a principle also likely to apply to affect appraisal. Cognitive capacity is also an important determinant of whether simple, heuristic or elaborate, substantive processing is used. Affect itself may result in capacity limits and attention deficits, predisposing judges toward using heuristic rather than substantive processing (Ellis & Ashbrook, 1988; Isen, 1984). Thus, affective state is itself a significant influence on processing preferences. Good moods seem to cue simple, heuristic thinking (Isen, 1984), while dysphoria often triggers slower, more careful and vigilant processing styles (Schwarz & Bless, 1991). Good or bad mood may also enhance specific motivation for mood-repair or mood-maintenance, and may increase motivation to be accurate. Such motivation for accuracy enhances the likelihood of substantive rather than heuristic processing, both in memory and in judgmental tasks (Martin, 1986). One important source of a motivation to be accurate in affect appraisal is the context itself: Some appraisals (e.g., those made publicly or likely to be scrutinized) clearly require a higher standard of accuracy.

Affect Congruence in Appraisals

According to the multiprocess framework, mood-congruence in affect appraisal occurs because mood comes to indirectly (through primed associations), or directly (through misattribution) provide relevant information to be used in computing an appraisal. The *affect-priming* account (Bower, 1981, 1991; Forgas & Bower, 1987; Forgas, 1991b; Isen, 1984) sees affect as indirectly influencing cognition through priming-related cognitions. The alternative, *affect-as-information* approach (Clore & Parrott, 1991; Schwarz & Bless, 1991), ascribes a direct informational role to affect. The multiprocess framework also suggests that affect-priming is most likely in the course of elaborate, substantive processing, whereas affect-as-information processes are more likely when simplified, heuristic processing is adopted. The dual informational and processing functions of affect in appraisals is summarized by Fig. 4.2. Mood-incongruent judgmental effects of the kind also described by Berkowitz are typically associated with motivational forces, such as a general motivation for accuracy (Martin, 1986) or specific motivational objectives superimposed on the judgmental process (Clark & Isen, 1982; Forgas, 1991a).

    In conclusion, it seems that affect appraisal must be considered in light of the various processing and informational consequences of emotional states. The multiprocess model outlined appears to provide a suitable integrative framework within which these complex, and often conflicting influences on appraisal can be

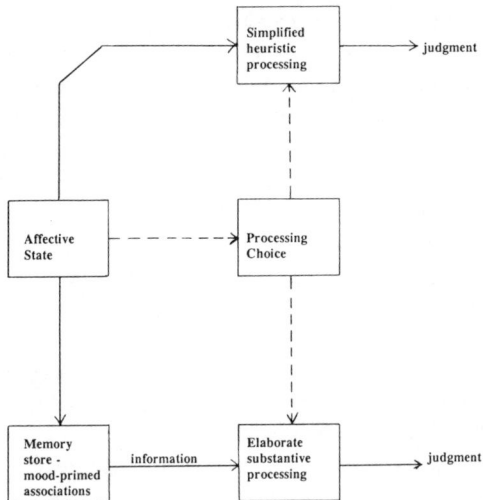

FIG. 4.2.   An illustration of the dual role of affective states in appraisal processes, influencing both the kind of processing strategies used by judges, and the kind of information they rely on in computing an appraisal (after Forgas, 1992a).

accommodated. As we have seen, affect appraisal involves at least two distinct informational effects (affect-priming and affect-as-information), each occurring in a different processing context (substantive vs. heuristic processing). Over the past several years, our research on affective influences on social judgments was able to demonstrate the processing conditions under which affect indeed has a reliable and predictable influence on social judgments and appraisal (cf. Forgas, 1991a, 1991b; 1992a, 1992b). Support for such a comprehensive multiprocess formulation comes from evidence collected by us as well as others, showing mood effects on a range of social judgments under different processing requirements (see Clore & Parrott, 1991; Fielder & Forgas, 1988; Forgas, 1991b; Forgas & Bower, 1987; Schwarz & Bless, 1991 for recent reviews). It seems that the incorporation of these multiprocess principles would suitably complement the CNA model, providing a testable theoretical framework within which higher order affect appraisal processes could be accommodated.

CONCLUDING REMARKS

The chapter by Berkowitz offers the kind of grand integration that is unfortunately only rarely seen in contemporary psychological theorizing. The chapter touches on many of the perennial great issues in our discipline, and marshalls an impressive range of arguments in support of the affect–action–appraisal framework as advocated in the CNA model. The first point I attempted to make in this discussion was precisely to emphasize the historical context and conceptual boldness of Berkowitz's enterprise. The second part of this chapter discussed some of the possible ambiguities inherent in Berkowitz's conceptualization of cognitive appraisal, his use of network principles, and several other aspects of what is called *higher order elaboration* within the CNA framework. These were, by and large, minor observations that in no way detract from the persuasive power of Berkowitz's overall argument. The final, third part was designed to suggest a possible complementary, theoretical framework suitable to deal with cognitive appraisal processes. This multiprocess model was initially developed as an integrative account of mood effects on social judgments, but it is clearly relevant to affect appraisal processes as well (Forgas, 1992a, 1992b). Just as judgmental models may have a contribution to make to affect-action theories of the kind proposed by Berkowitz, his model in turn has much to offer to those of us primarily interested in affective influences on social judgments. In particular, by persuasively arguing that behavioral preferences are indeed frequently not based on inferences, he calls attention to a large class of quasi-judgmental phenomena that are clearly beyond the scope of our current, predominantly cognitive theories.

So are we now any closer to understanding how or why people are likely to kick their cats after a tough day at work? I think the answer must clearly be affirmative. For too long, psychologists have searched for answers to questions such as these by selectively focusing on different parts of what must be seen as an indivisible process. One is reminded here of the three blind men in the parable, who, when they try to make out what an elephant is like by feeling various parts of its anatomy, inevitably come to very different conclusions about the nature of the beast. Similarly, psychologists focusing on cognitive processes not surprisingly believe that affect is all a matter of cognitive interpretation, whereas others doing behavioral experiments are more captivated by behavioral phenomena such as the anger/aggression syndrome. Both of these observations are true some of the time, identifying different aspects of what is, in reality, a single, unified process. It takes the kind of major integration that Berkowitz has undertaken to remind us of the wholeness and indivisibility of the phenomena we are dealing with. Although there will inevitably be some loose ends in an enterprise as ambitious as this, the theoretical framework provided by Berkowitz will undoubtedly become a classic contribution to the emotion literature. It will be interesting to see how the CNA model and the empirical research it will no doubt stimulate will change the way we think about anger and aggression over the next decade.

REFERENCES

Averill, J. (1982). *Anger and aggression: An essay on emotion.* New York: Springer-Verlag.
Bower, G. H. (1981). Mood and memory. *American Psychologist, 36,* 129–148.

Bower, G. H. (1991). Mood congruity of social judgments. In J. P. Forgas (Ed.), *Emotion and social judgments* (pp. 31–55). Oxford: Pergamon Press.

Brewer, M. (1988). A dual-process model of impression formation. In T. K. Srull & R. S. Wyer (Eds.) *Advances in social cognition* (pp. 1–36). Hillsdale, NJ: Lawrence Erlbaum Associates.

Clark, M. S., & Isen, A. M. (1982). Towards understanding the relationship between feeling states and social behavior. In A. H. Hastorf & A. M. Isen (Eds.), *Cognitive social psychology* (pp. 73–108). New York: Elsevier-North Holland.

Clore, G. L., & Parrott, G. (1991). Moods and their vicissitudes: Thoughts and feelings as information. In J. P. Forgas (Ed.), *Emotion and social judgments* (pp. 107–125). Oxford: Pergamon.

Ekman, P., Levenson, R. W., & Friesen, W. V. (1983). Autonomic nervous system activity distinguishes among emotions. *Science, 221,* 1208–1210.

Ellis, H. C., & Ashbrook, T. W. (1988). Resource allocation model of the effects of depressed mood state on memory. In K. Fiedler & J. P. Forgas (Eds.), *Affect, cognition and social behaviour* (pp. 25–44). Toronto: Hogrefe.

Fielder, K. (1991). On the task, the measures and the mood: Research on affect and social cognition. In J. P. Forgas (Ed.), *Emotion and social judgments* (pp. 83–107). Oxford: Pergamon.

Fielder, K., & Forgas, J. P. (Eds.). (1988). *Affect, cognition and social behavior.* Toronto: Hogrefe International.

Forgas, J. P. (Ed.). (1981). *Social cognition: Perspectives on everyday understanding.* London and New York: Academic Press.

Forgas, J. P. (1983). What is social about social cognition? *British Journal of Social Psychology, 22,* 129–144.

Forgas, J. P. (1989). Mood effects on decision making strategies. *Australian Journal of Psychology, 41,* 197–214.

Forgas, J. P. (1991a). Affective influences on partner choice: Role of mood in social decisions. *Journal of Personality and Social Psychology, 61,* 708–720.

Forgas, J. P. (Ed.). (1991b). *Emotion and social judgments.* Oxford: Pergamon Press.

Forgas, J. P. (1992a). Affect and social perception: Research evidence and an integrative theory. In W. Stroebe & M. Hewstone (Eds.), *European review of social psychology* (pp. 183–223). Chichester: Wiley.

Forgas, J. P. (1992b). Affect in social judgments and decisions: A multiprocess model. In M. Zanna (Ed.), *Advances in experimental social psychology* (pp. 227–275). New York: Academic Press.

Forgas, J. P. (1992c). On mood and peculiar people: Affect and person typicality in impression formation. *Journal of Personality and Social Psychology, 63,* 863–876.

Forgas, J. P. (in press-a). Affective asymmetry: Mood effects on the perception of atypical persons. *European Journal of Social Psychology.*

Forgas, J. P. (in press-b). On bad mood and strange couples: Affective influences on the perception of unbalanced relationships. *Personality and Social Psychology Bulletin.*

Forgas, J. P. & Bower, G. H. (1987). Mood effects on person perception judgements. *Journal of Personality and Social Psychology, 53,* 53–60.

Forgas, J. P., Bower, G. H., & Moylan, S. J. (1990). Praise or blame? Affective influences on attributions for achievement. *Journal of Personality and Social Psychology, 59,* 809–818.

Forgas, J. P., & Moylan, S. J. (1991). Affective influences on stereotype judgments. *Cognition and Emotion, 5,* 379–395.

Hilgard, E. R. (1980). The trilogy of mind: Cognition, affection, and conation. *Journal of the History of the Behavioral Sciences, 16,* 107–117.

Isen, A. (1984). Towards understanding the role of affect in cognition. In R. S. Wyer & T. K. Srull (Eds.), *Handbook of social cognition* (Vol. 3, pp. 179–236). Hillsdale, NJ: Lawrence Erlbaum Associates.

James, W. (1890). *Principles of psychology.* New York: Holt.

Kruglanski, A. W. (1989). *Lay epistemics and human knowledge: Cognitive and motivational bases.* New York: Plenum.

Kunda, Z. (1990). The case for motivated reasoning. *Psychological Bulletin, 108,* 331–350.

Laird, J. D., & Bresler, C. (1991). The process of emotional experience: A self-perception theory. In M. Clark (Ed.), *Review of personality and social psychology* (pp. 153–182). Beverly Hills: Sage.

Lazarus, R. S. (1984). On the primacy of cognition. *American Psychologist, 39,* 124–129.

Martin, L. L. (1986). Set/reset: Use and disuse of concepts in impression formation. *Journal of Personality and Social Psychology, 51,* 493–504.

Peeters, G., & Czapinski, J. (1990). Positive-negative asymmetry in evaluations. In W. Stroebe & M. Hewstone (Eds.), *European review of social psychology* (pp. 25–41). Chichester: Wiley.

Petty, R. E., Gleicher, F., & Baker, S. (1991). Multiple roles for affect in persuasion. In J. P. Forgas (Ed.), *Emotion and social judgments* (pp. 181–201). Oxford: Pergamon.

Schachter, S., & Singer, J. (1962). Cognitive, social and physiological determinants of emotional states. *Psychological Review, 63,* 379–399.

Schwarz, N., & Bless, H. (1991). Happy and mindless, but sad and smart? The impact of affective states on analytic reasoning. In J. P. Forgas (Ed.), *Emotion and social judgments* (pp. 55–73). Oxford: Pergamon Press.

Zajonc, R. B. (1980). Feeling and thinking: Preferences need no inferences. *American Psychologist, 35,* 151–175.

Zillmann, D. (1978). Attribution and misattribution in excitatory reactions. In J. Harvey, W. Ickes, & R. F. Kidd (Eds.), *New directions in attribution research,* (Vol. 2, pp. 00–00). Hillsdale, NJ: Lawrence Erlbaum Associates.

5 The Network Model of Emotion: Motivational Connections

Peter J. Lang
University of Florida

I am very pleased to comment on Berkowitz's theoretical treatise. I found many aspects of the work intensely interesting, and very worthy of discussion by the scholarly community. Furthermore, his emphasis on the primacy of association; his adoption of a network model and the concept of emotion prototypes; his view of instructional, intentional, or evaluative operations as modulatory of affect, rather than fundamental to its expression; his hypothesized connection between anger and background negative emotion; and more profoundly, his basic definition of emotions as action or response disposition, all move his theorizing very close to the bio-informational view (Lang, 1977, 1979, 1984, 1985; Lang, Bradley, & Cuthbert, 1990, 1992). There is much here to discuss. Because of space limitations, however, I react to only two basic questions. They are both implicit in any network model of emotion, and rose to mind often as I read Berkowitz's chapter. Indeed, they have frequently asked for answers as I considered my own research. First, are emotions fundamentally different from other information structures in memory, and if so, how? Second, on what basis do emotional states potentiate or inhibit other emotional responses and associated memorial information?

In responding, I am forced to take a path that may be unfamiliar to this audience of readers. That is, the answers do not lie near at hand in social or clinical psychology, but require a consideration of diverse fields, including information processing, psychophysiology, and what may seem like the back acres of animal behavior and the neurosciences. Thus, I hope my readers will hang onto their ecumenical hats, and that at the end they will find that the intellectual fare was worth the detour.

EMOTION AS COGNITION

My own application of the information network model to affective memory began with early studies of fear imagery. I wanted to know how such cognitive representations mediated therapeutic change in phobic patients. Research showed that repeated, vivid recollections of a fear experience led to significant diminution in fear behavior (Lang, 1968; Lang, Lazovik, & Reynolds, 1965; Lang & Lazovik, 1963). Although generally effective, this habituation, or working through in imagery, appeared to depend on the subject's physiological reactivity during the imagery experience. That is, all patients reported their fear images to be similarly distressing, particularly on early trials, but the patients who reliably profited from treatment were those who also showed an accompanying visceral arousal (Lang, Melamed, & Hart, 1970).

These findings led us to think about two kinds of emotional experiences, for example, experience that was *functional,* involving an active visceral response components (with implications for broad behavior change), and experience that was *nonfunctional*—saying all the right words, but no music on the polygraph.

With these data in mind, and stimulated by cognitive theorists such as Pylyshyn (1973), Kintsch (1974), and Anderson and Bower (1974), we attempted to model the conceptual content of a fear memory (Lang, 1977, 1979). It soon became apparent that our effort was not only relevant to fear, but that "other emotional states (e.g., anger, sexual arousal) [could] be analyzed from a similar conceptual framework," and furthermore, that it provided "a method for examining the interaction of emotional states" (Lang, 1977, p. 884).

THE BIO-INFORMATIONAL THEORY OF EMOTION

Emotions are viewed as action dispositions. They are instantiated when specific memory episodes (about context and behavior) are retrieved. Emotional episodes are coded in memory as networks of mutually connected information units. In network processing, activity in one unit is transmitted to adjacent units, and depending on the strength of activation, the entire structure may be engaged. The probability of whole network processing is increased with the number of units initially stimulated.

We presume the fundamental network to be neural. However, a network is also a useful organizational form at the conceptual level. In this view, emotions are made up of associated concept units (which, in turn, might be individual neural subnetworks). The higher level concepts can be classified into three types: stimulus, response, and meaning. Stimulus units are representations of perceptual events; response units code the three basic response systems or output procedures—behavioral acts, physiological mobilization, and expressive/evaluative language (Lang, 1978); meaning units refer to associated declarative (semantic) knowledge. This taxonomy is descriptively convenient; however, the actual subunits may well cut across the proposed categories. For example, Hebb (1949) described how visual stimulus representations might be based on the neural patterns instigated by eye movement responses.

Emotion networks can be described in natural language (e.g., French, German, English) as linked sets of propositions.[1] The conceptual contents of a possible anger network are listed here:

> Anger Episode—*Stimulus:* A car cuts you off and takes your parking space; the driver laughs; the offending driver is small in stature; *Meaning:* There are no more parking spaces; the same thing happened the day before; small people can be attacked with impunity; *Response:* "That pisses me off!" (verbal); vasodilation in facial tissue, blood pressure, heart rate and palmar sweating increase (visceral); Corrugator and masseter muscles tense, fist clenched and raised (behavioral).

This rendering, as a set of statements, should not be construed to mean that the information in an emotion network is solely, or even primarily linguistic. That is, stimulus and response events have more fundamental—ontogenetically and phylogenetically—neuroconceptual representation in memory. They are primitively activated by the external events and actions they represent. In man, these primary representations are more broadly cued (i.e., by verbal descriptions, moving and still pictures, diagrams, and other symbolic stimuli remote from the natural context).

It is important to reiterate, furthermore, that the basic connection between concepts is simple association. Thus, the emotional output of network processing does not depend on narrative structure or causal connectedness. We do not presume the necessary existence of a black box labeled, "office of the appraiser: evaluations on-line" that does if–then operations to an accompanying internal monologue: "This person is frustrating my efforts, its unjustified, he doesn't care about me, also he's not very big, and can't retaliate effectively; therefore, I will punish him." Indeed, it is held that simple emotion networks mediate affective behavior in organism with scant, if any, narrative capacity.

On the other hand, we do not suggest that human emotions are unaccompanied by causal schemas (e.g., see Leventhal, 1980), or that such stories are unimportant in life. An emotion's story might well be in memory before the affective event, as an available interpretation of new stimuli that match network concepts; alternatively, as Berkowitz (this volume) suggests, the story may be developed after the act, elaborating its meaning. It seems very likely that, given their historical and cultural ubiquity (Jaynes, 1976), there is a basic human need for narrative. Furthermore, stories may have significant survival value, organizing behavior and facilitating social cooperation. In the bio-informational view, however, the story is not fundamental to the mechanism of emotional action.

HOW DO EMOTIONAL MEMORIES DIFFER FROM
OTHER KNOWLEDGE STRUCTURES?

In a previous article (Lang, 1985, p. 160), I attempted to capture the layered nature of the emotion network in a three-dimensional graphic. From this perspective, an upper, language layer might contain, for example, the anger episode information as verbal code. This language data could be, as suggested earlier, parsed into a narrative form, according to stored rules of style, syntax, and grammar. A typical subject could also, based on associated knowledge, define the terms used, tell the story in different words, and explain the background and probable consequences of the event. That is, the subject would understand the network information as text in a natural language, and in theory, this could be accomplished without activating any imaginal or affective experience. Indeed, researchers in artificial intelligence have tried to build this sort of understanding into actual computers (e.g., Schank, 1982), and we recently witnessed a "Turing test" of current achievements on public television (with Daniel C. Dennett as moderator; Markoff, 1991).

Although the computer is a convenient metaphor for the human brain, and even now, software can be written to emulate some of that organ's computational functions; nevertheless, we should remember that the mind's computer is mounted on a biological chassis. Thus, as language input or text retrieved from memory, verbal information is seldom processed in this hypothetically restrictive fashion (i.e., only as language). In most people, words that symbolize perceptual events and actions automatically activate more fundamental representations of specific stimuli and responses. Furthermore, this second, more primitive network layer is connected to brain centers for afferent and efferent processing. Thus, through simple association, a text input can come to prompt the same action programs that are cued by real events.

A subject may say after reading a persuasive text (or hearing a dramatic reading) that it is "as if," or it "feels" something like, the described events were really happening. We propose that it is the associative spread of activation beyond the network's language level, engaging stimulus and response processors in the brain, which underlies such reports of media prompted imagery and affective experience. Considerable neurophysiological and psychophysiological evidence supports this hypothesis. On the sensory side, for example, recent EEG studies (Farah, 1988) have shown that visual images activate the same occipital area of the brain known to be involved in visual perception. From the efferent perspective, beginning with the classic research of Jacobson (1931), there is a vast research literature (see Cuthbert, Vrana, & Bradley, 1991; McGuigan, 1973) showing that instructionally evoked action images—from eye tracking to shooting baskets—prompt potentials in the appropriate muscle and organ systems.

In general, of course, the efferent effects of response information processing are so minute, a kind of "efferent leakage," that they can be measured only by the bioelectric amplifier. The subject's experience of an action context is only a feeling, that is, a disposition to behave that may have no overt sequelae (Frijda, 1986). Thus, effector systems are activated by the network, but the final instruction for overt behavior is "gated out"—presumably by context driven inhibitory information (e.g., "the savage polar bears being discussed aren't really here in Miami.") The barriers to action, however, can be fragile. Thus, responses move beyond the covert in good hypnotic subjects, whose eyes close automatically when they think about "how their eyes are heavy, how weights are attached to the lids, how they are moving inexorably down . . . down."

The associative processes described here are presumed to be automatic and not controlled—to use Schneider and Shiffrin's distinction (1977). In fact, they may defy intentionality. In the same way that Dostoyevski's brother, once told by the noted author not to think about "a white bear," could not stop thinking ursine thoughts (see Wegner, Schneider, Carter, & White, 1987), we have difficulty suppressing ideomotor connections. Furthermore, although language descriptions were used here to illustrate these effects, there are normally many input paths to an action network, including other media, such as pictures, films, plays, sound, and music. Thus, a televised Olympic jump may elicit an empathic, covert muscle action, though the viewer never leaves the comfort of the couch.

Processing the Network

We now have a partial answer to the first question, posed at the outset, concerning the basic difference between emotions and other information structures. Emotion networks differ from many other memories in that they are about action. They are not declarative knowledge—part of a semantic catalogue—but memories of behavioral episodes. They include procedures. More specifically, emotion networks contain response information, and activate associated efference (muscles, glands, and organ systems).

Using the tools of bioelectric recording, we have examined this basic proposition in a program of study that has already spanned two decades. The primary experimental stimuli have been evocative pictures and text (sentences or paragraphs about events that could be described as fearful, anger inducing, and the like). Verbal reports that thinking about this material is affectively arousing are taken as evidence that the input is understood as language (i.e., that subjects know the material can be judged and classified as emotional). Emotional processing, however, is indexed operationally by a pattern of autonomic and somatic activity in the subject, consistent with behavior that would be evoked by the events described in the text or picture.

There is no emotion without efference: The evidence accumulated for this hypothesis is necessarily inferential. It is based, however, on a broad database showing that physiological activity varies systematically (increasing or decreasing) with those independent variables that are expected to augment or diminish emotional reactions. These include:

1. Reports of subjective intensity and degree of functional disturbance. For example, when phobic patients or high fear normals (defined by questionnaire or interview) are exposed to written descriptions of pictures of phobic objects, they show large efferent changes (increased heart rate and skin conductance)—larger than subjects who report that these objects only make them uncomfortable, and much larger than subjects with no history of fear (e.g., see Lang, 1985, for a review).

2. The matching of stimulus and response representations. Working with normal college subjects (who respond to appropriate text with anger, fear, and the like, but are not pathologically primed), we were able to specify input factors that enhance or diminish emotional processing. It is an assumption of the model that the network is activated by input that matches elements in the memory network, and that the more matches, the greater the probability of efferent activation. Consistent with this view, we discovered that adding information to the text about responses ("fist clenched", "heart racing"), and furthermore, instructing subjects to attend to this action content, increased physiological reactivity (Lang, Kozak, Miller, Levin, & McLean, 1980). We also found that autonomic reactions were similarly facilitated if the external concept representation were more like the presumed actual, prompting stimuli (Lang, 1984; McLean, 1982), that is, by having the emotional scenario actually acted out before the subject (even though subjects knew the events were staged).

3. Degree of cognitive engagement and intentional control. To some extent, network activation is responsive to processing instructions. That is, when college subjects are told to only articulate the specific words in affective text, rather than to image the text as a personal experience, the affective physiological response is reduced (e.g., Vrana, Cuthbert, & Lang, 1989). Significantly, however, the autonomic reactance is not wholly eliminated, that is, despite a verbal orientation, the average subject still responds viscerally, slightly more to descriptions of emotional situations (a car crash) than neutral situations (sitting at home). As expected, individual differences among subjects are also important. In general, subjects who report a greater prevalence of "vivid" sensory imagery (as measured by questionnaire, Sheehan, 1967) respond with greater increases in heart rate and skin conductance than do poor imagers, to emotional texts (Miller et al., 1987) and emotionally evocative pictures. (Lang, Greenwald, Bradley, & Hamm, in press) Thus, it is possible that an imagery deficit could have contributed to the desensitization treatment failures, discussed earlier (Lang, Melamed, & Hart, 1970).

When emotional content is well learned, however, the variables considered here are reduced in importance. For example, while an imaginal cognitive style will somewhat facilitate autonomic reactance to fear text in simple phobics, severity of the fear accounts for substantial independent variance (Cook, Melamed, Cuthbert, McNeil, & Lang, 1988; NcNeil, Vrana, Melamed, Cuthbert, & Lang, in press). Furthermore, although normal subjects, when instructed to ignore a cue signaling an emotional memory, showed reduced autonomic reactions, this same "don't attend" instruction had no effect on more affectively primed anxiety patients, whose strong visceral responses occurred under all conditions of instruction (Patrick, Cuthbert, & Lang, 1989). When the cues match, emotion happens.

Emotion and Motivation: Neurophysiological Foundations

What Powers the Emotion Network?   The evidence is strong that affective memories are characterized by patterns of autonomic and somatic responses. Furthermore, in the absence of efference, it is unlikely that a verbally reported affect is *functional*. Nevertheless, physiological responding is not, in itself, an exclusionary index of emotion. For example, memories of an effortful task (e.g., running up stairs) are often accompanied by an efferent shadow of the original energy output—despite an absence of appreciable affect.[2] Affective images tend to differ from many other motor memories, however, in the intensity of retrieved efferent activation. They also appear to be more persistent, more readily instigated by degraded cues, and more refractory to instructional control. What powers these emotion networks? Why is the spread of activation from cognition to efference specially facilitated?

The fundamental answer to this question is that emotional networks include direct connections to the brain's primary motivational system. These are the same subcortical motivational circuits activated by unconditioned appetitive and aversive stimuli. They direct the general mobilization of the organism and the deployment of primitive approach and withdrawal behaviors. Furthermore, it is the same system that mediates the formation of conditioned associations based on primary reinforcement.

We assume that other memory structures do not include these direct links to primary motivational circuits. Thus, if we ask a teenager from a western country to name a population center in southern Vietnam, the memory network activated by the question may yield a specific verbal response, "Ho Chi Minh City," but it does not normally prompt a broad affective, action disposition. If the query is posed to a veteran of the Vietnam War, however, this same input could match content in a network that includes subcortical motivational connections. If the veteran suffers from posttraumatic stress syndrome these connections are high priority pathways to neural structures that mediate strong autonomic arousal and defensive (fearful or aggressive) behavior. Many of the associated responses are similar to those occasioned by the original trauma. They occur because the same subcortical circuits are reactivated that were motivationally relevant in the original aversive learning context.

In the next section, we consider this circuitry. Given Berkowitz's emphasis on anger and negative affect, we focus primarily on the aversive motivational system.

The Subcortical Subtext.   What is currently known about connections between representations of events and subcortical motivational structures comes mainly from animal research, particularly from studies of aversive learning in the rat. In this species, as in man, massive defensive reactions (autonomic and behavioral) are readily evoked by painful stimuli (e.g., electric shock). If such stimuli reliably occur contiguous with or immediately following a previously innocuous stimulus (e.g., an auditory tone), features of the defensive behavior come to be evoked by the second stimulus when presented alone. That is the new stimulus comes to activate a negative emotional response pattern we call fear.

Neurophysiological investigators are beginning to describe the neural basis of such conditioning phenomenon in information processing terms (e.g., "As a result of its association with the US, the CS thus gains access to a network that the US activates. Since the sterotyped emotional responses are coupled to the affective network, they result when that network is activated by either the CS or the US.") (LeDoux, 1990, p. 28). For LeDoux (1989), the primary affect network is subcortical—the bottom layer of the larger network structure that we described earlier.

Considerable information is now available about this emotion network's specific neurophysiology (see Fig. 5.1). In the current view, learning (e.g., of an emotional reaction) does not involve the formation of new neural pathways in the brain. Rather, it is likely that local changes are induced in existing circuits, by altering the neurochemistry of cells and changing the probabilities of synaptic firing. Using anatomical and electrophysiological tools, this chain of probable neural activation can be traced, starting from the input end in the sensory system—proceeding through the necessary connecting structures, defining the links least prodigal in synaptic connections—to the autonomic and motor effectors.

It was learned early in these investigations that, contrary to Pavlov's view (1927), the activation of simple emotional associations do not depend on prior cortical analysis of the conditioned cue (e.g., DiCara, Braun, & Pappas, 1970). Aversive learning to a simple tone will occur despite extensive lesions to sensory cortex. That is, the higher centers that accomplish *appraisal* or complex pattern recognition are not necessarily in the loop. Information about a stimulus, sufficient to the acquisition of a conditioned emotional response, requires processing only by the more primitive acoustic thalamus.

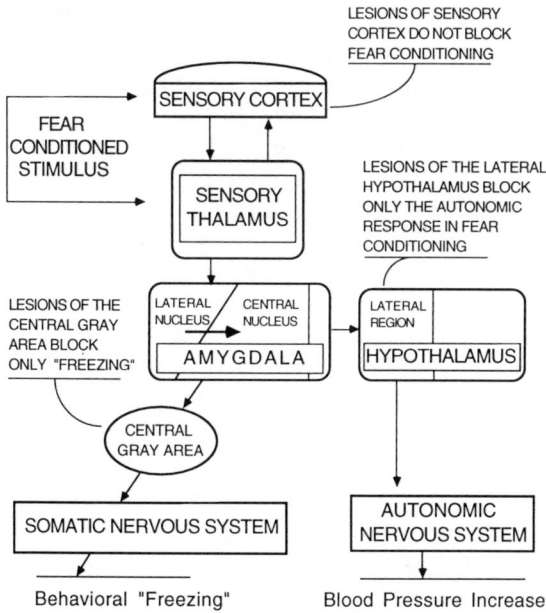

FIG. 5.1. Schematic representation of a part of the neural network involved in the transformation of an insignificant acoustic tone into a conditioned aversive input. The conditional stimulus is transmitted to the acoustic thalamus (through the auditory system and shell regions of the inferior colliculus [not shown]). The critical thalamic neurons are in the medial geniculate body the nearby posterior intralaminar nucleus. "The lateral nucleus of the amygdala receives the acoustic signal from the thalamus and transmits to the central amygdala. Efferent to the amygdala the pathway bifurcates. Projections from the central amygdala to the lateral hypothalamic area mediate the autonomic conditioned emotional response, whereas projections to the midbrain central gray region mediate the behavioral conditioned response" (LeDoux, 1990, p. 31). Based on the findings of LeDoux, Cicchetti, Xagorariss, and Romanski (1990).

The next critical connection to this neural network is from the medial geniculate body of the thalamus to the lateral, and then the central nucleus of the amygdala (LeDoux, 1990). The bilateral amygdala, located within the temporal lobes of the brain, has long been known as a critical structure in the mediation of emotional expression (see Ben-Ari, 1981). Both stimulation and ablation of this site reliably produce changes in a variety of affective/motivational behaviors in both animals and man—particularly in autonomic arousal and in fear and aggressive behaviors (Aggleton & Mishkin, 1986; Ursin, Jellestad, & Cabrera, 1981).

Systems and Patterns: Amygdala Connections.   In LeDoux's animal model of aversive learning, two dependent variables are assessed, one autonomic (mean blood pressure increase) and one somatic ("freezing," or immobility in the face of threat). By lesioning structures efferent to the central amygdala he determined that these two conditioned emotional responses are mediated by different subcortical structures, with the autonomic response dependent on an intact lateral hypothalamus, and the somatic component requiring an intact midbrain central gray area (see Fig. 5.1). Thus, it might be presumed that, despite the similar system activation, depending on the weighting of these local pathways, considerable variation in the pattern of affective output could be expected.

Plasticity of the subcortical circuits means that the network "learns" at this level of its anatomy and functioning. The amygdaloid complex is a critical structure in this learning. It is clear, furthermore, that amygdaloid connections are of specific relevance for the negative affect and aversion-driven behavior that is here under consideration. For example, Cahill and McGaugh (1990) showed that its destruction does not affect appetitively based conditioning; however, lesioning of the amygdala clearly blocks the acquisition of fear responses.

The amygdala circuit appears to be a general mediator of aversive responses (i.e., a key site in the general aversive motivational system). Consistent with this role, activation of the amygdala does not define a specific emotional response pattern. Indeed, as indicated in Fig. 5.1 for freezing behavior and cardiovascular arousal, there are independent routes from the central nucleus to different response systems, and presumably they can be modulated to produce highly varied outputs. Furthermore, the amygdala circuit has been implicated in a variety of other aversively motivated responses (i.e., in escape and avoidance learning; Ursin, 1965); in defensive/aggressive behavior (Blanchard & Blanchard, 1977; Roldan, Alvarez-Pelaez, & Fernandez de Molina, 1974), and as we examine in more detail later, in augmenting startle reactions (e.g., Davis, 1989).

This same aversive system also prompts varied hormonal and autonomic responses. For example, Iwata and LeDoux (1988) noted that heart rate and blood pressure decrease in response to a conditioned tone (previously accompanied by shock) when animals are physically restrained; on the other hand, these same autonomic responses increase when the conditioned signal is presented to freely behaving animals. These data recall similarly diverse context effects in human subjects, who show heart rate acceleration while imaging or thinking about unpleasant events (e.g., Vrana & Lang, 1990), but show significant deceleration when they report similar displeasure while looking at unpleasant pictures (e.g., Lang et al., in press).

Cortical Connections: Unpacking Affective "Appraisal."   In addition to activating descending motor circuits, output from the amygdala system projects to sensory cortex, association cortex, and the hippocampus—structures involved in complex pattern recognition and conceptual information processing. Furthermore, reciprocal circuits from these sites send information back to the lateral amygdala. Thus, the hypothesis that the higher order (semantic or conceptual) network is linked to the subcortical motivation circuit has, at the least, a clear anatomical base. Furthermore, given this two-way traffic lane, it is reasonable to assume that an affect might be initiated at either terminus. That is to say, crude, conditioned sensory input (e.g., a shadow across the visual field) might initiate thalamic activity that in turn raises the firing level of the aversive system that would subsequently be projected to association cortex. This aversive motivational input would potentiate associated knowledge structures in memory (e.g., a fear network based on predator attack). The concept network activated that modulates the action pattern would be one, either already primed by previous input, and/or one showing the closest match to other incoming sensations. In this case, emotion (subcortical activation) could be said to precede cognition (the conceptual network), as argued by Zajonc (1980; see also Öhman, Dimberg, & Esteves, 1989, on the preattentive evocation of emotion).

Given the functional anatomy, however, one can as easily imagine an alternative scenario. It is equally reasonable to assume that the initiating stimulus might require more complex primary processing (e.g., someone makes an insulting or demeaning comment). As a unit in a conceptual network, this percept would prime related higher order network matches. The cortical network would then activate lateral and central amygdala, again with collateral emotional autonomic and behavioral sequelae. Does cognition now precede emotion? Was the stimulus first "appraised" (e.g., Lazarus, 1984), before action was initiated? Although these are popular issues, we find on examination that the questions are either begged or mired in qualifications. If by cognition we mean only higher cortical processing (conscious thought and the like) then, in the first case, cognition is a late-comer to the party; in the second case, it could, perhaps, be said that thought precedes the affect. However, the neurophysiological work just reviewed shows great plasticity in the primitive circuitry (i.e., it is capable of considerable flexibility in information processing). Are not these subcortical associations part of the ongoing cognition? There are similar problems with appraisal, considering that affective association can be learned despite a lesioned cortex. One solution is to redefine the cognitive work of appraisal as the associative matching mechanism described here. It then has a fundamental role in much affective expression. We would by this course, however, give up every vestige of the term's origins in reasoned, subjective deliberation.

HOW DO EMOTIONAL MEMORIES ENHANCE OR INHIBIT OTHER AFFECTIVE RESPONSES?

Our view of motivation is similar to that of Konorski (1967; see also Mackintosh, 1983): Emotional behaviors—from complex affects to defensive and appetitive reflexes—are categorized according to reciprocal drive states. That is, they are either approach or withdrawal oriented (pleasant or unpleasant), and both these directional dispositions vary continuously in arousal, or intensity of activation. Elsewhere (Lang, Bradley, & Cuthbert, 1990, 1992), we have referred to these variables—affective valence and arousal—as determining the basic strategic stance of the organism. This means that to varying degrees, the motivational circuits tune the whole organism, either appetitively or defensively. For example, when a specific network with connections to the aversive system is engaged, other affectively negative information is also potentiated. This occurs because of the common associative connections of many different knowledge structures through the aversive system.

From this perspective, much of the variety in emotional expression is best described as tactical (i.e., as specific implementations of the strategic motivational disposition, accommodating particular contextual demands). Thus, aversive learning that originally prompted freezing as a response, might subsequently occasion attack or flight. In effect, any time the aversive system is activated, any network with which it is connected is moved toward the threshold of action. The network that ultimately captures the brain's central workspace—and thus determines a specific pattern of behavioral expression—will presumably be the one containing the greatest number of concept matches to the current stimulus context. This network instability, or probabilistic responsiveness to internal and external input variations, is intrinsic in recent *connectionist* modeling of neural networks (e.g., see McClelland & Rumelhart, 1981). The implication here is that aversive system output may look like fear, change to anger if targets are available, or a blend of both, with either anxiety or agitated depression as potential dominant affects later, as arousal diminishes.[3]

As the aforementioned account suggests, the bio-informational model readily accommodates Berkowitz's findings that hostile behavior has a higher probability of occurrence when subjects are already in an arousing, negatively affective state (see chapter 1, this volume). It is also consistent with results from studies of mood congruence and verbal behavior. That is, if a negative mood is evoked in subjects—or if they are intrinsically unhappy—there is higher probability that they will attend to and seem to better remember unpleasant than pleasant words (see Blaney, 1986, for a review).[4]

In the present view, any behavior motivated by the aversive system is potentiated when that system is active. In the subsequent section of this chapter, we present evidence that such affect matching is a fundamental mechanism, a general property of organisms, that can be demonstrated at the level of simple reflexes. Specifically, it is shown that an aversive/defensive reflex (the startle response) is augmented when an organism is already in an aversive state, and that the reflex is diminished, when the prior state does not match (i.e., it is positive and appetitive). Furthermore, the neurophysiological substrata of this phenomena will be explicated for animal subjects, relating it to the aversive learning circuits just considered. Finally, startle research with human subjects is reviewed, showing reflex modulation in emotion that closely parallels the animal model.

Affect and Startle Reflex

In all mammals, and most other species, any abrupt sensory event will prompt a general flexor movement of the body, bringing ongoing activity to a halt. This startle response appears to be a primitive, defensive reflex—perhaps serving an immediate protective function, avoiding organ injury (as in the eyeblink), and in acting as an interrupt, clearing the central processor to deal with possible threat. As we show, the neural path mediating this behavior is open to modulation by the same aversive motivational system that we have been considering. And indeed, when the system is activated—as in a fear state—the startle response is generally faster and of significantly greater amplitude.

The hypothesis that the startle response would be potentiated (augmented) during states of high motivation was first examined systematically by Brown, Kalish, and Farber (1951). These investigators noted that anxiety patients often show exaggerated startle responses. Presuming this to be a function of a high-drive state (Hull, 1943), they reasoned that aversively conditioned animals would show a similar enhanced startle when probes (shots from a toy pistol) were presented during the conditioned stimulus (CS) at extinction. Their experiment used male rats as subjects, a light–buzzer compound conditioned stimulus, and a shock unconditioned stimulus. Their results conformed to expectation: Animals did indeed react more forcefully—as measured by a stabilimeter in the floor of the cage—when the startle stimuli were presented during previously fear-conditioned signals (see also, Ross, 1961; Spence & Runquist, 1958).

The Brain's Fear–Startle Circuit.   Davis and his associates (e.g., Davis, 1989; Davis, Hitchcock, & Rosen, 1987) have extensively investigated the neural circuitry underlying the fear–startle connections. Davis held that classical CS-shock pairings produce a conditioned state of fear, and it is specifically the presence of this emotional state that augments the reflexive response to startle probes. His work has defined both the basic startle pathway and the site linking it to the aversive motivational system.

A diagram of the startle circuit is presented in Fig. 5.2. Startle probe input (e.g., an abrupt noise) first activates the cochlear nucleus, sending impulses to the lateral lemniscus, and then on to the reticular formation; the output path passes through spinal neurons to the reflex effectors. This is the basic obligatory circuit, directly driven by the parameters of the input stimulus (e.g., stimulus intensity, frequency, steepness of the onset ramp). The phenomenon of conditioned startle potentiation implies, however, a secondary circuit that modulates the primary reflex pathway. An important initial step in Davis program was to locate the neural site at which this priming occurs. Their method of investigation

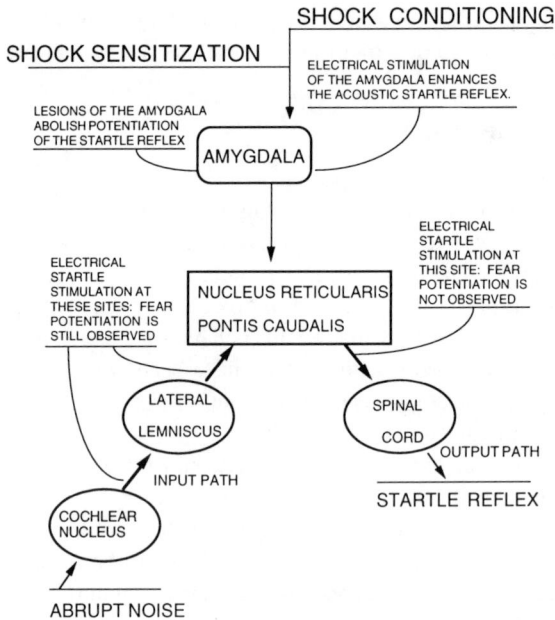

FIG. 5.2. Schematic representation of the primary neural path between a startle stimulus input and its effector output. Locations along
this path are shown where stimulation with microelectrodes will, or
will not, produce a potentiated startle response. This procedure isolated the neural structure (nucleus reticularis pontis caudalis) where
the modulating influence of previous aversive learning impacts on the
obligatory startle circuit. The central nucleus of the amygdala (the
same central structure in LeDoux's aversive learning network) has
monosynaptic projections in this reticular site. The fact that lesioning
of the amygdala blocks potentiation, and stimulation with microelectrodes potentiates the reflex (in the absence of prior fear conditioning), prompts the conclusion that this structure is a primary component of the aversive motational system (see Davis, 1989 for an
overview of the neurophysiology). Based on the findings of Davis
(1989); Boulis and Davis (1989); Hitchcock, Sananes, and Davis (1989).

was to intervene directly in the neural pathway, applying an electrical stimulus
with a microelectrode to evoke the startle response (see Berg & Davis, 1985).
Whereas obligatory reflexes were obtained all along the circuit path, the further
augmentation of the response because of fear conditioning only occurred if the
point of electrical startle stimulation was earlier in the circuit than the nucleus
reticularis pontis caudalis. It was thereby deduced that this reticular site is the
point at which the modulatory (i.e., motivational) and obligatory circuits
intersect.

Considerable evidence suggests that the modulatory circuit that potentiates the startle response is the same subcortical aversive system that has already been discussed. Specifically, it is clear that the central nucleus of the amygdala figures significantly in startle potentiation. First, there are direct, monosynaptic projections from the amygdala to the key reticular site (i.e., to the structure in the basic circuit on which modulation of the reflex depends); second, electrical stimulation of the amygdala (below the level for kindling) directly enhances startle reflex amplitude; and finally and most important, lesions of the amygdala abolish fear conditioned startle potentiation.

Thus, the animal data are clear, when the aversive system is activated, defensive behavior evoked by a new stimulus is potentiated. Furthermore, for at least one defensive reflex (i.e., the startle response), the underlying neural network is already well explicated. We know the mechanism through which an affective state can enhance a new emotional response.

Probing Human Emotion

Startle Inhibition.   Most human experimentation on the startle probe methodology has not previously been driven by motivational theories; the focus of investigation was the study of attention and the sensory system (e.g, see Anthony, 1985, and Graham, 1979, for reviews). Various stimuli, tasks, and/or instructional manipulations are used to guide subjects' attentional focus. While subjects are thus engaged, brief nontask-relevant startling stimuli are presented, with the expectation that the eyeblink component of the reflex will be attenuated to the degree that attentional resources are already allocated to the primary task. Taking this approach, Simons and Zelson (1985) studied differences in probe reflex inhibition, as subjects' processed foregrounds of varying interest value. Subjects viewed two content classes of photographic slides as a foreground task: (a) interesting content—a varying series of attractive nude males and females; and (b) dull content—a picture of a small wicker basket, repeatedly presented, to which it was presumed less attention would be allocated. Unpredictable auditory startle probes were administered during both slide contents. As expected, the blink reflex was significantly smaller for interesting than for dull slide content.

Although the investigators' focus was a sensory hypothesis, it is clear that the stimuli employed were not motivationally neutral. Pictures of attractive nudes are reasonably classified as appetitive and arousing stimuli. Furthermore, there is animal research suggesting that cues associated with positive incentives occasion inhibition of probe startle responses (Fechter & Ison, 1972; Ison & Krauter, 1975; Szabo, 1967). If, as Konorski (1967) earlier suggested, appetitive and aversive drive states are reciprocally inhibiting, this could be the mechanism that produced diminished probe reflexes. Thus, the results are open to an attentional explanation, but could be equally explained by the mismatch between motivational systems activated by foreground and probe stimuli.

The Affect–Startle Effect.   In a recent paper, Lang, Bradley, and Cuthbert (1990) hypothesized that the startle reflex probe could be used to test fundamental postulates of the theory of human emotion that is here under consideration. In brief, they suggested that evoked reflexes would be differentially modulated, depending on the affective valence of the individual's current motivational state. Thus, when the aversive system is activated (i.e., the brain is processing negative affective information and contacting the relevant subcortical, aversive system circuitry) the reflex will be augmented. This hypothesis presumes that (a) the startle response is an aversive/defensive reflex; and that (b) behaviors are synergistically amplified if an "affective match" exists between reflex and motive state. Furthermore, appetitive and aversive/defensive dispositions are held to be opponent states, reciprocally inhibiting non-matching behaviors. Thus, when appetitive information is the focus of processing, the startle reflex will show relative inhibition.

Looking at Pictures.   Vrana, Spence, and Lang (1988) undertook the first general test of this affect–startle hypothesis in the context of emotional perception. An adaptation of Simons and Zelson's paradigm was used, in which the subject viewed a series of photographic slides while acoustic probes were randomly presented, and the amplitude of the startle component of the eyeblink was measured. The slide stimuli were selected from the International Affective Picture System (IAPS; Lang, Ohman, & Vaitl, 1988) on the basis of normative affective ratings (see Fig. 5.1), and organized into three affective classes, unpleasant (e.g., poisonous snakes, aimed guns, pictures of violent death); pleasant (e.g., happy babies, appetizing food, attractive nudes); and neutral (e.g., umbrellas, hair dryers, and other common household objects). As shown in Fig. 5.1, a significant linear trend was observed over slide valence categories, with the largest startle blink responses occurring during unpleasant content and the smallest during the pleasant pictures.

This phenomenon has since been replicated in several independent experiments: Both Bradley, Lang, and Cuthbert (1990) and Greenwald, Bradley, Cuthbert, and Lang (1990) confirmed that, relative to neutral content, the phenomenon involves *both* a significant potentiation of responding during unpleasant slides, and a significant inhibition during pleasant pictures. Bradley, Cuthbert, and Lang (1991) replicated the phenomenon using monaural, rather than binaural acoustic probes; and furthermore, obtained evidence that this affect–startle effect may be lateralized (i.e., left ear probes, presumably conferring an advantage in right-brain processing, showed the strongest relationship with affective valence). Jansen and Fridja (1991), using evocative video film clips, and Hamm, Stark, and Vaitl (1990), using IAPS slides, obtained the affect–startle effect in European subjects. Finally, Bradley, Cuthbert, and Lang (1990) found the same pattern of affective modulation using visual rather than acoustic startle probes, disconfirming an alternative hypothesis that affective differences were secondary to differences in modality-directed attention (Anthony & Graham, 1985).

Other data from the research just discussed (Bradley et al., 1990, 1991) further support the view that the affect–startle effect is specific to emotional valence. Thus, both pleasant and unpleasant slides elicited similar large skin conductance responses and reports of greater arousal and interest value, than did neutral slides. Furthermore, subjects spent more time looking at both types of affective slides than neutral pictures when allowed to control viewing time. Only the startle blink varied linearly over slide valence categories, increasing monotonically in magnitude from pleasant, to neutral, to unpleasant contents, supporting the hypothesis that the startle reflex is potentiated or inhibited, depending specifically on whether it matches the valence of ongoing emotional perception.[5]

Emotional Imagery: The Network Modulates the Reflex.   It was previously suggested that different media potentially activate the same affective networks in the brain. Thus, if startle modulation is driven by the emotional state itself (i.e., it is not exclusively a phenomenon of emotional perception), these effects should be observed under other conditions of network activation. In an investigation of this hypothesis, Vrana and Lang (1990) studied probe responses to emotional memories. In this case, there was no proximal affective stimulus. At the beginning of the experiment, subjects learned pairs of sentences, one was neutral in content, and one described a fearful event. Recall of the sentences was subsequently cued by tone signals, and probe stimuli were presented during memory processing. Larger reflex responses were observed when subjects remembered sentences with fearful content than when neutral sentences were recalled. Furthermore, this differential effect varied with the processing task. Probe responses were smaller when subjects were told just to articulate the sentences silently than when they were instructed to vividly imagine the sentence content.

Cook, Hawk, Davis, and Stevenson (1991) also studied probe responses during emotional imagery. On the basis of a prior testing, sentences were created that taped a variety of common emotional episodes (i.e., situations associated with fear, anger, sadness, happiness, etc.). Probe responses during imagery of unpleasant emotions were systematically larger than during pleasant affects. Other studies of emotional imagery have also found this same affect–startle effect (e.g., Bradley, Lang, & Cuthbert, 1991; Cuthbert, Bradley, York, & Lang, 1990).

The data also suggest that subjects with pathologically strong affects show more marked startle modulation. Thus, individuals with many fears (as defined by questionnaire) show a greater reflex potentiation in fear imagery than subjects with fewer fears (Cook et al., 1991); similarly, Hamm, Globisch, Cuthbert, and Vaitl (1991) reported larger probe responses in phobic subjects (looking at phobic pictures) than in nonphobics. Furthermore, Vrana (see Bradley & Vrana, in press) observed a systematic reduction in phobic imagery-potentiated blink reflexes after desensitization therapy.

These data are consistent with the view that, in human beings, the processing of conceptual information with emotional content activates subcortical neural circuitry similar to that explicated by animal models of emotional associative learning. A fear state imposed in human subjects by media or memory imagery augments the startle reflex in the same way as does a classically conditioned stimulus in rodents. This connection is further supported by human conditioning studies. That is, college subjects respond to electric shock sensitization (Greenwald, Bradley, Cuthbert, & Lang, 1990), threat of shock (Grillon, Ameli, Woods, Merikangas, & Davis, 1991), and classical shock conditioning (Hamm, Greenwald, Bradley, & Lang, 1991; Hamm et al., 1990) with the same systematic increases in startle reflex response found in animals (Davis, 1989).

SUMMARY AND CONCLUSIONS

This quest for answers, prompted by Berkowitz's chapter, took us on a long journey. It necessarily required a trek across several disciplines, as we considered findings from clinical, social, and cognitive psychology, as well as animal behavior and the neuroscience.

We began with early studies of fear imagery, as used in behavior modification. In this context, the proximal stimulus is a verbal description of a fearful event, which prompts a "fear experience" in phobic patients. Our research suggested, however, that such reported emotional experience had implications for behavior (i.e., could mediate substantive change in avoidance or fear distress) only to the extent that these reports were associated with measurable efference (i.e., coincident output patterns of somatic and autonomic activity). Subsequent studies focused on determining the cognitive processes that generated these functional action dispositions (as opposed to merely understanding text content).

Our early analysis suggested that affects can be meaningfully construed as networks of information that define an episode in memory. This hypothesized memory network includes representations of relevant stimuli, of patterns of responding, and of related declarative knowledge. Because of the associative connections between these representations, the network as a whole can be activated by input that matches only some of the network concepts. Furthermore, this conceptual response information is linked to action programs for the efferent system. Thus, general network activation results in measurable effector output.

The conceptual content of an affect network is highly idiosyncratic: Stimulus information that one subject processes as emotion may not affect another, and because affects are basically episodes, response output will also vary greatly, depending on the contextual imperatives of the original learning. We suggested, however, that these affective memories are, from the perspective of motivational strategy, much simpler. The network's coherence, its associative strength, derives from its connections to one of only two motive systems—appetitive or aversive. These systems are based on subcortical circuits that determine associative reinforcement learning.

In answer to the first question posed at the outset: Affective networks differ from other memory structures in that they have direct associative links to the limbic circuits that drive behavior. Both motive systems mediate a broad arousal reaction, hormonal and cardiovascular, which can support strong, rapid reactions. The evidence suggests, however, that aversive and appetitive systems are in other ways independent, facilitating, in the first case, defensive, withdrawal behaviors (negative affects), and in the second case, consummatory, nurturant, approach behaviors (positive affects). To some extent, these systems may operate reciprocally (i.e., engagement of one system inhibits responses linked to the other). Thus, our answer to the second question: Affects potentiate affective responses with matching valence; a valence mismatch diminishes responding.

Neuroscientists are now able to tell us much about this subcortical, aversive motivation system, at least as it is organized in lower mammals. We know that the subcortical circuitry is itself plastic. Simple affective associations are learned and retained in the absence of cortical sensory processing. Without benefit of appraisal, connections are established between sensory thalamus and the aversive learning circuits in the amygdala that mediate defensive responding. On the other hand, in intact animals, connections go back and forth between the amygdaloid complex and higher centers. Thus, associated information at the cortical level can influence—enhance, modulate, reduce—activity in the motivation circuit.

The assumption of general motivation circuits—priming a variety of aversive affects, or alternatively, a spectrum of appetitive dispositions—is consonant with the animal research. In this chapter, we have emphasized neurophysiological studies of the startle response, showing that this simple defensive reflex is reliably enhanced when the amygdaloid aversive system is activated (e.g., by prior conditioning). This same startle potentiation effect has now also been shown in human beings. As for the rat, human subjects trained to fear stimuli that augur shock show larger startle probe responses to conditioned than control stimuli. Furthermore, research with human beings also suggests that activation of any aversive network—via external stimulation or memory imagery—has same effect of enhancing startle reactions. That is, if the aversive motivational circuitry is engaged, other aversive connections are facilitated. These same studies suggest a broader affective congruence. That is, startle reflexes appear to be diminished when subjects process appetitive information, although this phenomenon has not yet been studied in the animal model.

In conclusion, we can do no better than reiterate Berkowitz's message: "Any truly comprehensive analysis of emotions must be far-ranging and broad in scope. Such a general formulation obviously should be compatible with what is known about the neurophysiology of emotions and probably would also do well to make reference to neurophysiological processes" (p. 37). As we have tried to show, the bio-informational approach has already made modest progress on this road.

We also applaud Berkowitz's admonition to reconsider emotion theories narrowly modeled on "cognitive" processes. I would like to add this clarification. Among many social and clinical psychologists, a *cognition* is a rational (right or wrong) proposition, some reasoned analysis, or a self-instruction. For this group, cognitive activity refers to a sort of internal monologue, framed in natural language, and although some of its operations may be unconscious, they are modeled on subjective reports of conscious thought. I believe that it was in this sense that the term was employed by Berkowitz. For cognitive scientists, however, *cognition* is a broader term, synonymous with "information processing." A cognitive event is simply some computation accomplished by the brain. From this perspective, there is nothing less cognitive about an automatic, associative connection than, for example, language processing, except that the former might be considered more primitive, or perhaps—more fundamental. Using the term in this larger sense, I would then modify Berkowitz's closing sentence: To understand emotion, we need to know the basic cognitive operations, the associative connections to effector activity and behavior, and the structure and function of the mediating physiology.

ACKNOWLEDGMENTS

Preparation of this chapter was supported in part by National Institute of Mental Health Grants MH37757, MH41950, and MH43975, and Grant AG09779 from the National Institute of Aging. Thanks to Margaret M. Bradley, who read early drafts of this commentary and offered many helpful suggestions.

ENDNOTES

[1]Influenced by the cognitive psychology of the time, earlier formulations of bio-informational theory (Lang, 1977, 1979) suggested that networks should be construed as having a basic propositional suborganization. We are now less convinced of its generality. "Given the connectionist arguments (McClelland & Rumelhart, 1985), all elements, including the lowest order concepts in our model, might be viewed as distributed patterns of values in some hypothetical general brain code" (Lang, 1987, p. 410).

[2]In the 1940s, Shaw (1940) reported an experiment in which subjects first lifted a series of small lead weights and subsequently imagined this same task. Bioelectric potentials were recorded from the lifting muscles of the forearm. He noted that there was a linear relationship between the amplitude of electromyographic activity during imagery, and the original heft (calibrated in grams) of the remembered lead weight. The intervening years added considerably to this general literature.

[3]The model presented here does not presume there are invariant autonomic and/or somatic

patterns associated with specific emotions (fear, anger, joy, etc.) as is still argued, for example, by Levenson (1992). The tactical demands of the specific context, and the subject's unique physiological structure, temperament, and specific learning history, inevitably modulate both the behavioral disposition and the physiological logistics of affective expression.

[4]The bio-informational view differs from Bower's (1981) later development of an emotional network model in that it does not assume the existence of separate emotion nodes. In the case of a well-learned, affective pattern, the units of the network are in aggregate the emotion prototype. Its facilitation of, or inhibition by, other affects is determined by the degree of associative match between the networks' concept units (see Lang, 1985, pp. 144–147), and more fundamentally (as we show here) through mutual or discordant connections to the aversive or appetitive motivational systems. Barnard and Teasdale (1991) have more recently addressed the same issues of mood congruence in their Cognitive Subsystems Theory. Their approach is derived from psycholinguistics. They conceive an elaborate organization of data processors (including a truly impressive boxology) that operate primarily in the semantic domain. They do not, however, directly address motivational issues, nor is the approach greatly constrained by psychophysiological or neurophysiological data.

[5]Cuthbert, Bradley, and Lang (1990) examined probe responses to equivalently pleasant slides that were high and low in arousal; a similar comparison was made for unpleasant slides. Skin conductance, a useful measure of sympathetic activation, increased monotonically with reported arousal, irrespective of valence. Startle modulation also increased with arousal, but the direction of effect was again specific to emotional valence. Thus, the most arousing pleasant stimuli produced the greatest reflex inhibition; on the other hand, the most arousing unpleasant stimuli produced the greatest reflex potentiation.

These data are consonant with Konorski's conception of opponent aversive and appetitive arousal systems, in that the different reflex modulation patterns are enhanced by increases in excitation of either affective type. They also follow Watson and Tellegen's (1985) positive and negative affect dimensions, defined by a 45° rotation of the valence–arousal circumplex (see Fig. 5.1). This model suggests that magnitude might increase for action affects such as fear and anger, but would be less influenced by sadness, helplessness, or depression, which are equally unpleasant, but may involve low activation. Similarly, little reflex inhibition would be found in contented relaxation, whereas sexual pleasure, elation, or enthusiasm should produce clear reflex attenuation (see Lang et al., 1992, Lang, Bradley, & Cuthbert, in press).

These results have a broader implication—for mood congruence and other modulatory influences between emotions. They imply that these effects depend on the intensity as well as the valence of emotion. That is, for congruent affects there is a "transfer of excitation" (Zillmann, Katcher, & Milavsky, 1972) and associated behaviors, but with incongruence, the incompatible behaviors will be surpressed. Finally, although we have speculated about activation and startle modulation, and the apparent stability of the affect–startle effect with variation in tactical affective physiologies (e.g., see Vrana & Lang, 1990, p. 195), there is as yet little data on the effects of specific behavioral dispositions on probe response (e.g., during overt approach or withdrawal, in states of inhibition or restraint, with active or passive coping—all of which have interesting theoretical implications.)

REFERENCES

Aggleton, J. P., & Mishkin, M. (1986). The amygdala: Sensory gateway to the emotions. In R. Plutchik & H. Kellerman (Eds.), *Emotion theory, research, and experience*, (Vol. 3, pp. 281–299). New York: Academic Press.

Anderson, J. R., & Bower, G. H. (1974). A propositional theory of recognition memory. *Memory and Cognition, 2*, 406–412.

Anthony, B. J. (1985). In the blink of an eye: Implications of reflex modification for information processing. In P. K. Ackles, J. R. Jennings, & M. G. H. Coles (Eds.), *Advances in psychophysiology* (Vol. 1, pp. 167–218). Greenwich, CT: JAI Press.

Anthony, B. J., & Graham, F. (1985). Blink reflex modification by selective attention: Evidence for the modulation of "automatic" processing. *Biological Psychology, 21,* 43–59.

Barnard, P. J., & Teasdale, J. D. (1991). Interacting cognitive subsystems: A systemic approach to cognitive–affective interaction and change. *Cognition and Emotion, 5,* 1–39.

Ben-Ari, Y. (1981). *The amygdaloid complex.* Amsterdam: Elsevier/North-Holland.

Berg, W. K., & Davis, M. (1985). Associative learning modifies startle reflexes at the lateral lemniscus. *Behavioral Neuroscience, 99,* 191–199.

Blanchard, R. J., & Blanchard, D. C. (1977). Aggression behavior in the rat. *Behavioral Biology, 21,* 197–224.

Blaney, P. H. (1986). Affect and memory: A review. *Psychological Bulletin, 99,* 229–246.

Boulis, N. M., & Davis, M. (1989). Footshock-induced sensitization of electrically elicited startle reflexes. *Behavioral Neuroscience, 103,* 504–508.

Bower, G. H. (1980). Mood and memory. *American Psychologist, 36,* 129–148.

Bradley, M. M., & Vrana, S. R. (in press). The startle probe in emotion and emotional disorders. In N. Birbaumer & A. Ohman (Eds.), *The organization of emotion.* Toronto: Hogrefe-Huber.

Bradley, M. M., Cuthbert, B. N., & Lang, P. J. (1990). Startle reflex modification: Emotion or attention? *Psychophysiology, 27,* 513–523.

Bradley, M. M., Cuthbert, B. N., & Lang, P. J. (1991). Startle and emotion: Lateral acoustic stimuli and the bilateral blink. *Psychophysiology, 28,* 285–295.

Bradley, M. M., Lang, P. J., & Cuthbert, B. N. (1990). Habituation and the affect–startle effect. *Psychophysiology, 27,* S18. [Abstract]

Bradley, M. M., Lang, P. J., & Cuthbert, B. N. (1991). The Gainesville murders: Imagining the worst. *Psychophysiology, 28,* S14. [Abstract]

Brown, J. S., Kalish, H. I., & Farber, I. E. (1951). Conditioned fear as revealed by magnitude of startle response to an auditory stimulus. *Journal of Experimental Psychology, 32,* 317–328.

Cahill, L., & McGaugh, J. L. (1990). Amygdaloid complex lesions differentially affect retention of tasks using appetitive and aversive reinforcement. *Behavioral Neuroscience, 104*(4), 532–543.

Cook, E. W. III, Hawk, L. H., Davis, T. L., & Stevenson, V. E. (1991). Affective individual differences and startle reflex modulation. *Journal of Abnormal Psychology, 100,* 5–13.

Cook, E. W. III, Melamed, B. G., Cuthbert, B. N., McNeil, D. W., & Lang, P. J. (1988). Emotional imagery and the differential diagnosis of anxiety. *Journal of Consulting and Clinical Psychology, 56,* 734–740.

Cuthbert, B. N., Bradley, M. M., York, D. J., & Lang, P. J. (1990). Affective imagery and startle modulation. *Psychophysiology, 27,* S24. [Abstract]

Cuthbert, B. N., Bradley, M. M., & Lang, P. J. (1990). Valence and arousal in startle modulation. *Psychophysiology, 27*(4A) S24. [Abstract]

Cuthbert, B. N., Vrana, S. R., & Bradley, M. M. (1991). Imagery: Function and physiology. In P. K. Ackles, J. R. Jennings, & M. G. H. Coles (Eds.), *Advances in psychophysiology* (Vol. 4, pp. 1–42). Greenwich, CT: JAI Press.

Davis, M. (1989). Neural systems involved in fear-potentiated startle. *Annals of the New York Academy of Sciences, 563,* 165–183.

Davis, M., Hitchcock, J., & Rosen, J. (1987). Anxiety and the amygdala: Pharmacological and anatomical analysis of the fear potentiated startle paradigm. In *Psychology of learning and motivation* (Vol. 21). New York: Academic Press.

DiCara, L., Braun, J. J., & Pappas, B. (1970). Classical conditioning and instrumental learning of cardiac and gastrointestinal responses following removal of neocortex in the rat. *Journal of Comparative and Physiological Psychology, 73,* 208–216.

Farah, M. (1988). Is visual imagery really visual? Overlooked evidence from neuropsychology. *Psychological Review, 95,* 307–318.

Fechter, L. D., & Ison, J. R. (1972). The inhibition of the acoustic startle reaction in rats by food and water deprivation. *Learning and Motivation, 3,* 109–124.

Frijda, N. H. (1986). *The emotions.* New York: Cambridge.

Graham, F. K. (1979). Distinguishing among orienting, defense, and startle reflexes. In H. D. Kimmel, E. H. van Olst, & J. F. Orlebeke (Eds.), *The orienting reflex in humans* (pp. 137–167). Hillsdale, NJ: Lawrence Erlbaum Associates.

Greenwald, M. K., Bradley, M. M., Cuthbert, B. N., & Lang, P. J. (1990). The acoustic startle response indexes aversive learning. *Psychophysiology, 27,* 36. [Abstract]

Grillion, C., Ameli, R., Woods, S. W., Merikangas, K., & Davis, M. (1991). Fear-potentiated startle in humans: Effects of anticipatory anxiety on the acoustic blink reflex. *Psychophysiology, 28,* 588–595.

Hamm, A. O., Globisch, J., Cuthbert, B. N., & Vaitl, D. (1991). Startle reflex modulation in simple phobics and normals. *Psychophysiology.* [Abstract]

Hamm, A. O., Greenwald, M. K., Bradley, M. M., & Lang, P. J. (1991). *Emotional learning, hedonic change, and the startle probe.* Manuscript submitted for publication.

Hamm, A. O., Stark, R., & Vaitl, D. (1990). Startle reflex potentiation and electrodermal response differentiation: Two indicators of two different processes in pavalovian conditioning. *Psychophysiology, 27,* S37. [Abstract]

Hebb, D. O. (1949). *The organization of behavior: A neuropsychological theory.* New York: Wiley.

Hitchcock, J. M., Savanes, C. B., & Davis, M. (1989). Sensitization of the startle reflex to footshock: Blockade by lesions of the central nucleus of the amygdala or its efferent pathway to the brainstem. *Behavioral Neurosciences, 103,* 509–518.

Hull, C. L. (1943). *Principles of behavior.* New York: Appleton-Century.

Ison, J. R., & Krauter, E. E. (1975). Acoustic startle reflexes in the rat during consummatory behavior. *Journal of Comparative and Physiological Psychology, 89,* 39–49.

Iwata, J., & LeDoux, J. E. (1988). Dissociation of associative and nonassociative concommitants of classical fear conditioning in the freely behaving rat. *Behavioral Neuroscience, 102,* 66–76.

Jacobson, E. (1931). Electrical measurements of neuromuscular states during mental activities. Variation of specific muscles contracting during imagination. *American Journal of Psychology, 96,* 115–121.

Jansen, D. M., & Frijda, N. (1991). *Modulation of acoustic startle response by film-induced fear and sexual arousal.* Manuscript submitted for publication.

Jaynes, J. (1976). *The origin of consciousness in the breakdown of the bicameral mind.* Boston: Houghton-Mifflin.

Kintsch, W. (1974). *The representation of meaning in memory.* Hillsdale, NJ: Lawrence Erlbaum Associates.

Konorski, J. (1967). *Integrative activity of the brain: An interdisciplinary approach.* Chicago: University of Chicago Press.

Lang, P. J. (1968). Fear reduction and fear behavior: Problems in treating a construct. In J. M. Schlien (Ed.), *Research in psychotherapy,* (Vol. 3, pp. 90–103). Washington, DC: American Psychological Association.

Lang, P. J. (1977). Imagery in therapy: An information processing analysis of fear. *Behavior Therapy, 8,* 862–886.

Lang, P. J. (1978). Anxiety: Toward a psychophysiological definition. In H. S. Akiskal & W. L. Webb (Eds.), *Psychiatric diagnosis: Exploration of biological predictors* (pp. 365–389). New York: Spectrum.

Lang, P. J. (1979). Presidential address, 1978: A bio-informational theory of emotional imagery. *Psychophysiology, 16,* 495–512.

Lang, P. J. (1984). Cognition in emotion: Concept and action. In C. E. Izard, J. Kagan, & R. B. Zajonc (Eds.), *Emotions, cognitions, and behavior* (pp. 192–228). New York: Cambridge.

Lang, P. J. (1985). The cognitive psychophysiology of emotion: Fear and anxiety. In A. H. Tuma &

J. D. Maser (Eds.), *Anxiety and the anxiety disorders* (pp. 131–170). Hillsdale, NJ: Lawrence Erlbaum Associates.

Lang, P. J. (1987). Image as action: A reply to Watts and Blackstock. *Cognition and Emotion, 1,* 407–426.

Lang, P. J., & Lazovik, A. D. (1963). Experimental desensitization of a phobia. *Journal of Abnormal and Social Psychology, 66,* 519–525.

Lang, P. J., Bradley, M. M., & Cuthbert, B. N. (1990). Emotion, attention, and the startle reflex. *Psychological Review, 97,* 377–395.

Lang, P. J., Bradley, M. M., Cuthbert, B. N. (1992). A motivational analysis of emotion: Reflex-cortex connections. *Psychological Science, 3,* 44–49.

Lang, P. J., Greenwald, M. K., Bradley, M. M., & Hamm, A. O. (in press). Looking at pictures: Affective, facial, visceral, and behavioral reactions. *Psychophysiology.*

Lang, P. J., Kozak, M. J., Miller, G. A., Levin, D. N., & McLean, Jr., A. (1980). Emotional imagery: Conceptual structure and pattern of somato–visceral response. *Psychophysiology, 17*(2), 179–192.

Lang, P. J., Lazovik, A. D., & Reynolds, D. J. (1965). Desensitization, suggestibility and pseudotherapy. *Journal of Abnormal Psychology, 70,* 395–402.

Lang, P. J., Melamed, B. G., & Hart, J. D. (1970). A psychophysiological analysis of fear modification using an automated desensitization procedure. *Journal of Abnormal Psychology, 76,* 220–234.

Lang, P. J., Öhman, A., & Vaitl, D. (1988). *The international affective picture system* [photographic slides]. Gainesville, FL: The Center for Research in Psychophysiology, University of Florida.

Lazarus, R. S. (1984). On the primacy of cognition. *American Psychologist, 39,* 124–129.

LeDoux, J. E. (1989). Cognitive–emotional interactions in the brain. *Cognition and Emotion, 3,* 267–289.

LeDoux, J. E. (1990). Information flow from sensation to emotion: Plasticity in the neural computation of stimulus value. In M. Gabriel & J. Moore (Eds.), *Learning and computational neuroscience: Foundations of adaptive networks* (pp. 3–52). Cambridge, MA: Bradford Books/MIT Press.

LeDoux, J. E., Cicchetti, P., Xagoraris, A., & Romanski, L. (1990). The lateral amygdaloid nucleus: Sensory interface of the amygdala in fear conditioning. *The Journal of Neuroscience, 10,* 1062–1069.

Levenson, R. W. (1992). Autonomic nervous system differences among emotions. *Psychological Science, 3,* 23–27.

Leventhal, H. (1980). Toward a comprehensive theory of emotion. In L. Berkowitz (Ed.), *Advances in experimental social psychology* (Vol. 13, pp. 139–207). New York: Academic Press.

Mackintosh, N. J. (1983). *Conditioning and associative learning.* New York: Oxford.

Markoff, J. (1991). Man or Machine? *The New York Times,* Nov. 9, pp. 1, 10.

McClelland, J. L., & Rumelhart, D. E. (1985). Distributed memory and the representation of general and specific information. *Journal of Experimental Psychology: General, 114,* 159–189.

McClelland, J. L., & Rumelhart, D. E. (1981). An interactive activation model of context effects in letter perception: Part 1. An account of basic findings. *Psychological Review, 88,* 375–407.

McClelland, J. L., & Rumelhart, D. E. (1988). *Explorations in parallel distributed processing: A handbook of models, programs, and exercises.* Cambridge, MA: MIT Press/Bradford books.

McGuigan, F. J. (1973). Electrical measurement of covert processes as an explication of "higher mental events." In F. J. McGuigan & R. A. Schoonover (Eds.), *The psychophysiology of thinking.* (pp. 343–376). New York: Academic Press.

McLean, A., Jr. (1982). Emotional imagery: Stimulus information, imagery ability and patterns of physiological response. *Dissertation Abstracts International, 42*(11) 4884–B.

McNeil, D. W., Vrana, S. R., Melamed, B. G., Cuthbert, B. N., & Lang, P. J. (in press). *Emotional* imagery in simple and social phobia: "Normal" fear and pathological anxiety. Manuscript submitted for publication.

Miller, G. A., Levin, D. N., Kozak, M. J., Cook, E. W. III, McLean, A., & Lang, P. J. (1987). Individual differences in emotional imagery. *Cognition and Emotion, 1,* 367–390.

Öhman, A., Dimberg, U., & Esteves, F. (1989). Preattentive activation of aversive emotions. In T. Archer & L. G Nilsson (Eds.), Aversion, avoidance and anxiety (pp. 169–193). Hillsdale, NJ: Lawrence Erlbaum Associates.

Patrick, C. J., Cuthbert, B. N., & Lang, P. J. (1989). Automaticity of emotional processing in anxious and non-anxious patients. *Psychophysiology, 26,* S47. [Abstract]

Pavlov, I. P. (1927). *Conditioned reflexes.* Oxford: Oxford University Press.

Pylyshyn, Z. W. (1973). What the mind's eye tells the mind's brain: A critique of mental imagery. *Psychological Bulletin, 80,* 1–24.

Roldan, E., Alvarez-Pelaez, R., & Fernandez de Molina, A. (1974). Electrographic study of the amygdaloid defense response. *Physiology and Behavior, 13,* 779–787.

Ross, L. E. (1961). Conditioned fear as a function of CS–UCS and probe stimulus intervals. *Journal of Experimental Psychology, 61,* 265–273.

Schank, R. C. (1982). *Dynamic memory: A theory of reminding and learning in computers and people.* Cambridge Press: New York.

Schneider, W., & Shriffrin, R. M. (1977). Controlled and automatic human information processing. *Psychological Review, 84,* 1–66.

Sheehan, P. W. (1967). A shortened form of Betts' questionnaire upon mental imagery. *Journal of Clinical Psychology, 223,* 380–389.

Simons, R. F., & Zelson, M. F. (1985). Engaging visual stimuli and reflex blink modification. *Psychophysiology, 22,* 44–49.

Spence, K. W., & Runquist, W. N. 1958). Temporal effects of conditioned fear on the eyelid reflex. *Journal of Experimental Psychology, 55,* 613–616.

Shaw, W. A. (1940). The relation of muscular action potentials to imaginal weight lifting. *Archives of Psychology, 247,* 50.

Szabo, I. (1967). Analysis of the muscular action potentials accompanying the acoustic startle reaction. *Acta Physiologica of the Hungarian Academy of Sciences, 27,* 167–178.

Ursin, H. (1965). Effect of amygdaloid lesions on avoidance behavior and visual discrimination in cats. *Experimental Neurology, 11,* 298–317.

Ursin, H., Jellestad, F., & Cabrera, I. G. (1981). The amygdala, exploration and fear. In Y. Ben-Ari (Ed.), *The amygdaloid complex* (pp. 317–329). Amsterdam: Elsevier/North-Holland.

Vrana, S. R., & Lang, P. J. (1990). Fear imagery and the startle probe reflex. *Journal of Abnormal Psychology, 99,* 189–197.

Vrana, S. R., Cuthbert, B. N., & Lang, P. J. (1989). Processing fearful and neutral sentences: Memory and heart rate change. *Cognition and Emotion, 3,* 179–195.

Vrana, S. R., Spence, E. L., & Lang, P. J. (1988). The startle probe response: A new measure of emotion? *Journal of Abnormal Psychology, 97,* 487–491.

Watson, D., & Tellegen, A. (1985). Toward a consensual structure of mood. *Psychological Bulletin, 98,* 219–235.

Wegner, D. N., Schneider, D. J., Carter, S. R., & White, T. L. (1987). Paradoxical effects of thought suppression. *Journal of Personality and Social Psychology, 53,* 5–13.

Zajonc, R. B. (1980). Feeling and thinking. *American Psychologist, 35,* 151–175.

Zillman, D., Katcher, A., & Milavsky, B. (1972). Excitation transfer from physical exercize to subsequent aggressive behavior. *Journal of Experimental Social Psychology, 8,* 247–259.

6

A Componential, Self-Regulative Systems View of Berkowitz's Cognitive–Neoassociationistic Model of Anger

Howard Leventhal
Rutgers University

In this chapter, agreement is expressed with Berkowitz's analysis in five areas:

1. Emotions are complex.
2. Emotions involve both psychological and physiological factors.
3. Pain and distress generate anger.
4. The emotion mechanism is multilevel.
5. One level of the emotion processing system is network-like in structure.

I criticize Berkowitz's equation of cognition with conscious, deliberative decision making and propose as a substitute three levels of cognitive process, all three active in the generation and maintenance of emotional states. In a final section, I elaborate on two aspects of emotion models: (a) emotions as an assembly of multiple components at each level of processing (e.g., expressive and somatic), which suggests that phenomena such as the generalization of arousal and state dependent memory depend on cross situational sharing of components rather than specific affects; and (b) the mind as a neural network in an endocrinological bath, which suggests that endocrine and immune products play a major role in organizing emotional states and moods. Their effects on the organization of emotion are critical for an understanding of the phenomena (generalization and state dependent memory) that Berkowitz describes.

My reading of Leonard Berkowitz's interesting and scholarly chapter stimulated three lines of response. First, I acknowledge a few of the many points of agreement. Second, I focus on an issue of disagreement, Berkowitz's conceptualization of cognition. Third, I discuss an overlapping yet somewhat different perspective on emotion theory that emphasizes the organizational aspect of emotional reactions. In this latter discussion I focus on two themes: (a) emotions are multicomponent structures and not homogeneous entities; and (b) the endocrine and immune systems play a critical role in the organization of emotional states. Although these ideas may seem familiar to the reader, they are different than the notions held by me (Leventhal, 1979, 1980, 1984) and others (e.g., Schachter & Singer, 1962) from the 1960s. Specifically, I differentiate the components of emotion from its levels (cognitive, expressive, autonomic) and suggest that the identification of components the more important for emotion theory. I also propose that our knowledge of receptor sites and the systemwide distribution of endocrines requires revision of the network model.

AREAS OF AGREEMENT

My list of items of agreement is brief, as I have selected from a longer list those items that are of particular relevance to the sections that follow. Perhaps the most important is Berkowitz's emphasis on the complexity of emotion mechanisms. Emotion words (e.g., "anger," "fear," "joy," "disgust," etc.) identify a complex set of reactions ranging from subjective states through overt actions. The use of labels, however, creates the illusion of *thingness,* as though emotions were specific entities such as tables or chairs. Emotions and moods are dynamic states and not things, and highly complex mechanisms are engaged in their construction. The illusion of thingness conveyed by single terms and the implication that we are dealing with entities may have encouraged investigators to propose overly simple, and occasionally univariate solutions to the complex problems of the initiation, organization, consequences, and maintenance of emotional and mood states. It may also have encouraged the separation of literatures which Berkowitz so rightly decries.

A second issue of agreement is that emotion models need take into account physiological as well as psychological processes (Berkowitz, p. 37). Care must be taken, however, to avoid mindless reductionism when using data from another nonpsychological level of description. In the domain of emotion theory, physiological concepts and data can be used to identify stimuli to emotional processing, to define possible limits for psychological processes, that is, how rapidly (or slowly) will a process unfold, and to help us choose the more plausible psychological model from among a larger set. But one must keep in mind that we are attempting to create a psychological model (Marr, 1982). Thus, physiological data are not to be used to explain away psychological findings.

Third, it is clear that a wide range of painful and emotionally distressing events provoke fight/flight reactions (see also Gray, 1990). The evocation of the fight/flight reaction by painful and distressing stimuli has been documented in a wide range of species and can be elicited in both neonate and mature animals (Leventhal & Tomarken, 1986). Even though the body of data supporting the fight/flight notion is overwhelming, I do not doubt that Berkowitz is correct in suggesting that social scientists and psychologists have resisted it. Given the empirical support, it seems difficult to understand the resistance until one realizes that this notion suggests we are something less than fully rational beings.

Fourth, a multilevel mechanism underlies the evocation and organization of emotional reactions. As used in this context, multilevel refers to levels of a psychological model or psychological mechanism for the processing of inputs and construction and organization of emotional reactions. We are not here using the concept of levels to mean levels of description (e.g., physiological, psychological, sociological, etc.)

Fifth, we agree with Berkowitz in suggesting that at least one level of the emotion processing system can be construed as "networklike" in structure, and another as propositional and more open to conscious control. The characteristics we attribute to these levels overlap with but are not identical to those postulated by Berkowitz.

These five points represent a substantial overlap in perspective. There are, however, areas of disagreement and suggestions for modification of the network model, and I address them now.

AREAS OF DISAGREEMENT AND/OR CONFUSION

The greatest point of disagreement, or perhaps confusion on my part, pertains to Berkowitz's use of the term *cognition*. He, along with Zajonc (1980), and perhaps Lazarus (1984), equates cognition with conscious appraisals (p. 4), situational construals (p. 5), and deliberative, or controlled, processes that may serve to justify rather than motivate aggressive action (p. 4). Cognition typically serves, therefore, as a barrier to automatic, aggressive impulse (p. 6). Berkowitz clearly gains two advantages by incorporating these processes within the concept of cognition: (a) it sharpens the contrast between controlled and deliberative processes with the automatic reactions attributed to associative networks; and (b) it makes clear that the elicitation of anger need not depend on complex appraisals of unwarranted harm, nor must the execution of aggressive behavior be dictated by a conscious, systematic plan designed to remove a threat or right a perceived injustice. Whereas both of these gains are of value in arguing the pros and cons of social policies for the control of aggression and anger and meting out of punishment, these positive values are outweighed, in my judgment, by serious losses when we attempt a rigorous analysis of emotional mechanisms.

Multiple Levels of Cognition:
The Perceptual–Motor Model

In prior expositions of our perceptual–motor model of emotion (Leventhal, 1979, 1980, 1984; Leventhal & Scherer, 1987) as well as in more recent writings (1991), we have used the term *cognition* as a global label for a hierarchy of at least three types of mental processes that intervene between stimulus and emotional response. The three levels of cognitive process that we have defined are, *sensory–motor, schematic,* and *conceptual or propositional.* Each level refers to a different mediational system comprised of representational and procedural processes for decoding stimuli and constructing and organizing emotional reactions to specific stimulus inputs. Although all three of these mediating mechanisms are simultaneously active, each makes a distinct contribution to the initiation, creation, and maintenance of emotion and mood.

Sensory–Motor Processes.   Sensory–motor processes were seen as the pre-wired mechanism (see Berkowitz, p. 11), the initial vocabulary (Leventhal, 1980), or seeds for the formation of more complex mediating structures. I suggested most recently (Leventhal, 1991) that these perceptual–motor structures appear to have many of the properties of modules (Fodor, 1983) that allow the neonate to detect and represent facial and vocal stimulus patterns and produce expressive responses that mimic the expressive reactions of caregivers (Field, Woodson, Greenberg, & Cohen, 1982). The modularity hypothesis recognized the selectivity of these representational and procedural (productive) processes. Thus, the facial and vocal stimulus patterns that are selected for attention represent a highly limited set of inputs from the wide range of stimuli that can be accessed by the visual and auditory systems. Similarly, the mimickry represents the selection of a limited number of response patterns from a much wider domain. Neonatal reactions of distress and anger to constraints or *to disconfirmations of expectancies* are additional forms of modular, expressive motor mediation. The complexity of organization and temporal maintenance of these responses indicates that they are far too complex to be classified as simple reflexes. In short, this is a "simple" or base level of cognitive mediation.

Schematic Processes.   The second of our three levels, the schematic, is a close match to Berkowitz's associative network. Schemata are patterned structures formed by linkages between eliciting stimuli (both social and internal), expressive reactions, postural and systemic (autonomic) responses, and contextual stimuli. The sensory–motor reactions described in the immediately prior section provide the seeds for the development of schemata. Because these sensory–motor reactions are communicative and interpersonal they permit the production of temporally extended episodes of human interchange. Thus, the infant's expressive reply to a caregiver's expressive display initiates a response leading to a counter response, and so on, or a temporally extended interplay that has been described as a "dance" (Trevarthen, 1984) and allows for the incorporation of a wide range of stimuli and responses into an *emotion schema*. Although some portion of these associations may be inwired, that is, somatic reactions may be innately linked with particular expressive reactions as suggested by the studies from Davidson's laboratory (Davidson, Ekman, Saron, Senulis, & Friesen, 1990), the social interplay will affect the intensity and range of responses incorporated into the schema (Leventhal, 1986). Pathways for such learning are outlined by Rolls (1990).

As both Berkowitz, and Bower and Cohen (1982) make clear, these emotional memory networks, or emotion schemata, are representations of prior emotional experiences. They are likely to be episodic (i.e., representations of specific instances of intense, emotional activity), but it is also likely that they can be prototypic (i.e., representations of a past history of emotional experience). Single episodes are likely to be represented when extremely intense and absorbing: Examples would be those involved in the formation of phantom pain (Leventhal, 1982) or episodes of extreme fright.

The schematic level of the perceptual–motor model defines the associationist component of Berkowitz's model and in both models it is a mediator of impulse. Thus, the activation of a schema seems to be responsible for the enhancement of aggressive reactions to distress whether that distress is elicited by elevated temperature, by smells, by tastes, or by other negative affects such as depression and fear. Schematic processes seem to combine sensitization and classical conditioning though they lack the directionality associated with traditional CS–CR associations. Thus, each component of a schemata appears to serve as stimulus and response, though their bidirectionality may not be entirely symmetrical.

Conceptual Processes.   The third, the conceptual level of cognition was conceived as the store of abstract, propositional memories about prior emotion episodes, and procedures for reacting to these episodes. Because conceptual cognition is abstract and not directly dependent upon situational or perceptual stimulation, it has two important properties that differentiate it from schematic mediation: (a) it is more susceptible to conscious control or regulation; and (b) it is the mediator of extended, temporal representations or scripts (Abelson, 1976). Conceptual cognition plays a critical role, therefore, in controlled thinking and talking about emotional episodes and in controlled execution of decisions and procedures for regulating situations and emotion. And given the time-spanning capacity of controlled processes, in contrast to the shorter span of conditioned, schematic processes, conceptual mediation is critical for the storage of information involved in an individuals reactions to ongoing emotional episodes. And as with sensory–motor and schematic mediation, conceptual cognition has both representational and procedural functions.

Areas of Disagreement Concerning the Definition of Cognition

How does the aforementioned psychological hierarchy map with that suggested by Berkowitz? First, it is congruent with his suggestion that cognition (of a conceptual type) is a key information store that is utilized in generating verbalizations about emotion. It is also congruent with his observation that conceptual cognition and its associated verbal output is the basis of much of the data used by emotion theorists. As a consequence, we also agree that serious questions can be raised respecting the extent to which the conceptual story about emotion will match observations of schema driven (i.e., automatic, emotional reactions). Thus, the study by Shaver, Schwartz, Kirson, and O'Connor (1987), exceptional though it may be in describing prototypes based on subjects' prior observations of the emotional reactions of themselves and others, requires careful scrutiny as to validity (i.e., or the match between concepts and performance based schemata).

We take issue, however, with Berkowitz's argument that the primary, and indeed the only function of conceptual cognition is to serve as a "check" on network elicited impulse. Berkowitz's distinction between associative and cognitive structures assigns to cognition the role of checking action (i.e., when one becomes aware of an anger impulse, conceptual cognition is the source of conscious decisions to "lean over backward"). This formulation ignores two possibilities. The first is that conceptual procedures may be automatic (i.e., a variety of procedures for "leaning over" or ways of coping may become automatic and thoughtless!). And when coping procedures are automatic, they may be elicited without the immediately prior awareness of emotion; one can "lean over backward" before noticing that one is angry, and one can hide one's head in the sand as an automatic, reaction that anticipates and avoids emotional upset. The second, is that the unfolding sequence of anger, an angry attack followed by a series of counterthrusts and attacks, may also be automatic and programmed at a conceptual (script) level. Thus, the series of representations and procedures (i.e., the sequence of scenes that define a conceptual script) can be highly automated. Although Berkowitz's model is sensitive to the distinction between automatic and controlled process it pays too little attention to the temporal, script-storing function of conceptual cognition.

But it is at the network level (i.e., schematic cognition), where there may be the greatest need for change in the neoassociationistic model. The network structure is the major organizing factor of emotion in Berkowitz's model. I assume the network, as he conceives it, incorporates sensory–motor units as nodes, and integrates these core processing units with more complex, acquired cognitions (stimulus and response associations). But how is this network organized? Is it organized solely by the formation of associations between elements in a "neutral" medium, the brain as a computer?

THE ORGANIZATION OF EMOTION

The impulsive property of emotional reactions and their observed functions as interruptions (Mandler, 1975; Scherer, 1984) and disrupters of problem-solving behaviors often leads us to forget that emotions are organized activities constructed by an underlying, organized mechanism (Leeper, 1948). Berkowitz's description of angry impulses as reactions that can be directed to any available target, whether or not the target is a justified recipient of attack, is partially consistent with the perspective of emotion as disruption as he views anger as a reaction that disrupts other ongoing activities. But he also sees it as a product of a complex, underlying system in which environmentally and internally elicited negative affects play a key role in the elicitation of the anger impulse. Thus, Berkowitz recognizes that the angry impulse is more than a reflexive lashing out; the response itself is well organized and more complex than a reflex, as it lasts for long periods of time and can affect reactions in subsequent and unrelated situations if it is not curbed by cognition's conscious and conscientious eye.

In my judgment, Berkowitz' neoassociationist model fails to adequately account for two of the empirical effects cited by him, the generalization of arousal, and state dependent learning. Both assume an organized emotional process that is sustained over considerable time spans. Network models require two important modifications if they are to account for these phenomena: (a) a more clear recognition of the componential nature of emotional processes; and (b) incorporation of endocrinological factors as network organizers.

The Componential Nature of Emotion

Although Berkowitz clearly recognizes the complexity of the mechanism underlying the construction of emotional reactions, it is my impression that he would be satisfied with an approach that singles out different levels of response (e.g., subjective feelings, expressive reactions, and autonomic response), and differentiates mental processes as cognitive and network. In my judgment, a model that differentiates specific components at each level as well as identifying different levels would benefit the analysis of the aggression problem.

For example, studies of the neurological substrate of emotional behavior suggests the distinct contribution of left frontal activation to approach behaviors and right frontal and parietal to avoidance behaviors (Davidson, Ekman, Saron, Senulis, & Friesen, 1990) and the differentiation of punishment and reward centers in limbic system (Gray, 1990). Specific functions for the control of other complex, emotionally motivated behaviors also seem to be localized (e.g., for the control of sexual activity, food consumption, and thermo-regulation on the positive side and attack, behavioral inhibition and disgust [nausea/vomiting] on the negative side). Particular emotions appear to be assemblages of these components. For example, anger may include specific *expressive response* components

141

such as the baring of teeth, flattening of ears, and changes in the hair follicles, and systemic/autonomic components such as heart rate acceleration and systolic blood pressure rise, to support vigorous action, all of which may be partially integrated and subsumed by a powerful *approach* tendency. Emotional reactions associated with appetitive drives such as sex and hunger will incorporate many of these same components (e.g., a strong approach tendency and systemic/ autonomic changes to support action, though the pattern is somewhat different from that seen in anger).

A differentiated model of this sort raises specific questions about generalization effects and memory effects, two of the phenomena Berkowitz feels important for understanding aggression. Thus, when we ask what it is that generalizes in studies such as that by Zillmann, Katcher, and Milavsky (1972), an answer that differentiates the generalization of both activation for approach and systemic preparation for action, rather than generalization of arousal, might provide a more precise response and lead to differential predictions for different postarousal tasks (e.g., those requiring avoidance and high levels of autonomic activity versus those requiring approach and high levels of autonomic activity). Similarly, when one asks questions about the impact of affect on memory, one might speculate that those components important for determining the direction of action (e.g., approach vs. withdrawal), would make a substantial contribution to retrieval effects, as different knowledge systems would be needed for these two opposing action systems (Leventhal, 1991). One hypothesis derivable from this analysis is that the memory store for aggression and pleasure would be partially overlapping. Other approaches (e.g., Gilligan & Bower, 1984) would emphasize memory linkages based on a specific type of affect and/or punishment versus reward rather than a component of emotion such as active approach. One might hope that increased theoretical precision would allow for more meaningful analysis.

A componential analysis also helps make sense of the apparently impulsive, nonfunctional properties of aggressive attack (e.g., the direction to irrelevant targets of aggressive reactions stimulated by multiple prior inputs). As Berkowitz suggests, these impulsive reactions may be nonfunctional for the elimination of an environmental threat, or as ways of settling a score, but they may be functional in reestablishing homeostasis in an action system or at the systemic level of such a system. Thus, the organism's overt action could be a way of returning a motor or autonomic component to baseline, rather than being an action taken to satisfy an angry impulse.

Endocrine Organization of Emotional Processes

My final point concerns Berkowitz's use of a network model that is based on a computer analogy. Although one must distinguish between hardware and software, it is all too clear that many network analogies draw upon both. Hardware imagery clearly influences how we think about the psychological process of *tuning*, which is important for the generalization of aggressive behavior. The computer model represents external and internal cues, including subjective states, as nodes whose activation spreads throughout the system. The computer analogy further suggests that activation, both its spread and maintenance, depends on the strength of connections between nodes and continued activity (i.e., continued external input or internal thought), to maintain the activity; the digital circuitry of the electronic machine is either on or off.

The human organism, however, is a chemical/electronic structure, and not a collection of wires or pathways etched in silicon. Indeed, our (neural) networks might best be conceived as resting in a bath; hence, a more appropriate image is that of your desktop computer functioning under water! Of course, the bath is not simply water: The neural network is bathed in a dynamic endocrine system the contents of which shift over time. The changing levels of endocrines, interleukins, and neurotransmitters acting on receptor sites on neurons and organs generate different organizations of neural activity, or *system–states* (Leventhal, 1991; Leventhal & Patrick-Miller, in press), affecting representations (memory formation and retrieval) and availability of procedural skills. In short, the organization of the behavioral system, and of the systems ability to form associations, is shaped by the chemical milieu as well as by direct (i.e., neural) communication.

An extremely important feature of system-states is the multiple time constants for change in its constituents. Some of endocrines are quickly taken up or metabolized, whereas others can stay about for minutes, hours or days. Although a complicating factor for the neural modeller, the varied time constants provide grist for the emotion theorist suggesting hypotheses about the generalization of some components of affective processes over far longer time frames than those involved in direct neural communication. Indeed, an individual's failure to recognize that aggressive reactions may generalize to irrelevant settings may reflect a lack of awareness of differential time constants in somatic and cerebral systems. Thus, somatic states that may support the generalization of anger, are sustained by endocrine activity that may be long lasting and relatively inaccessible to awareness. Consciously available angry feelings that would seem to be the appropriate basis for generalization of anger, are short lived as they are sustained by neural activity whose neurotransmitters have a relatively brief time frame. Indeed, humoral activation can be toxic for the very reason that its activity can be sustained without continued cognitive awareness.

CONCLUSION

My response to Berkowitz's chapter was designed to develop specific ideas and general themes that allow us to go beyond the neoassociationistic model he proposes. I began, therefore by emphasizing five areas of agreement:

1. The complexity of emotion mechanisms.
2. The need to take into account both physiological and psychological proeesses, with care taken to avoid mindless reductionism.
3. The role of pain and emotional distress in provoking fight/flight reactions, a notion that social scientists and psychologists have resisted.
4. The importance of a multilevel system for understanding the evocation and organization of emotional reactions; and
5. Agreement that at least one level of the emotion processing system is "network like" in structure.

These five points represent a substantial overlap in perspective.

To go beyond the model, I was critical of Berkowitz's tendency to equate cognition with conscious, deliberative decision making. I suggested instead, that the emotion system is comprised of at least (and possibly more than) three levels of cognitive process: sensory–motor, a simple innate processing system; schematic, an automatic, network like structure; and conceptual, a propositional, time-binding system for representing events whose associated regulative procedures can be conscious and deliberate, or automatic. Each level has its way of structuring or representing external and internal stimuli and its own set of associated response procedures. And whereas all three levels are active in the generation and maintenance of emotional states, their contribution to experience and observed behavior may vary with different affects, persons, and situations. This differentiation of cognitive process allows for automatic and anticipatory control of aggressive impulses as well as conscious, "bending over backward."

My final effort at expanding the model elaborated two themes: the componential nature of affective processes, and the role of endocrinological processes in the evocation and organization and maintenance of emotion and mood. I argued that emotion labels create the illusion that emotions are things or entities rather than dynamic states generated by complex mechanisms. By differentiating emotions into multiple components at the expressive and somatic levels of processing, new questions are raised about processes such as the generalization of arousal, and whether specific components such as approach–avoidance rather than emotional entities such as anger and depression are responsible for state dependent effects in memory.

Finally, we presented a revised view of networks; rather than analogizing mental networks to complex computers, we prefer to see the mind as a neural network in an endocrinological bath. The endocrines in this bath combine with receptor sites on both neural and nonneural cells, organizing system-states for different emotions and moods. As this milieu varies in its makeup as a function of eliciting conditions and different half-lives or temporal constants, the organization of the emotion system changes in significant ways over time. I believe this underrepresented feature of emotional organization will play an important role in understanding many of the temporally extended phenomena (e.g., generalization of arousal, etc.) that Berkowitz describes. In summary, although I take issue with some features of Berkowitz's neo–associationist model, it clearly stimulated and helped organize a few new associations for me.

REFERENCES

Abelson, R. P. (1976). Script processing in attitude formation and decision making. In U. S. Carroll & J. W. Payne (Eds.), *Cognitive and social behavior* (pp. 33–45). Hillsdale, NJ: Lawrence Erlbaum Associates.

Bower, G. H., & Cohen, P. R. (1982). Emotional influences on learning and cognition. In M. S. Clark & S. J. Fiske (Eds.), *Affect and cognition* (pp. 263–289). Hillsdale, NJ: Lawrence Erlbaum Associates.

Davidson, R. J., Ekman, P., Saron, C. D., Senulis, J. A., & Friesen, W. V. (1990). Approach–withdrawal and cerebral asymmetry: Emotional expression and brain physiology I. *Journal of Personality and Social Psychology, 58*, 330–341.

Field, T. M., Woodson, R., Greenberg, R., & Cohen, D. (1982). Discrimination and imitation of facial expression by neonates. *Science, 218*, 179–181.

Fodor, J. A. (1983). *The modularity of mind*. Cambridge, MA: MIT Press.

Gilligan, S. G., & Bower, G. H. (1984). Cognitive consequences of emotional arousal. In C. E. Izard, J. Kagan, & R. B. Zajonc (Eds.), *Emotions, cognition, and behavior* (pp. 547–588). Cambridge: Cambridge University Press.

Gray, J. A. (1990). Brain systems that mediate both emotion and cognition. *Cognition and Emotion, 4*(3), 269–288.

Lazarus, R. S. (1984). On the primacy of cognition. *American Psychology, 39*, 124–129.

Leeper, R. (1948). A motivational theory of emotion to replace "emotion as disorganized response." *Psychological Review, 55*, 5–21.

Leventhal, H. (1979). A perceptual–motor processing model of emotion. In P. Pliner, K. Blankstein, & I. M. Spigel (Eds.), *Advances in the study of communication and affect: Perception of emotion in self and others* (Vol. 5, pp. 1–46). New York: Plenum Press.

Leventhal, H. (1980). Toward a comprehensive theory of emotion. *Advances in Experimental Social Psychology, 13*, 139–207.

Leventhal, H. (1982). The integration of emotion and cognition: A view from the perceptual–motor theory of emotion. In M. Clark, & S. Fiske (Eds.), *Affect and cognition: The 17th annual Carnegie symposium on cognition* (pp. 121–156). Hillsdale, NJ: Lawrence Erlbaum Associates.

Leventhal, H. (1984). A perceptual–motor theory of emotion. *Advances in Experimental Social Psychology, 17*, 117–182.

Leventhal, H. (1986). Symptom reporting: A focus on process. In S. McHugh & T. M. Vallis (Eds.), *Illness behavior: A multidisciplinary model* (pp. 219–237). New York: Plenum Press.

Leventhal, H. (1991). Emotion: Prospects for conceptual and empirical development. In R. J. Lister & H. J. Weingartner (Eds.), *Perspectives on cognitive neuroscience* (pp. 325–348). New York: Oxford University Press.

Leventhal, H., & Patrick-Miller, L. (in press). Emotion and health: The mind is in the body! In M. Lewis, & J. Haviland (Eds.), *The handbook of emotion*. New York: Guilford.

Leventhal, H., & Scherer, K. R. (1987). The relationship of emotion to cognition: A functional approach to semantic controversy. *Cognition and Emotion, 1*, 3–28.

Leventhal, H., & Tomarken, A. J. (1986). Emotion: Today's problems. *Annual Review of Psychology, 37*, 565–610.

Mandler, G. (1975). *Mind and emotion*. New York: Norton.

Marr, D. (1982). *Vision: A computational investigation into the human representation and processing of visual information.* New York: W. H. Freeman.

Rolls, E. T. (1990). A theory of emotion, and its application to understanding the neural basis of emotion. *Cognition and Emotion, 4*(3), 161–190.

Schachter, S., & Singer, J. (1962). Cognitive, social, and physiological determinants of emotional state. *Psychological Review, 69,* 379–399.

Scherer, K. R. (1984). On the nature and function of emotion: A component process approach. In K. R. Scherer & P. Ekman (Eds.), *Approaches to emotion* (pp. 293–317). Hillsdale, NJ: Lawrence Erlbaum Associates.

Shaver, P., Schwartz, J., Kirson, D., & O'Connor, C. (1987). Emotion knowledge: Further exploration of a prototype approach. *Journal of Personality and Social Psychology, 52,* 1061–1086.

Trevarthen, C. (1984). Emotions in infancy: Regulators of contact and relationships with persons. In K. R. Scherer & P. Ekman (Eds.), *Approaches to emotion* (pp. 129–157). Hillsdale, NJ: Lawrence Erlbaum Associates.

Zajonc, R. B. (1980). Feeling and thinking: Preferences need no inferences. *American Psychology, 35,* 151–175.

Zillmann, D., Katcher, A. H., & Milavsky, B. (1972). Excitation transfer from physical exercise to subsequent aggressive behavior. *Journal of Experimental Social Psychology, 8,* 247–259.

The Role of Cognition and Effort in the Use of Emotions to Guide Behavior

Leonard L. Martin
John W. Achee
David W. Ward
Thomas F. Harlow
University of Georgia

In this chapter, we address two issues raised by Berkowitz regarding the role of cognition in emotion. One issue is essentially semantic, whereas the other is more substantive. The semantic issue deals with Berkowitz's use of the term *cognitive*. He restricts it (unnecessarily, we think) to processes that are conscious, effortful, deliberate, and rational, and refers to processes that do not possess these qualities as noncognitive. The second issue we address involves Berkowitz's suggestion that negative emotions produce in people a tendency to engage in aggressive behavior that can only be overcome with effortful processing. We argue that (a) most cognitive processing is not conscious, effortful, deliberate, and rational; and that (b) the link between negative emotions and aggressive behavior can be altered with effortless, nonconscious processing relatively early in the information processing sequence.

IS ALL COGNITION EFFORTFUL?

The view of cognition as conscious, deliberate, effortful, and rational is not an uncommon one (see Zajonc, 1980). However, the current tact is to classify behaviors not in terms of being automatic versus controlled or cognitive versus noncognitive, but in terms of the combination of features they possess (Bargh, 1989; Shiffrin, 1988). A process may be unintentional, for example, yet still demand cognitive effort for its completion. Or, a process may be intentional yet demand relatively little cognitive effort (for a more complete discussion of this issue, see Uleman, 1989). Even so, both types of processes can legitimately be called cognitive.

In fact, it is in terms of this view of cognition that we couched the results of the Martin, Seta, and Crelia (1990) experiments discussed by Berkowitz. In these three experiments, we blatantly primed concepts in subjects and subsequently asked the subjects to form an impression of a person whose actions were interpretable in terms of the primed concepts. We found that the impressions of subjects who did not exert a great deal of cognitive effort (because they were either distracted, socially loafing, or low in need for cognition) showed assimilation, whereas the impressions of subjects who did exert cognitive effort showed contrast. We concluded that this type of contrast (i.e., reset contrast) demands the expenditure of more cognitive effort than does assimilation because it represents a correction (or overcorrection) of an initial assimilative process. Thus, reset contrast is analogous to the kind of effortful restraint process described by Berkowitz with regard to anger and aggression.

There are two caveats to this analogy, however. Even though assimilation demands less cognitive effort than does reset contrast, it is still a cognitive process. It involves the interpretation of behavioral information in terms of a concept. On the other hand, it appears that neither the assimilation nor the contrast is open to introspective awareness. In debriefing after our experiments, the subjects routinely denied that the manipulations influenced their impressions and suggested instead that they rated the target person as they did because they really felt he was that way.

Thus, it would appear that assimilation and reset contrast are nonconscious cognitive processes. More generally, we feel that the term cognition can be used to refer to mental work whether that work be conscious, rational, deliberate, and effortful, or none of these.

IS EFFORT NEEDED TO OVERCOME THE EFFECTS OF NEGATIVE EMOTIONS?

One of Berkowitz's strong claims is that there is a built-in association between negative affect and the anger–aggression syndrome. He argues that "People who are feeling bad, whatever the reason . . . are theoretically apt to feel angry, have hostile thoughts, and be disposed to attack a suitable available target." (p. 10). However, when people become "highly conscious of what they [are] feeling and what they [are] tempted to do, these persons presumably [engage] in 'higher order' thinking so that they [consider] the possible appropriateness of their emotions and urges in the given circumstances and then [decide] to restrain themselves" (p. 35). In short, Berkowitz suggests that the occurrence of a negative stimulus event produces a direct, automatic incitement to aggressive behavior that can only be overcome by a conscious, effortful correction process.

We agree that some motor reactions are closely linked with the occurrence of specific emotions. Postures and facial expressions, for example, may provide the best evidence for this kind of direct link (Ekman & Friesen, 1975). But even if the link for postures and expression is direct, we cannot conclude that the link is direct for more complex behaviors, such as aggression. We argue instead that effortless, nonconscious cognitive mediation can change the implications of a given emotion, and thus alter its link to specific behaviors. This altered link can be considered a redirection of the emotion that occurs before there is a behavioral predisposition that has to be corrected. This point is probably best made with an example.

Consider the role of negative arousal in attitude change. If we apply the automatic-link hypothesis to the dissonance paradigm, we would expect that the presence of inconsistent cognitions would give rise to a negative drive state and that this drive state would automatically induce in people a tendency to change their attitude.[1] This means that in the absence of a conscious, effortful correction process, people would change their attitudes. To carry the analogy further, we would have to conclude that when people are provided with a misattribution of their arousal (e.g., a pill), they still experience a predisposition to change their attitude, but they consciously decide that it is inappropriate to do so. Consequently, they effortfully restrain their automatically induced predisposition.

This scenario seems implausible to us. It seems more likely that the attribution manipulation leads to different interpretations of the drive state, and that these interpretations, in turn, make the drive state either relevant or irrelevant to attitude change. Thus, subjects in the dissonance paradigm do not have to engage in effortful processing to suppress an initial predisposition to change their attitudes. There is no predisposition when the arousal has been attributed to a pill. To use the cliché from the old western movies, the predisposition has been headed off at the pass.

In summary, we believe that there are processes that might legitimately be called cognitive, but that are not rational, deliberate, or open to introspective awareness, and these processes can operate early in the information processing sequence to change the link between emotion and specific behaviors. One implication of this view is that anger (or negative affect more generally) can elicit behaviors other than aggression even when subjects do not engage in a conscious, effortful correction process. We are not arguing that people need to interpret their feelings in a Schacterian sense. We are arguing that they need to interpret the implications of their feelings. Even when it is clear what people are feeling, they still need to know what it means when they are feeling that way. And, we believe that the meaning or implications of one's feelings are context-dependent.

HOW FEELINGS INFORM

We begin with the assumption that feelings carry information and thus operate as input to other processes (cf. Wyer & Carlston, 1979). Information is drawn from feelings in much the same way that it is drawn from overt behavior, through a self-perception process (Bem, 1967). The hypothesis that people draw information from their moods has been formalized by Schwarz and Clore as the mood as information hypothesis (e.g, Clore, 1992; Schwarz & Clore, 1983, 1988; see also Martin, Harlow, & Strack, in press; Wyer & Carlston, 1979; Wyer & Srull, 1989). According to Bem (1967), people infer that they like coffee if they observe themselves frequently drinking coffee. According to the mood as information perspective, people infer that they like coffee if they observe themselves experiencing pleasant sensations when they drink coffee. In other words, we say that we like coffee because we feel good when we drink it.

How does this informational view of affect explain behavioral effects? To answer this, we must first ask where affect comes from and what function it serves.

MOODS, PROCESSING GOALS, AND BEHAVIORAL DECISIONS

There is evidence that the attainment of a goal or approach to a goal is associated with positive affect, whereas nonattainment or lack of approach is associated with negative affect (Carver & Scheier, 1990; Hsee & Abelson, 1991; Ortony, Clore, & Collins, 1988). There is also evidence that the reverse relation holds. That is, people in positive moods are more likely than those in negative moods to judge that they have attained their goals (Heady & Veenhoven, 1989). This latter finding suggests that people may interpret their positive affect as a sign that they have attained or made progress toward their goals, and interpret their negative affect as a sign that they have not attained or have not made progress toward their goals.

To the extent that this is true, people in positive moods would be more likely than those in negative moods to cease their current goal-directed behavior (Carver & Scheier, 1990). Such a finding would be consistent with the mood as information perspective if one assumes that in the course of performing a task, people (either implicitly or explicitly) ask themselves a question like, "Have I reached my goal?" If so, then people in positive moods would answer with a yes, whereas people in negative moods would answer with a no. In other words, people may evaluate their decision to stop striving toward their goal more favorably when they are in positive moods than when they are in negative moods.

Suppose, however, that in the course of performing a task, people asked themselves (either implicitly or explicitly) "Am I enjoying this task?" As with the previous question, people in positive moods would answer with a yes, whereas people in negative affective moods would answer with a no answer. This time, though, the behavioral implications of the answers are different. If people take their positive affect as evidence that they are enjoying the task and take their negative affect as evidence that they are not enjoying the task, then people in positive moods would persist longer than would people in negative moods (assuming that people continue doing what they enjoy).

In short, if people's processing objectives (e.g., the question they ask themselves) can change the implications of their affective states, then both positive and negative moods can cause people to continue or cease a behavior. This hypothesis was tested in two experiments by Martin, Ward, Achee, and Wyer (in press). The experiments were identical to one another up to the last task the subjects were asked to perform. So, we begin by describing the features the experiments have in common.

In both experiments, subjects reported for what they thought was an experiment about rating movies. They were told that they would, in fact, be rating movies, but that they would also be performing a number of other, unrelated tasks. They were told that the full reason for performing the various tasks would be explained to them at the end of the experiment.

Subjects were shown either a set of humorous film clips or a set of sad film clips. As the subjects finished viewing each clip, they filled out a questionnaire labeled "Pilot Movie Ratings." The questionnaire asked routine questions about the film clip, such as whether the subjects had seen the movie before, if they knew its title, if anything in particular stood out in the film clip, and if they thought someone could tell what the movie was about based just on the clip they saw. After the subjects viewed and rated the last film clip, they rated their moods.

Following the mood ratings, subjects performed a 1 minute distractor task in which they drew a map of their campus. They were told that the experimenters were interested in the way people represent information about their environment. The actual purpose of this distractor task was to put some time between the subjects' mood ratings and their performance of the target task. Pilot data had indicated that without this distractor, subjects would discount their moods as the basis for their subsequent behavioral decisions (cf. Berkowitz & Troccoli, 1990). After the subjects had drawn the map for 1 minute, they were given the instructions for the target task. At this point Experiments 1 and 2 diverged.

In Experiment 1, subjects heard the target task described as an impression formation task. They were provided with 69 index cards, and each card described a behavior in which a target person had ostensibly engaged (e.g., returned money to the lost and found). Subjects were told to read the behaviors and then indicate on a series of ratings scales their impression of the person.

The subjects were also told that they did not have to read all of the behaviors. More specifically, half the subjects were told that they could stop when they felt they had enough information on which to base their impressions. The remaining subjects were told that they could stop when they no longer enjoyed reading the behaviors. The amount of time the subjects spent on the impression formation task (i.e., reading the index cards) was the main dependent variable.

We found, consistent with our predictions, that when subjects had been told to stop when they had enough information, those in positive moods stopped sooner than did those in negative moods. On the other hand, when subjects were told to stop when they no longer enjoyed the task, those in negative moods stopped sooner than did those in positive moods. These results are depicted graphically in Fig. 7.1.

These effects appear to have arisen from the operation of a nonconscious, noneffortful, redirection process (as opposed to the kind of conscious, effortful correction process Berkowitz has proposed). We have two sources of indirect evidence for this. First, all of our subjects were asked to complete a need for cognition inventory prior to watching the happy or sad films. Thus, we were able to block our subjects in terms of the extent to which they engage in and enjoy effortful cognitive processing. When this individual difference was entered as a factor in the analysis, it did not interact with the mood and question manipulation. The effects we observed were equally likely for subjects who tend dispositionally to exert cognitive effort as for subjects who tend dispositionally to not exert effort. Thus, the re-direction process is apparently not very cognitively demanding.

The second source of evidence came from our debriefing sessions. Before we explained the hypothesis to the subjects, we asked them to speculate about the nature of the experiment. The subjects were generally reluctant to do so, and of those that did, not one subject guessed the hypothesis correctly, and not one made any reference to the instructions they had been given for the impression formation task. A few subjects suggested that the experimenters were interested in seeing how watching movies influenced people's moods. But, even these subjects did not draw a connection between their moods and their performance on the impression formation task. So, we feel confident that the processes that gave rise to our results were not open to introspective awareness.

In summary, the results of Experiment 1 are consistent with the hypothesis that a noneffortful, nonconscious process can alter the impact of people's moods

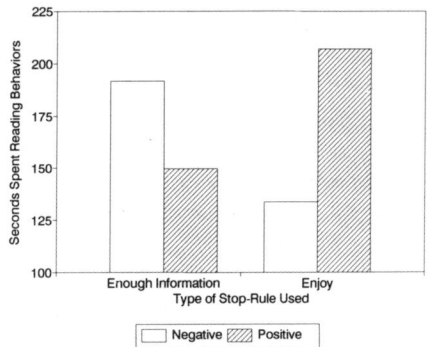

FIG. 7.1. Number of seconds spent on the impression formation task as a function of mood and processing objectives

on their behavioral decisions. All subjects performed the same impression formation task, and subjects in the positive and negative conditions were in equivalent
moods. Yet, the amount of time the subjects spent performing the impression
formation task differed as a function of their moods and the question they asked
themselves. This effect occurred equally in subjects high in need for cognition
and those low in need for cognition, and it occurred in the absence of introspective awareness.

These findings were replicated and extended in a second experiment in which
we explored the effects of moods and processing goals on a memory-based (as
opposed to a stimulus-based) task. Subjects in positive or negative moods were
asked to generate a list of birds from memory. Some of the subjects were told to
stop generating the birds when they felt it was time to stop, and some were told to
stop generating the birds when they no longer enjoyed the task.

As before, the main dependent variable was the length of time the subjects
spent on the listing task. Consistent with the results of Experiment 1, when
subjects were asked to stop when they no longer enjoyed the task, those in
negative moods stopped sooner than did those in positive moods, but when
subjects were asked to stop when they thought it was time to stop, those in
positive moods stopped sooner than did those in negative moods. These results
are depicted graphically in Fig. 7.2.

As in Experiment 1, we had subjects in equivalent positive or negative
moods, performing the same task, yet differing in the amount of time they spent
on the task as a function of the question they asked themselves. Also, in replication of Experiment 1, we found that the interaction between mood and processing
objectives (i.e., the self-question) was not influenced by the subjects' level of
need for cognition, and not one subject indicated any awareness of the link
between their moods, their instructions, and their performance on the bird-listing
task. So, Experiment 2, like Experiment 1, seems to provide evidence of an
effortless, unconscious re-direction of the effects of mood on behavior.

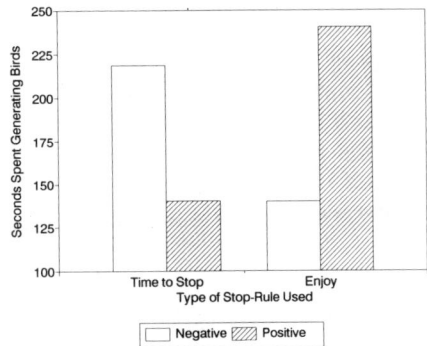

FIG. 7.2. Number of seconds spent on the listing task as a function of mood and process-ing objectives

GENERALITY OF OUR MODEL

What are the implications of these two experiments for Berkowitz's theory? We address this question in the context of two general claims made by Berkowitz. He argued first that anger is a "special emotion." It has a direct link to aggression. People who are angry are predisposed to be aggressive. However, he later asserts that any kind of negative affect can produce a predisposition to aggress. With this statement, he seems to be undermining the special status of anger. Interestingly, we agree with both statements. Anger does stand in a special relation to aggressive behavior, and any kind of negative affect can lead to aggression.

The two statements are not inconsistent if one keeps in mind that moods and emotions may differ in the specificity of the information they provide. Moods are more diffuse than are emotions (Isen, 1984). Thus, moods can potentially provide information relevant to a wider range of behavioral decisions than can emotions. Evidence of the mood–emotion distinction can be seen in judgment studies that have manipulated moods as opposed to specific emotions.

Clore, Schwarz, and Kirsch (1983) put subjects into either positive or negative moods by guiding them through hypnotically induced fantasies. These fantasies were either pleasant or unpleasant and were about either a date or a vacation. Following this guided fantasy, subjects were asked to judge the favorableness of either a person or a vacation. Results indicated that subjects evaluated both the person and the vacation more positively when they were in good rather than bad moods, and this was true independent of the content of the mood-inducing fantasy. Thus, the mood effect was general.

Gallagher and Clore (1985), on the other hand, induced specific emotions in subjects and then asked the subjects to make judgments for which these emotions either were or were not relevant. More specifically, subjects were (hypnotically) induced to feel either anger or fear, and were asked either to read a scenario and indicate the degree of blame they accorded the person in the scenario or they were asked to estimate the number of people who suffer negative life events. The effects turned out to be quite specific. Angry subjects gave higher blame ratings than did fearful subjects, but fearful subjects gave higher risk ratings than did angry subjects.

These results are understandable if one considers the specific information carried by each emotion. When we want to know whether to blame someone, one relevant piece of information is how angry we feel. On the other hand, when we want to determine the amount of risk in a situation, anger is uninformative. Fear, on the other hand, is informative for assessment of risk but not for assessment of blame.

So, emotions provide more specific information than do moods. This suggests that it may be easier to alter the behavioral implications of moods than the behavioral implications of emotions. In other words, it may be easier to redirect a negative mood away from aggression than to redirect anger away from aggression. On the other hand, we suspect that it is not impossible to do so. More specifically, we hypothesize that with the right processing objective (e.g., self-question), the meaning of feeling angry can be something other than "Be aggressive." In other words, anger may not inform people to aggress. Rather, it may inform them more generally that forceful action is needed. And, the nature of this forceful action may depend on people's processing objectives relative to their anger.

Such processes are clearly operative at the anecdotal level. For example, Jimmy Connors said that he intentionally makes himself angry during tennis matches in order to improve his game. He tries harder and is more focused when he is angry. Similarly, people who have broken diet after diet may finally get sufficiently angry at themselves that they resolve to stay on their next diet, and then do so. The anger motivates them to success. And finally, anger over political actions (e.g., war, abortion, race relations) can move people to action, much of it nonviolent.

If our model really does apply to anger and aggression, then it should be possible to redirect anger into something other than aggression, and this redirection could occur effortlessly and nonconsciously. We have not tested this hypothesis empirically, but we suspect that something like the following scenario might work. Imagine angering subjects by giving them an arbitrarily difficult task to perform. Then, ask them one of the following questions:

1. Is it fair of me to give you this task?
2. Are you satisfied with your own performance on the task?

We would hypothesize that the anger aroused by the test will lead to an aggressive tendency with the former question, but will lead to increased motivation on the task with the second question.

CONCLUSION

In summary, we believe that there are processes that might legitimately be called cognitive, even though these processes are not effortful, rational, deliberate, or open to introspective awareness. We also believe that these processes can operate to change the course of emotional behavior early in the information processing sequence. More specifically, these processes are assumed to influence the link between emotion and specific behaviors prior to the occurrence of a behavioral predisposition. This is something other than a conscious, effortful correction of a behavioral tendency that has already been elicited.

We do not feel, however, that our data are inconsistent with Berkowitz's general model. We give more credit to nonconscious processing than he does, but our data do not rule out the possibility that effortful, conscious correction can take place, and the processes we discussed could easily be located in the area of Berkowitz's model called the associative network. We would make one caveat, however. We suspect that the redirection processes we discussed involve *procedural knowledge* (Anderson, 1983) as opposed to simple declarative knowledge represented in semantic networks (which is what Berkowitz emphasizes in his discussion). But again, this is not inconsistent with the general model. Berkowitz includes the term *lower-order primitive processing* in his model (see his Fig. 1.1), but he does not elaborate upon this processing. We believe that the inclusion of nonconscious, procedural knowledge into Berkowitz's model would greatly enhance the model's flexibility and generality.

ENDNOTES

[1]We have no reason to believe that Berkowitz expects his model to apply to the dissonance paradigm. We make this application in the hopes of making our own position clearer.

REFERENCES

Anderson, J. R. (1983). *The architecture of cognition.* Cambridge, MA: Harvard University Press.

Bargh, J. A. (1989). The power behind the throne of judgment: Varieties of automatic influence in social perception and cognition. In J. S. Uleman & J. A. Bargh (Eds.), *Unintended thought* (pp. 1–24). New York: Guilford.

Bem, D. (1967). Self-perception: An alternative interpretation of cognitive dissonance phenomena. *Psychological Review, 74,* 183–200.

Berkowitz, L., & Troccoli, B. T. (1990). Feelings, direction of attention, and expressed evaluations of others. *Cognition and Emotion, 4,* 305–325.

Carver, C. S., & Scheier, M. F. (1990). Origins and functions of positive and negative affect A control-process view. *Psychological Review, 97,* 19–35.

Clore, G. L. (1992). Cognitive phenomenology: Feelings and the construction of judgment. In L. L. Martin & A. Tesser (Eds.), *The construction of social judgments* (pp. 133–163). Hillsdale, NJ: Lawrence Erlbaum Associates.

Clore, G. L., Schwarz, N., & Kirsch, J. (1983). *Generalized mood effects on evaluative judgments.* Paper presented at the annual meeting of the Midwestern Psychology Association. Chicago, IL.

Ekman, P., & Friesen, W. V. (1975). *Unmasking the face.* Englewood Cliffs, NJ: Prentice Hall.

Gallagher, D., & Clore, G. L. (1985). *Emotion and judgment: Effects of fear and anger on relevant and irrelevant cognitive tasks.* Paper presented at the annual meeting of the Midwestern Psychology Association. Chicago, IL.

Heady, B., & Veenhoven, R. (1989). Does happiness induce a rosy outlook? In R. Veenhoven (Ed.), *How harmful is happiness?: Consequences of enjoying life or not* (pp. 106–127). Rotterdam: Universitaire Pers.

Hsee, C. K., & Abelson, R. P. (1991). Velocity relation: Satisfaction as a function of the first derivative of outcome over time. *Journal of Personality and Social Psychology, 60,* 341–347.

Isen, A. M. (1984). Toward understanding the role of affect in cognition. In R. S. Wyer & T. K. Srull (Eds.), *Handbook of social cognition* (Vol. 3, pp. 179–236), Hillsdale, NJ: Lawrence Erlbaum Associates.

Martin, L. L., Harlow, T. F., & Strack, F. (1992). The role of one's bodily sensations in the interpretation of social events. *Personality and Social Psychology Bulletin, 18,* 412–419.

Martin, L. L., Seta, J. J., & Crelia, R. (1990). Assimilation and contrast as a function of people's willingness and ability to exert cognitive effort while forming an impression. *Journal of Personality and Social Psychology, 59,* 27–37.

Martin, L. L., Ward, D., Achee, J., & Wyer, R. S. (in press). The motivational consequences of affective information. *Journal of Personality and Social Psychology.*

Ortony, A., Clore, G. L., & Collins, A. (1988). *The cognitive structure of emotion.* Cambridge: Cambridge University Press.

Schwarz, N., & Clore, G. L. (1983). Mood, misattribution, and judgments of well-being: Informative and directive functions of affective states. *Journal of Personality and Social Psychology, 45,* 513–523.

Schwarz, N., & Clore, G. L. (1988). How do I feel about it? Informative functions of affective states. In K. Fiedler & J. Forgas (Eds.), *Affect, cognition, and social behavior* (pp. 44–62). Toronto: Hogrefe.

Shiffrin, R. M. (19880. Attention. In R. C. Atkinson, R. J. Herrnstein, G. Lindzey, & R. D. Luce (Eds.), *Stevens' handbook of experimental psychology* (2nd ed., pp. 739–811). New York: Wiley.

Uleman, J. S. (1989). A framework for thinking intentionally about unintentional thought. In J. S. Uleman & J. A. Bargh (Eds.), *Unintended thought* (pp. 425–449). New York: Guilford.

Wyer, R. S., & Carlston, D. (1979). *Social cognition, inference, and attribution.* Hillsdale, NJ: Lawrence Erlbaum Associates.

Wyer, R. S., & Srull, T. K. (1989). *Memory and cognition in its social context.* Hillsdale, NJ: Lawrence Erlbaum Associates.

Zajonc, R. B. (1980). Feeling and thinking: Preferences need no inferences. *American Psychologist, 30,* 151–175.

8 Those to Whom Evil Is Done

Keith Oatley
*Ontario Institute for Studies in Education
and University of Toronto*

In his poem "September 1, 1939" (Auden, 1977) ends the second stanza:

> Those to whom evil is done
>   Do evil in return.

These are lines, said Brodsky (1987), which "every living person has to tattoo in his/her brain" (p. 321). The strength, I think, of Berkowitz's argument derives from his experimental evidence showing something of how this process may work. Those who suffer harm find it difficult to avoid then punishing someone— whether or not this person is responsible for the hurt. This process seems to have all the properties of a mechanism, perhaps a blind one. The existence of the process prompts us to conclude, as Berkowitz seems to intend if I read him aright, that anger and aggression are pathologies of human existence; not merely regrettable, but malignant cancers in the body politic.

Berkowitz says that experimental work on the causation of aggression has been isolated from research on emotions. He argues for a rapprochement between the two fields of research on aggression and research on emotions. Although I agree that there has been isolation and that there should be integration, I believe the rapprochement between the two fields may require some modification of Berkowitz's basic assertion that pain causes anger which causes antisocial aggression.

Let me first agree, from the perspective of a researcher on emotions, with most of what Berkowitz says. The theory he advances is important in that it does bring together data that have previously been unintegrated. There is recent corroborative evidence from emotion research that anger can be produced by rather basic events like pain or frustration (Stein & Levine, 1989)—not merely by interpersonal events such as the perception of some insult. Recently too, Oatley and Duncan (unpublished) studied outpatients with a diagnosed organic gastroin-testinal disorder who had abdominal pains. Some 25% of episodes of abdominal pain in such patients were associated with an episode of anger that was suffi-ciently clear to be conscious and to be noted in a structured diary in which we had asked them to record emotion incidents.

We see this kind of research, on people keeping structured diaries of incidents of emotion in everyday life, as epidemiological. We collect data on where and why incidents of emotion occur, to whom, how often, and so on (Oatley & Duncan, 1992). Such data are complementary to experimental data of the kind that Berkowitz collects. The emotion incidents that we study have the disadvan-tage of depending on self-reports and of being correlational. Therefore, they can not unambiguously show causation. By contrast, experimental data, although they can indicate causes, have other limitations. They may indicate that some phenomenon is statistically significant, but they don't show whether it is impor-tant. Moreover, an experimental result can indicate that a manipulation can have a causal effect, but from such studies alone we can not know whether this is a primary cause of the outcome event in ordinary life. We need—and I think Berkowitz would agree—to converge on a phenomenon from several directions, thus establishing its validity. On the idea that frustration and pain can cause anger, there are the beginnings of converging evidence. Not only does this causal mechanism exist as Berkowitz has shown, but it is sufficiently frequent in some parts of everyday life to be important.

There is another welcome convergence between Berkowitz's approach and research on emotions in the area of the associationistic properties of emotions. One point concerning these associationistic ideas, however, is that the original formulation of Bower (1981) that recall is state-dependent, so that information of any kind learned in one emotional state will be preferentially recalled in this same state, has been questioned by Bower (1987) himself because the phe-nomenon is not robust. A better hypothesis, accounting for more of the evidence, is that past incidents which are themselves closely associated with an emotion are recalled when the same kind of emotion occurs again. This is the hypothesis of emotion congruency. Berkowitz discusses this question—but still wishes to re-tain the state-dependent explanation, whereas on my reading a congruency ap-proach, and a model based on it such as that of Conway and Bekerian (1987), would fit his data better.

The most serious divergence between Berkowitz's argument and the one that is emerging from emotion research is that whereas Berkowitz takes anger and aggression to be largely antisocial, perhaps anachronistic, many cognitive theo-rists of emotion see emotions generally as functional.

Berkowitz situates his research in the tradition of William James, and the neo-Jamesian studies of Schachter and Singer (1962). Despite the pervasiveness of this line of thinking in American psychology, an argument can be made that it is inappropriate for Berkowitz to relate his work to it. Berkowitz's own formulation, I think, contradicts the basic formulation of this tradition. According to James (1890), the sequence of emotional arousal is this: An event occurs and this is followed by a reaction to it. An emotion is the perception of the bodily processes of this reaction. Berkowitz, however, proposes a quite different idea, which is not just a revision or addition to James' theory as he suggests. It specifically contradicts the whole basis of Jamesian thinking on emotions. Berkowitz suggests the following sequence. An event (e.g., pain) occurs which elicits an emotion (e.g., anger), and this in turn has two main effects: (a) it generates an impulse to action; and (b) it activates an emotion-coded semantic network.

Although I have some reservations about emotion-coded semantic networks, I believe that Berkowitz is correct in this formulation—but it is anything but Jamesian. For James, emotions did not cause actions or effects: They were endpoints. They gave color to experience. Not only did James have nothing to say about the functions of emotions other than suggesting this coloring property, but also his formulation led researchers away from the idea that emotions might have any other functions. Unfortunately, James' theory or its variants had much of the field to themselves—at least as judged by American textbooks of psychology.

If anything, I think, Berkowitz is Darwinian in his conception. Darwin (1872/1965) postulated that emotional expressions could be elicited by stimuli that had diffusely activating properties. He also thought that these effects were largely involuntary, and included impulses to action. At the center of Darwin's formulation was the idea that emotional expressions are primitive. That is to say, they derive from patterns that once had a function in evolution or individual development, but they occur in human adults whether or not they are of any use. Berkowitz should relate his approach to Darwin's, I believe, because in Berkowitz's formulation people who have been angered by some pain attack a target person whether or not that person could have been responsible for the pain. Berkowitz proposes an additional implication, consistent with Darwin's approach: The urges to action that anger induces are destructive, perhaps evil in our society. But because we also can think about our emotions, we can, perhaps, inhibit some of them. This addition is consistent with the approach of Darwin who discussed this same idea in general terms, and used the term *repression* for the attempt at inhibition.

To me the evidence in the literature on emotions indicates that Darwin was far closer to the truth than ever James or his followers have been. Even so, Darwin's ideas have been modified and extended considerably by modern research. Darwin's primary concern in his 1872 book was to trace continuities from adult humans back to other animals, and from adulthood back to infancy. In doing this he conceptualized emotions as rather like the anatomical fossils that became such an important part of post-Darwinian biology, or like the anatomical vestiges that exist in human bodies, for instance like the small bones at the base of the spine that are rudimentary tails. Emotions were, for Darwin, of this same kind: They pointed to evolutionary continuity, but they were essentially behavioral vestiges, not necessarily having any current function.

We are prompted by Darwin's account, however, to take a step in thinking that he himself did not take. If we now accept his evolutionary theory, we need not simply suppose that our primary interest is in emotions as vestiges, and as evidence for evolution. We could postulate that emotions might also have some current usefulness, some important functions in adult life. Emotions occur and are salient in so many species. It would be strange, indeed, if all of these were vestiges of obsolete mechanisms. Once one has accepted the theory of natural selection, it strains credulity to suppose that emotional behavior has somehow been shielded from selective pressures. We are led to postulate current functions for emotions in all, or most, of the species in which they occur. This, I think, summarizes the current position among theorists of emotions—human emotions have current adaptive functions.

Could anger have such functions? This I think becomes an all-important question raised by the work of Berkowitz, and by the work on anger carried out by emotion researchers.

It is easy to see anger and aggression as largely destructive—often they are. Whole cultures have seen anger and aggression in this way, and have not only disapproved of them, but also been largely successful in suppressing or avoiding them, see for example Brigg's (1970) account of the Utku, an Inuit people, or Nance's (1975) account of the Tasaday.

By contrast, in Euro-American culture, anger and aggression are tolerated and even mythologized. We accept that something bad necessarily provokes anger and aggression. As Berkowitz points out, a pain, a frustration, a wide variety of events experienced as bad, can have this effect. In the stories that are told and retold on film and television, this theme has become a major staple, until its iterations have become tedious—the theme is the one indicated in the lines from Auden's poem with which I began this piece: A person does something bad. This then provokes the protagonist (either the injured party or someone acting on the injured person's behalf) to unlimited violent aggression against the original perpetrator. This same theme is played out in international relations. In witnessing such cultural phenomena, it is easy to think that anger is childish, an anachronism, a still-living fossil, which with modern technology seems frighteningly capable of bringing our evolution to a final halt.

In the individualistic society of American and Europe, anger has acquired other functions, however, though these are not much celebrated in Hollywood. In our kind of society, although the individual is seen as the center, the source of action, the basis of experience, individuals have not stopped needing others— and fortunately, we have not stopped cooperating with others. Thus, Averill (1982) found that, in Massachusetts at least, most incidents of anger concerned a person the subject knew and liked. For 63% of incidents the motive was to assert authority or independence, or to improve the subject's self-image. Most people find anger to be subjectively unpleasant, but despite this, 62% of Averill's subjects who had become angry, and 70% of subjects who had been targets of someone's anger rated the angry incident as having been beneficial to their relationship. In London, England too, a similar finding was made by Jenkins, Smith, and Graham (1989) on a large representative community sample from which 139 families were selected for study. Speaking of marital quarrels that had lasted 10 minutes or more with raised voices, 79% of the women in these families said they thought at least some good came from these quarrels.

I take the explanation of Averill's (1982) and Jenkins et al.'s (1989) findings to be the following (Oatley, 1992). In Euro-American society we see ourselves as entering into quasi-contractual arrangements with others such as friendship, marriage, parenthood, employment, and so on. As these arrangements extend over time, and involve repeated interactions, sooner or later the other person (or institution) fails to live up to an expectation. In our society such failures, experienced as insults, as provocations, as inconsiderateness, as being let down, as illegitimate actions, are the prototypical instigations of the emotion of anger. The function of anger, then, is to readjust the relationship and to modify the expectations that each person has of the other. In Western industrial societies renegotiation is the norm in such episodes.

The implication for Berkowitz's hypothesis is this, I believe. Anger is instigated by events. Perhaps the best single descriptor of an event capable of eliciting anger is frustration. Moreover, as Berkowitz argues, anger in turn elicits both an impulse to aggression, and a set of thoughts. This mechanism is very basic. In itself it is indeed primitive. In young children we can see this mechanism in a raw form, and aggression may be immediate. But like every other aspect of childhood this is a building block in a culture. What we make of it varies considerably both individually and culturally. In the Inuit society described by Briggs (1970), expressed anger is very rare among adults and is not used by parents in socializing children. It is not that anger does not occur. It is seen as socially incompetent, perhaps much as Americans would see extreme shyness and embarrassment in an adult as socially incompetent. The term for anger in the Utku language can be translated as childish, and Briggs found her 17-month stay as an adopted member of an Utku family difficult because they regarded her occasional displays of anger, which would be normal in the Canadian society from which she came, as deeply disconcerting. They made it difficult for the Utku to cross the cultural bridge to her, because she behaved so inappropriately. In fact, a pivotal moment in her stay with these people occurred when she became angry at some Canadian holiday visitors because they had inconsiderately damaged one of the two canoes the Utku group possessed, and then wanted to borrow the other one. Briggs' anger, even though displayed in defence of their interests, resulted in the Utku finding it difficult to have much to do with her as such a volatile person.

The Utku suffer cold and hardship in ways that most Americans would find unacceptable and irritating to a degree. One is reminded of Berkowitz's experiments in which subjects in Wisconsin suffer the pain and cold of having arms immersed in cold water, or held in uncomfortable postures. In Utku life cold, pain, and discomfort are experiences of every day life. They lead not to anger and irritation—so far as Briggs could see—but to humorous tolerance, such experiences being the ordinary run of hardships that one has to put up with.

As I understand it, Berkowitz's model allows for this kind of cultural variability. What I would like to point out, however, is that he may be overestimating the extent to which some aspects of his experimental results are human universals. In Euro-American society, any pain, any frustration, any infringement, is liable to be seen as a threat to our individuality, to our autonomy, to our control over events. Berkowitz offers thoughts about aggressive impulses in a quotation from an earlier paper, "suffering is seldom ennobling. . . . Afflicted persons can restrain their hostile and aggressive tendencies, perhaps by becoming aware. . . . Here as in so many other ways, it is thought that makes us better" (Berkowitz, 1990, p. 500). This seems to express a longing for another kind of society, for a kind of culture that is more gentle than the one in which we live, perhaps more like Utku society. I share this longing also.

It seems, however, unlikely that given our cultural trajectory there will be constructed from materials at hand, the kind of society that Berkowitz is thinking of. Might it not be more appropriate to accept anger and aggression as among the central attributes of individualism, sometimes but not always, evil.

Within our kind of society, then, we must find ways of affirming cooperation, including the cooperation that occurs when two angry people find they have both had inappropriate expectations, and perhaps exploring the functional and constructive effects of this in our thought and literature. In our individualistic society, anger and aggression are usually means for adjusting the relations between autonomous individuals.

REFERENCES

Auden, W. H. (1977). *The English Auden: Poems, essays and dramatic writings*. London: Faber.

Averill, J. R. (1982). *Anger and aggression. An essay on emotion*. New York: Springer.

Berkowitz, L. (1990). On the formation and regulation of anger and aggression: A cognitive–neoassociationistic analysis. *American Psychologist, 45,* 494–503.

Bower, G. H. (1981). Mood and memory. *American Psychologist, 36,* 129–148.

Bower, G. H. (1987). Commentary on mood and memory. *Behavior Research and Therapy, 25,* 443–455.

Briggs, J. L. (1970). *Never in anger: Portrait of an Eskimo family*. Cambridge, MA: Harvard University Press.

Brodsky, J. (1987). *Less than one: Selected essays*. Harmondsworth: Penguin.

Conway, M. A., & Bekerian, D. A. (1987). Situational knowledge and emotions. *Cognition and Emotion, 1,* 145–191.

Darwin, C. (1965). *The expression of emotions in man and the animals.* Chicago: University of Chicago Press. (Original work published 1872)

James, W. (1890). *The principles of psychology.* New York: Holt.

Jenkins, J. M., Smith, M. A., & Graham, P. (1989). Coping with parental quarrels. *Journal of the American Academy of Child and Adolescent Psychiatry, 28,* 182–189.

Nance, J. (1975). *The gentle Tasaday.* New York: Harcourt Brace Jovanovich.

Oatley, K. (1992). *Best laid schemes: The psychology of emotions.* New York: Cambridge University Press.

Oatley, K., & Duncan, E. (1992). Incidents of emotion in daily life. In K. T. Strongman (Ed.), *International review of studies on emotion* (pp. 249–293). Chichester: Wiley.

Schachter, S., & Singer, J. (1962). Cognitive, social and physiological determinants of emotional state. *Psychological Review, 69,* 379–399.

Stein, N. L., & Levine, L. J. (1989). Making sense out of emotion: The representation and use of goal-structured knowledge. In N. L. Stein, B. L. Leventhal, & T. Trabasso (Eds.), *Psychological and biological approaches to emotion* (pp. 45–73). Hillsdale, NJ: Lawrence Erlbaum Associates.

9 On the Scientific Study of Angry Organisms

W. Gerrod Parrott
Georgetown University

Surely, one of the most intriguing aspects of human emotion is how some occurrences can seem readily understandable, whereas others can seem utterly irrational. Anger takes second place to no emotion in exhibiting this property. We find anger not only in the justified fury of a victim of a robbery but also in the insults and kicks directed at a malfunctioning auto by a frustrated vacationer, not only in righteous indignation over atrocities but also in irritable outbursts at family members at the end of a hard day. It is the apparent inconsistency that intrigues—some angers are based on well-supported accusations whereas others seem based on impulse, or whim, or nothing at all.

Theories of emotion need to account for this apparent inconsistency, and one can divide contemporary strategies for doing so into two basic types. One, the hallmark of *dual systems* approaches to emotion, is to conceive emotion as having some noncognitive origin that may or may not subsequently lead to cognitive activity. The other, the hallmark of *cognitive appraisal* approaches to emotion, is to consider emotion as necessarily involving an appraisal of the situation that may or may not be biased. For the former approach, the problem is to account for the systematic relations between certain appraisals and certain emotions, as well as for such issues as linkage between cognitive and emotional development, the fact that further thought can modify emotions, and so forth. For the latter approach, the problem is to account for instances of impulsive or irrational emotion, as well as for the related issues of the (occasional) difficulty of controlling one's emotions, infrahuman emotion, physiological aspects of emotion, and the like.

The tension between these two approaches defined the central issues in the theory of emotion in recent years. Certainly, much of the debate is concerned

167

with which approach best accounts for the facts and best facilitates new research. But the debate involves more than just empirical findings—at stake is a view of human nature, and perhaps, even a view of the nature of psychological science. The dual systems approach characterizes emotionality as something akin to a primitive animal that lurks beneath our conscious, rational selves; it tends, like behaviorism, to emphasize those aspects of emotion that humans share with infrahuman species—organisms, as they were once commonly called. The cognitive appraisal approach instead characterizes people as being oriented toward interpretation and meaning, albeit sometimes in immature, self-centered, or self-serving ways. Furthermore, the dual systems approach tends to be more compatible with an approach to science that, like the physical sciences, stresses causality and determinism, whereas the cognitive appraisal approach's evocation of motives, reasons, and agency seems to turn away from the model of the physical sciences. The choice between the two approaches is therefore a matter not only of best accounting for the facts, but also of adopting a view of human nature and of the scientific enterprise.

Berkowitz's target article for this volume proposes a theory of anger and, more generally, emotion that is squarely in the tradition of the dual systems approach. In this chapter, I wish to show how his theory fits into this tradition, to demonstrate some problems with taking this approach, and to suggest ways in which the cognitive appraisal approach might better explain the same phenomena.

Before embarking on this plan, however, I would like to point out an important contribution of Berkowitz's work, one that stands, regardless of the ultimate verdict on its conclusions. I stated previously that it is necessary for theories to account for apparent inconsistencies in the nature of emotion. Emotion theorists, however, often seem to forget this necessity, and, as the cognitive approach to psychology replaced the behaviorist approach, some aspects of emotion indeed have tended to be emphasized while others were elided. Berkowitz's persistent attention over the years to the role of pain in producing anger and aggression has played a valuable role in keeping this important phenomenon on the agenda during a time when it may otherwise have been neglected. He has functioned as a gadfly in the best sense, and if the critique I offer here occasionally seems to bite in a gadflyish manner, let me emphasize that it does so only out of the hope that progress can be facilitated by such reciprocal tabanid activity, especially in the study of such a multifaceted phenomenon as emotion.

THE COGNITIVE NATURE OF IMPULSIVE ANGER

Berkowitz attempts to explain instances of anger that do not seem to be provoked by deliberate wrongdoing. His theory is a prototype of the dual systems approach. He proposes that anger starts in a relatively primitive system that works according to the principles of stimulus–response psychology. An unpleasant stimulus gives rise to the aggression-related responses of feeling angry, thinking hostilely, and attacking to cause injury. Awareness of these responses yields rudimentary anger. This primitive system may subsequently recruit another system that follows the principles of cognitive psychology. Berkowitz goes to great length to contrast these two types of systems. Unlike the cognitive system, the associationistic one is said to be "more automatic and involuntary," not to require learning, to produce raw feelings, to lead to quick reactions and impulsive outbursts, not to be directly controlled by free choice, to be present in young infants, and to give rise to responses without intervening appraisals. Only subsequently are these responses said to give rise to "complicated thoughts" and the application of social rules, or to become interpreted to form an experience of anger.

Berkowitz's distinction between these two systems seems to suffer from several conceptual difficulties, however. One problem is that the properties attributed to the associationistic system are really not all that different from the properties that cognitive psychologists routinely ascribe to such "complicated cognitions" as language, memory, and problem solving. I have previously made this point with respect to Zajonc's (1980) version of dual systems theory (Parrott & Sabini, 1989; Parrott & Schulkin, in press), and the same point seems to apply to Berkowitz's theory. Numerous aspects of cognition appear to be innate (consider language, or size perception). Furthermore, many cognitive processes, both innate and learned, are automatic, involuntary, and quick (consider the uncontrollability of the responses of a practiced reader engaged in the Stroop task, or the unconscious and unstoppable activation of complex ideas and memories that underlies cognitive priming). The cognitive sophistication of infants is now well-documented, so unless one equates cognition with language there is no problem in supposing that appraisals figure in their emotions (for some evidence see Parrott & Gleitman, 1989, or the summary in Lazarus, 1991, chap. 8). In short, many complex cognitive operations have just the properties Berkowitz ascribes to the primitive anger system. This fact suggests that primitive aspects of emotion can be explained cognitively, without recourse to postulating a primitive animal within.

The point here is not that "cognition can be defined either broadly or narrowly." The point is that one no longer is compelled to account for impulsive emotional responses in stimulus–response terms; one is free to draw on the concepts of cognitive psychology in accounting for even these relatively primitive emotional phenomena. This is not to deny that there are some complex cognitions that are reflective, conscious, deliberate, and verbal; but to characterize all or even most cognitive processes in this manner is to create a false dichotomy between cognitive and noncognitive.

When one applies this cognitive perspective to Berkowitz's model, it seems unclear whether the primitive anger system can be distinguished at all clearly from the cognitive system. Even what Berkowitz calls "rudimentary anger" appears to require such complicated operations that it is difficult to imagine it occurring without cognition. According to his model, aversive events give rise to a set of physiological, motor, and cognitive reactions that make up rudimentary anger. But even if we consider only the sensory types of aversive event Berkowitz focuses on—such as holding one's arm in the air or in cold water—does it make sense to assert that these events give rise to hostile thoughts and feelings and yet are primitive and noncognitive? I do not think that this assertion can stand.

The case of hostile thoughts seems straightforward. What kind of thoughts are these such that they can be hostile and can involve memories and ideas (as Berkowitz asserts) and yet be noncognitive? Such a reaction may be automatic and quick (for some people, at least), but it seems no less cognitive than is the process of cognitive priming.

The case of feelings requires more explanation, because it is still common in psychology to assume that feelings are sensory and biological, hence, primitive and noncognitive. Whereas some types of feelings are purely sensory (e.g., feeling pressure), many emotional feelings do not seem to be. Rather, they arise from awareness of evaluations, cognitive activity, and current cognitive and action tendencies (Parrott, 1988; cf. Frijda, 1986; Reisenzein & Schönpflug, 1992). That this is so is suggested by some interesting phraseology in Berkowitz's chapter. Whereas Berkowitz asserts that rudimentary feelings of anger grow out of internal sensations or body sensations (suggesting a Jamesian approach to emotional experience), nevertheless, he goes on to make some statements that are difficult to reconcile with this assertion. When discussing how rudimentary anger biases memory, Berkowitz writes that "particular feelings have come to be linked in memory with certain ideas, *especially through their semantic relatedness*" (italics added). If feelings are merely internal sensations then this is a very odd assertion—internal sensations have semantic content?—but if feelings of anger are instead thought of as including appraisals, then it makes sense to describe them as being semantically related to memories. Later, when discussing self-regulation, Berkowitz seems to suggest that becoming aware of feelings of anger might lead people to consider whether such feelings were inappropriate. Again, if feelings are just sensations, how can a sensation be inappropriate? Either emotional feelings must involve beliefs as well as sensations, or else some nonsensory aspect of emotion must be appraised when making judgments of social appropriateness. (Otherwise it would make as much sense to consider the social appropriateness of feeling back pain as that of feeling angry.) The cognitive approach to emotional feelings would actually help Berkowitz make some of his points. In the section on priming he must argue at length to establish that priming can generate feelings as well as thoughts, a point that follows easily from the cognitive approach.

Berkowitz concluded his target chapter by telling "emotion researchers, . . .

especially those of the conventional cognitive persuasion, that there is far more in heaven and earth and even in the psychology of emotions than is dreamt of in their philosophy." As should now be clear, one theme of this commentary is that emotion researchers of the conventional behavioral or physiological persuasion need to learn that there is far more to the cognitive approach than is dreamt of in their philosophy.

THE CONCORD BETWEEN ANGER IMPULSES AND CONSCIOUS AWARENESS

It seems significant that, when impulsive hostile thoughts occur, there never seems to be a dissociation between these impulses and what Berkowitz would call "complicated cognition." It is true that we may retrospectively recall a moment of impulsive hostility and ask ourselves, "What came over me? How could I have been so crabby, unfair, and mean-spirited?" In this sense, Berkowitz is absolutely right that there does seem to be a tendency for more anger and aggression under aversive conditions—his rejection of contemporary cognitive approaches to emotion for being "too cognitive and rationalistic" may be wrong with respect to the "cognitive", but may be on target with respect to the "rationalistic."

Nevertheless, at the time the impulsive hostility occurs, our entire being, complicated cognition and all, seems united in our anger toward our targets. When we lash out, there is no consciousness of a detached self witnessing the fury of the primitive animal within. When people are impulsively angry, they just as impulsively think in ways consistent with being angry. When they cease to believe that they have a right to be angry, they stop being angry. So what is remarkable about impulsive anger is not that it can spring into being without *any* beliefs that one has been wronged, but that it can spring into being based on such *flimsy* beliefs that one has been wronged. The interesting questions, then, concern not how people become angry without believing they have any right to be, but rather how people become inclined to construe situations in ways consistent with anger. What circumstances have this effect and why? Why do so many find their suffering more tolerable if they can somehow blame someone else for it rather than blame themselves or no one at all?

HOW DOES AVERSIVE STIMULATION LEAD TO ANGER?: A COGNITIVE ACCOUNT

The primary difference between the dual systems approach and the cognitive appraisal approach is in accounting for why aversive stimulation might lead to increased anger. The dual systems approach posits a direct, noncognitive link, whereas the cognitive appraisal approach must posit an intervening, cognitive step in which aversive stimulation somehow biases cognitive appraisals in a manner that then makes anger more likely. Roughly speaking, a cognitive account of aversively stimulated anger might postulate that such stimulation has the effect of lowering the threshold for the perception of blameworthiness. To illustrate such an account in more detail, it is helpful to employ two principles that have come from the cognitive movement. One is that stimuli can be interpreted very differently in different contexts. The other is to consider some of the processing that might occur between "aversive" stimulus and angry response.

Let us consider an example. In everyday life, one may react more angrily in response to a friendly interruption when one is in pain than when one is not in pain, but there is a nontrivial sense in which this stimulus has a different meaning on these two occasions. What may seem a friendly interruption when one is not in pain may seem entirely different when one is in pain. In pain, the interruption seems to be just one more thing to cope with when one already has too much to cope with; it seems another demand for resources that just are not available at the moment, because they are deployed in minimizing one's suffering; its demands on one's attention and resources therefore actually increases one's suffering. When in pain, one's priorities are narrowed such that the only thing that seems important is escaping the pain; therefore, most causes of interruptions seem less important. When one is in pain, time can seem to move more slowly, which can further contribute to becoming impatient with others. Because one's pain seems so salient to oneself, one finds it hard to believe that it is not also obvious to others, in which case the interruption seems to imply that the interrupter believes one's increased suffering is unimportant. When one feels unable to deal politely with a stimulus that one only wishes to make go away, the costs of angry behavior may well seem to be worth the benefit they provide. (Quick *Gedankenexperiment:* imagine two interruptions, one to announce need for help with statistical programming, the other to announce the arrival of one's pain medication from the pharmacy—which interrupter gets snapped at? Or, better, do the two interrupters arouse equally intense impulsive flashes of primitive annoyance?)

In short, pain modifies the meaning of events by affecting a variety of personal and social factors that serve as a context for them. The effect is to lower the threshold for the perception of wrongdoing and thereby to increase the probability of anger. It is important to realize the wide latitude that exists in most situations for construing responsibility and blameworthiness. There is also a great variety of cognitive and motivational processes that bias the judgment of events, ranging from simple egocentrism to complex motivated strategies of ego defense (Solomon, 1976). The present account is admittedly only a rough sketch, but I hope it suggests an alternative way of accounting for the sort of phenomena that are of central interest to Berkowitz.

Among the virtues of the sort of approach I have sketched, there is one that seems particularly interesting. One difficulty with Berkowitz's account concerns the conception of the aversive events that are said to cause anger. Part of the appeal of any theory that links aversive events—or even more generally, feeling bad—to anger is that it seems to provide a neat explanation for a messy phenomenon. If we made a list of things that seem to increase irritability, it might include: being sleep deprived, being under time pressure, being in pain, sensing that one's situation is hopeless, having hypoglycemia, and feeling unappreciated. These things appear to have nothing in common save their aversiveness, so a theory that links aversiveness to anger would seem to have something in its favor. Yet, to have such powerful generality, the concept of aversiveness must be quite abstract, since whatever makes a toothache aversive is surely rather different from whatever makes being unappreciated aversive. Yet Berkowitz's model treats all aversive events as if they are essentially cold pressor tasks. By doing so he really addresses only a fraction of the sources of irritability; therefore he fails to explain the generality that makes this topic so interesting.

The cognitive approach, however, offers more than an account of how pain increases the probability of anger. Similar analyses could be offered for each of the other aversive things that increase irritability. Some of the contextual changes would be similar and others would be different, but a general notion of aversiveness could be arrived at. The list of mechanisms would be long and not very elegant and might differ somewhat for different cultures and different people, but such is the reality of psychology. In various ways the aversive things would be understood as modifying a person's sense of well-being, as giving rise to a sense that a limit has been reached, that one cannot tolerate any more stress, that one has had enough, that drastic measures are warranted. The factors that make people irritable are the factors that make them believe that their situation is sufficiently intolerable that the benefits of anger and aggression appear to outweigh whatever costs they incur. Such an approach to understanding the link between pain and irritability, I believe, has more potential for accounting for the generality of the concept of aversiveness than does the dual systems approach.

THE DISTINCTION BETWEEN OBJECTIVE
AND SUBJECTIVE APPRAISAL

An important part of Berkowitz's argument is directed at establishing that anger can be aroused by events that are neither arbitrary nor unjustified. He views this conclusion as refuting cognitivist claims that anger results from an appraisal of wrongdoing by another. But it is important to recognize that there is a difference between a reasonable person's judging that no wrongdoing has occurred and the victim's impulsive angry reaction that somebody is to blame. That is, there is a critical difference between perceiving in the heat of the moment that an act is blameworthy and claiming that any reasonable person who knew the facts would agree that the act was blameworthy.

This is the distinction that Averill (1983) made when showing how his subjects consistently distinguished between anger and annoyance. Averill explained the distinction by analogy to the difference between knowledge and belief. I would explain it in terms of the distinction between objectivity and subjectivity drawn by Sabini and Silver (1982). Averill's subjects seemed to reserve the term *anger* for instances when they believed that others would see the situation their way, that is, when they believed their judgment of wrongdoing to be objective; they used the term *annoyance* when they were less certain that their personal reactions would be socially validated, that is, when they believed (or were only willing to claim) their perception of wrongdoing to be subjective.

In this framework, one would say that Berkowitz's evidence for anger in reaction to justified frustrations refutes the claim that anger requires objective wrongdoing, but does not refute the claim that anger requires the subjective perception of wrongdoing. The empirically testable question that now arises is whether this sort of subjective perception occurs in the experiments Berkowitz cites. I do not know the answer.

What I do know is that people are capable of feeling angry despite knowing (or, at least, suspecting) that their anger has no objective basis. In my research on envy I find that this complex emotion often involves some form of angry resentment (Parrott, 1991). Sometimes this resentment is directed at a specific person or group that the envious person believes to have been responsible for the unfairness of the envied advantage. Such resentment, which I call *agent-focused resentment,* entails a belief that wrongdoing occurred, and is easily compatible with the typical cognitivist account of anger. But other times there is resentment accompanied by the belief that no wrongdoing has occurred. Such resentment, which I call *global resentment,* involves a subjective conviction that unfairness somehow exists anyway. Global resentment is directed not at any particular person but, rather, at the situation, or at fate, or at life itself, which is perceived to be somehow unfair.

That such an emotion is possible is itself interesting. My undergraduate informants report envious resentment directed at friends who have wealthy parents, or at those who effortlessly do well in school, or at those who have parents who remain happily married, or at those who were born with desirable facial features or body shapes. The objects of such envy did nothing wrong to obtain these advantages, of course; they were just lucky. Envious people often do not believe that the objects of their envy are in any way responsible for their advantage, and may even believe the envied person is exceptionally generous in sharing his or her good fortune. Nevertheless, the envy is of an angry, resentful type, as if the principles of justice and equality ought to apply to all aspects of life, as if even the rewards of fate should be based on merit, not luck.

Because of the ambiguity of many real-life situations, however, there is often some possibility of interpreting events so as to construe the envied person as being blameworthy. Sure, the handsome person did not deliberately cause others to be less attractive, but could he not have been nicer about it, must he look so happy? Literature contains many explorations of this tension between objective and subjective unfairness, as Richard Smith discussed in an intriguing essay (Smith, 1991). Part of Hamlet's indecisiveness is due to some of his motives for killing Claudius being legitimate whereas others are personal and not a proper justification for taking revenge. Before acting he has to sort out his motives and determine that there are sufficient grounds for having the legitimate motives. Considerations of objective and subjective unfairness enter into the verdict on those who envied Melville's Billy Budd, Pushkin's Mozart, and Shakespeare's Julius Caesar.

Such resentment provides everyday evidence that people are capable of subjective resentment and anger despite some degree of awareness that this hostility lacks an objective basis. Perhaps, people do not wholly care about the socially sanctioned assessment of right and wrong. Perhaps, feeling inferior can be added to our list of anger facilitating aversive events. And perhaps, all these aversive events might be understood as making one temporarily less able or willing to consider other's points of view, and thereby less concerned about or cognizant of discrepancies between one's subjective appraisal and an objective one.

That Berkowitz does the sort of research that would uncover anger and aggression in the absence of objective wrongdoing suggests to me an admirable ability to produce in the laboratory phenomena that might reveal significant elements of human nature. His theory, however, characterizes this anger as innate and uncognized, as occurring the same way in humans and in rats. As such, it seems to miss many of the ways in which such phenomena might illuminate human nature.

THE SCIENTIFIC STUDY OF EMOTION

The approach sketched in this chapter suggests that it will be impossible to have broad laws that can permit one to deduce when anger will occur. The factors that influence how a person will construe an event are subtle and many. Averill's pioneering work on anger (e.g., Averill, 1979) showed us where this path leads—empirical work is important, but only in tandem with an appreciation of legal concepts, of how social norms are applied to particular situations, of conflicting cultural attitudes toward anger, of the social construction of emotion. The path leads not so much toward Laws of Behavior as to the *Summa Theologiae* and the Roman Stoics.

To many, such an approach to human emotion may seem utterly unscientific, a rejection of crucial values of experimental psychology, but I am increasingly persuaded that it is the only type of psychological science worth pursuing. General laws predicting certain types of responses to certain types of stimuli rarely hold up, and when they do it is despite shedding no light on the intervening processes (which are usually the most interesting part). A good example occurs with respect to my research on mood and memory, which was referred to by Berkowitz. Under certain conditions subjects in good moods can be shown to recall memories that are more negative than those recalled by subjects in bad moods (Parrott & Sabini, 1990). One hypothesis of why this occurs is that people sometimes try to regulate their moods, and might try to counter their mood by recalling memories incongruent to it. This hypothesis may seem counterintuitive for two reasons. First, subjects in the experiments had no awareness of regulating moods, and prevalent conceptions of mood regulation maintain that self-control is a controlled process, not an automatic one. Second, the incongruent recall occurred for subjects in good moods as well as for those in bad moods, and the prevalent assumption is that only subjects in bad moods have a motive to dispel their moods—subjects in good moods should be motivated to maintain their moods.

My own deliberations on these issues have persuaded me that these assumptions about the nature of mood and mood regulation are just wrong (Parrott, 1993). Self-regulation often becomes habitual and automatic over years of practice, requiring little effort or awareness. People have motives to inhibit good moods and to maintain bad moods just as surely as they have the hedonic motives more commonly supposed (e.g., a person with work to do may find it necessary to inhibit a good mood so as to concentrate on work). One consequence of appreciating these motives (and there are dozens of them) is that predicting mood regulation is no longer straightforward. A person in a good mood may be motivated either to maintain the mood or to inhibit it. Which motive predominates depends on a bewildering number of things, ranging from the task at hand and the social circumstances to the person's beliefs about moods and philosophy of life.

So it is with anger. Meaning and context are important—loud noises may often seem aversive and tend to stir up anger, but probably not when they emanate from sirens on ambulances coming to one's rescue (or at least not as much as do vastly softer sounds of gum chewing in the library). Innate tendencies may be alterable—Berkowitz himself points out that rats with certain learning histories no longer show the usual aggression in response to painful stimulation. In the human case there seems much greater potential for learning to modify the natural tendency of pain to induce anger. We are left again with a topic in which general laws of behavior are difficult to propose independent of knowledge about history, culture, meaning, and context.

In his recent book *Cosmopolis,* Stephen Toulmin (1990) advanced the interesting thesis that the preference for universal, context-free scientific laws arose as a solution to problems that existed in seventeenth century Europe. He argued that the need for such an approach to science has now passed, and that civilization is now poised for a return to the values of Renaissance humanism, with its greater tolerance of uncertainty, contextualism, and the discovery of local, temporary relations. Such a shift may or may not be occurring, but were it to occur I think it would foster the approach to research best suited for understanding human emotion.

REFERENCES

Averill, J. R. (1979). Anger. In H. E. Howe, Jr. & R. A. Dienstbier (Eds.), *Nebraska symposium on motivation* (Vol. 26, pp. 1–80). Lincoln: University of Nebraska Press.

Averill, J. R. (1983). Studies on anger and aggression: Implications for theories of emotion. *American Psychologist, 38,* 1145–1160.

Frijda, N. H. (1986). *The emotions.* Cambridge: Cambridge University Press.

Lazarus, R. S. (1991). *Emotion and adaptation.* New York: Oxford University Press.

Parrott, W. G. (1988). The role of cognition in emotional experience. In W. J. Baker, L. P. Mos, H. V. Rappard, & H. J. Stam (Eds.), *Recent trends in theoretical psychology* (pp. 327–337). New York: Springer-Verlag.

Parrott, W. G. (1991). The emotional experiences of envy and jealousy. In P. Salovey (Ed.), *The psychology of jealousy and envy* (pp. 3–30). New York: Guilford.

Parrott, W. G. (1993). Beyond hedonism: Motives for inhibiting or maintaining good and bad moods. In D. M. Wegner & J. W. Pennebaker (Eds.), *Handbook of mental control* (pp. 278–305). Englewood Cliffs, NJ: Prentice-Hall.

Parrott, W. G., & Gleitman, H. (1989). Infants' expectations in play: The joy of peek-a-boo. *Cognition and Emotion, 3,* 291–311.

Parrott, W. G., & Sabini, J. (1989). On the "emotional" qualities of certain types of cognition: A reply to arguments for the independence of cognition and affect. *Cognitive Therapy and Research, 13,* 49–65.

Parrott, W. G., & Sabini, J. (1990). Mood and memory under natural conditions: Evidence for mood incongruent recall. *Journal of Personality and Social Psychology, 59,* 321–336.

Parrott, W. G., & Schulkin, J. (in press). Psychophysiology and the cognitive nature of the emotions. *Cognition & Emotion.*

Reisenzein, R., & Schönpflug, W. (1992). Stumpf's cognitive–evaluative theory of emotion. *American Psychologist, 47,* 34–45.

Sabini, J., & Silver, M. (1982). *Moralities of everyday life.* New York: Oxford University Press.

Smith, R. H. (1991). Envy and the sense of injustice. In P. Salovey (Ed.), *The psychology of jealousy and envy* (pp. 79–99). New York: Guilford.

Solomon, R. C. (1976). *The passions: The myth and nature of human emotions.* Notre Dame: University of Notre Dame Press.

Toulmin, S. (1990). *Cosmopolis: The hidden agenda of modernity.* New York: The Free Press.

Zajonc, R. B. (1980). Feeling and thinking: Preferences need no inferences. *American Psychologist, 35,* 151–175.

10

More Thoughts About the Social Cognitive and Neoassociationistic Approaches: Similarities and Differences

Leonard Berkowitz
University of Wisconsin-Madison

> *"Come on, Pitt," Drummond said dryly. "You know as well as I do that people in the grip of powerful emotions don't think like that—or half our crimes of impulse would never be committed, probably three quarters. They don't think; they feel—overwhelming rage, or fear, or simply confusion and a desire to lash out at someone and blame them for the pain they are suffering."*
>
> —Anne Perry (Highgate Rise, *1991, pp. 55)*

I can't imagine authors of the target articles not liking the chapter–commentary–and reply format employed by this series. Not only are the writers very likely to be flattered by the time and attention the commentators have given to their writing, but in their concluding responsive chapter they also see themselves as cleverly answering whatever mistaken arguments the commentators may have offered in objection to their analysis. I myself am pleased by this target chapter–comment format for both of these reasons, but in addition, I have also learned and benefited from many of the points raised by the commentators and have also enjoyed the opportunity to think more about a number of the issues they have emphasized.

SOME OF THE BENEFITS

I readily acknowledge these benefits. To mention only some of the more obvious ones: Oatley showed me that my theoretical formulation is somewhat closer to Darwin's conception of emotions than to James' better known theory, and I also

179

found the research observations cited in several of the chapters (including, but not only, the cross-cultural material reported by Averill, and the results of Lenny Martin's intriguing experiments) quite interesting. Furthermore, whereas I was familiar with the theoretical approaches taken by most of the commentators, such as the Lang; Leventhal; and Ortony, Clore, and Collins models, I also appreciated the additional information all of these theorists provided about their particular perspectives. Indeed, the commentaries about the status of contemporary theorizing in the study of emotions are generally very informative.

Reading the Lang and Leventhal chapters was especially instructive. Where traditional cognitive theorists, such as (notably) Clore, Ortony and their colleagues, discuss emotional structures solely in semantic terms, Lang and Leventhal go beyond the verbal level, and maintain, persuasively for me, that a truly comprehensive account of emotions must be organized on a number of levels. Although these two writers do not use the same words and slice emotional patterns in somewhat different ways, both seem to agree that emotions are structured along sensory–perceptual and expressive–motor (or response output) dimensions as well as the semantic–conceptual dimensions favored by the more traditional cognitive formulations, such as the one offered by Ortony and his associates. It seems to me that truly comprehensive accounts of emotion would do well to go beyond even the multiprocess models advanced by some theorists such as Forgas (1992) and incorporate the kind of multilevel analysis advocated by Lang and Leventhal.

It was also worthwhile to have so many of the commentators identify the imprecisions and poorly worded statements in my target chapter. Most notably, virtually all of them questioned my overly simplistic discussion of the role of cognitive processes. Although I certainly knew that cognitive theories of emotion do not necessarily assume that the various emotional states are the result of only deliberate, conscious thought and analysis, some of my statements in the target chapter easily give the impression that this is my view of the cognitive theories. Perhaps I was so intent on highlighting what I regarded as the central differences between my own cognitive–neoassociationist (CNA) approach and the more familiar, traditional cognitive formulations that I failed to adequately describe the subtleties and complexities in the latter theorizing. Then, too, several of the commentators show that I occasionally was not as clear as I should have been in spelling out the details of my CNA model. As just one case in point, in his thoughtful summary and critique of my formulation, Forgas suggested that "the CNA [analysis] predicts fairly rigid, invariant associations" between negative affect and the anger/aggression syndrome, whereas the associations postulated by the associative network models in cognitive psychology "are essentially plastic, moulded (sic) by past experiences and learning." Maybe the problem here is also a matter of my emphasis. Believing that the associationistic doctrine implies probability rather than a fixed and definite connection, I had meant to suggest there was something of a likelihood, not certainty, that negative feelings would activate the various components of the anger/aggression syndrome. More importantly, consistent with Miller's (1941) discussion of the frustration—aggression hypothesis, I also think (and tried to say) that the strength of the association between unpleasant feelings and anger/aggression-related reactions can be modified, weakened, or strengthened, by experience and learning— although the association presumably is not only learned. By the way, this last phrase means, contrary to what Parrott has implied, that associations (such as the probabilistic connection between negative affect and anger/aggression reactions) can be inborn as well as acquired. And then, too, although I evidently hadn't said this explicitly enough, my model does assume, with Forgas, that associations operate in the later, relatively elaborate construction of the affective experience (see Berkowitz & Heimer, 1989) as well as in the conjectured initial phase of the development of anger. I should have made these points (and others) clearer.

SOME THOUGHTS ABOUT THE DIFFERENT THEORETICAL APPROACHES

Nonetheless, although I agree with many of the commentators' remarks and realize that the cognitive–neoassociationist analysis of anger can be improved in important ways, I believe it is important to spell out the differences in the theoretical assumptions made by the neoassociationist perspective followed in the target article and those made by the traditional cognitive approach to emotions, the approach generally holding that appraisals, attributions, or other forms of a fairly high level of mental activity are all-important. (My chapters in this volume are not intended to take issue with those theorists, regarded by themselves and others as cognitively oriented, whose underlying thinking is compatible with the main thrust of my arguments even though they prefer to couch their ideas in cognition-sounding terms.) After identifying these conceptual disparities, I attempt to show that, in several vital respects, those adopting the traditional cognitive orientation to emotions have little if any evidence that their assumptions are necessarily more valid than the neoassociationists' assumptions. This being so (in my judgment, anyway) and believing that neoassociationistic ideas can contribute to our understanding of emotions, I then call for an integration of the two approaches.

To start, let us consider just what is involved in the cognitive approach to social psychology as well as the typical cognitive analysis of emotions.

What is the Social Cognitive Approach?

Social psychologists have been talking about *social cognition* for several decades now, generally agreeing that this is the dominant perspective in the discipline. It is also now commonplace for the authors of social psychology texts to claim (mistakenly) that social psychology has always been cognitive in its orientation. Although it is not very clear what these statements mean exactly, because few discussions of the cognitive approach provide the same detailed specification of what are its defining features, I think it is helpful to review the kinds of ideas that seem to be linked to the traditional cognitive orientation so that we can make its underlying assumptions explicit. This survey occasionally contrasts what is here viewed as the traditional cognitive perspective with the assumptions held by contemporary associationism, the approach that I (following Landman & Manis, 1983) term *neoassociationism*.

The Necessity of Intervening Mental Activity

Cognitive social psychology obviously emphasizes the part played by thinking in human conduct. Some writers in this area, guided by the Lewinian tradition, then contend that people's thoughts (which may be either conscious or unconscious) necessarily determine how they will respond to the situation they are in. Ross and Nisbett (1991) expressed this conception of the person as thinker in their discussion of "the social psychological perspective" (or better still, the cognitive perspective in social psychology). According to them, "To predict the behavior of a given person successfully, we must be able to appreciate the actor's construal of the situation—that is, the manner in which the person understands the situation as a whole" (p. 11). They maintained that social psychology was never behavioristic because "Its most astute practitioners always understood that it is the situation as construed by the subject that is the true stimulus" (p. 11).

Similarly, in their comprehensive survey of cognitive social psychology, Fiske and Taylor (1991) explicitly held that intervening mental activity mediates between the external situation on one hand and felt emotions and behavior on the other. Thus, they suggested, emotional states in themselves do not directly affect behavior. For cognitive social psychology, Fiske and Taylor said, "the person in-between the presumed cause and the result is viewed as a *thinking organism;* this view contrasts with viewing the person as an emotional organism or a mindless automation" (p. 10). In other words, people's thoughts, not their aroused internal states, are the direct cause of what they do when they are emotionally excited.

The well-known dispute between Zajonc and Lazarus as to whether affect can arise independently of cognitions is, of course, relevant to this conception of the primacy of mental activity in human emotions and behavior. Fiske and Taylor essentially sided with Lazarus in this argument, holding that mental processes must be involved in moods and emotions. They proposed that "relatively simple affective responses" of the kind discussed by Zajonc (1980), such as preferences, affective judgments, and liking, might be "nonintellective" reactions, as Zajonc had maintained. But for many (probably including themselves), they said, the more complex moods and emotions "intrinsically depend on cognitively driven appraisal processes" (p. 456). The majority of the cognitively oriented commentators basically take the same stance.

But to return to the more general matter of humans as thinkers, although those taking a strong cognitivist position clearly give greater weight to the mediating role of mental activity, neoassociationists are aware that cognitive processes play a significant part in human reactions. The social cognitivists' picture of their theoretical opponents applies more to Watsonian or Skinnerian behaviorism than to contemporary neoassociationism and doesn't even fit the more recent, liberalized form of S–R theorizing advocated by Neal Miller (1959). Miller and others sharing his modern S–R associationistic approach recognize that it is the meaning of the external stimuli, and not their objective nature, that greatly determines how the actors will respond to them. Miller also departed from Watsonian/Skinnerian behaviorism in noting that psychological theories referring to unobservable intervening variables, including variables pertaining to interpretations and expectations, were generally more economical than theories postulating elaborate S–R chains. Notions of meaning and of interpretation are not foreign to contemporary associationistic formulations. Indeed, as Landman and Manis (1983) pointed out, present day neoassociative theories posit cognitive structures, organized arrangements of knowledge. Associative network conceptions of emotion, whether Bower's well known formulation (e.g., Bower & Cohen, 1982) or my own CNA model, are good examples.

Construction of Internal Representations

Other discussions of the cognitive perspective have gone beyond the emphasis on the primacy of mental activity. One especially noteworthy example can be found in the Markus and Zajonc (1985) review of cognitive social psychology's basic concepts and assumptions. Saying that "today's social psychology" is basically "the study of the social mind" rather than the study of social behavior (p. 137), they noted that from the cognitive perspective, "The essential link in the behavioral process became an *active cognitive construction of the environment*. . . . The implicit idea is that we can understand social behavior only if we understand the precise nature of these [constructed] representations" (p. 138).

Other writers have also highlighted this matter of "active cognitive constructions." And so, to cite only two other examples, Neisser's (1967) pioneering text from the 1960s held that cognitive psychology is concerned with all of the processes by which sensory input is transformed, reduced, and elaborated, while more recently, Isen and Hastorf (1982) said cognitive psychology is interested in the processes by which knowledge is constructed and represented.

Landman and Manis (1983) regarded this perspective's emphasis on the mental construction of internal representations as one of its chief features. With them, we can say that cognitive social psychology has: (a) a concern with the psychological process(es) that is/are (b) involved in the *active transformation and internal representation* of the external sensory input. The social cognition approach basically holds, then, that a constructed representation of some external occurrence, in which the objective nature of the event has been mentally transformed into some representation that is qualitatively different, necessarily intervenes to determine the reaction to this event. This is the core assumption differentiating what I have termed the traditional cognitive perspective from the neoassociationistic framework.

Neoassociationism's Assumptions

Neoassociationism obviously doesn't believe an actively constructed internal representation always intervenes between situation and response. Much more than the cognitive school of thought, it is ready to postulate "passive or automatic mechanisms of processing" and doesn't confine itself exclusively to the "more active principles endorsed by constructionist (i.e., cognitively oriented) theorists" (Landman & Manis, 1983, p. 71). And furthermore, in maintaining that there can be relatively passive and automatic emotional, behavioral, and even cognitive reactions to external occurrences, neoassociationism has more of a bottom up orientation, "assigning greater functional importance to stimulus features . . ." (Landman & Manis, p. 70). Although the advocates of this position do posit cognitive structures, as I've already noted, they are generally more likely than cognitivists to say that "perception, memory, and other cognitive activities [can be] built up from the features of the input, or [can be] more 'data driven' than 'theory driven' " in their formation and operation (p. 70).

Are One or More Psychological Systems Involved in Emotions?

When we think of all these differences between the two theoretical frameworks, it is easy to arrive at yet another difference stressed by several emotions researchers: that having to do with the number of distinct psychological systems that are presumably involved in emotional reactions. Where the traditional cognitive approach typically holds that emotions grow out of the operation of a single, relatively unitary system, the neoassociationistic perspective basically postulates two or more separate systems, one relatively passive and bottom-up in operation, and others (one or more) of a cognitive, top-down nature. Parrott has emphasized this difference in his commentary, and seems to argue that words historically linked to associationist thinking should be avoided, at least partly because they imply a dual system theory of emotions. Clore, Ortony, and their colleagues are somewhat more liberal in this regard. They indicate a willingness to grant the possibility of two or more operative systems, but they clearly prefer to think of one cognitive system as being virtually all-important. On the other side, the Lang and Leventhal formulations summarized in this volume, Zajonc's (1980) well-known separation of affective and cognitive systems, and my own neoassociationistic framework all assume that widely different psychological mechanisms contribute to the formation and operation of emotions.

DIFFERENT INTERPRETATIONS OF TWO PHENOMENA

I think it is worthwhile seeing how these two different perspectives are applied to two sets of phenomena of interest to cognitive social psychologists: priming effects and the influence of moods on judgments. (To be clear, this discussion equates neoassociationism generally with network/spreading activation models, much as Landman and Manis do and as I have done in the target article.) As I said before, I try to show that the cognitive approach doesn't necessarily and always provide a better explanation of these phenomena.

The Case of Priming

Word Preferences

Many of the commentators noted that cognitive processes can be automatic, involuntary, and quick. With most social psychologists sharing their approach, they are apt to point to priming effects as a good example of this rapid automaticity. I wonder, however, if the widespread insistence on calling priming a cognitive, but not an associative, concept (as Parrott, for one, did in his remarks) isn't partly due to an automatic, involuntary, and quick bias against conceptions smacking of associationism. Thus, Parrott apparently argues that only terms preferred by those calling themselves cognitive theorists should be used in talking about priming.

Other writers in the cognitivist tradition have also preferred not to think of the priming effect in associative terms and have attempted to explain this phenomenon by appealing to supposedly cognitive mechanisms. Thus, Wyer and Srull (e.g., Wyer & Srull, 1986) advanced a "storage bin" model, holding that, as Fiske and Taylor put it, "recently primed concepts are at the top of the mental heap" (p. 263). Some of these theoretical accounts of priming actually are conceptually very close to the neoassociationistic interpretation, for example the "synapse model" summarized by Fiske and Taylor (1991, p. 263), but it is the rare cognitively oriented writer who recognizes this similarity and even mentions associations. Higgins and King (1981) were unusual in that although they chose to employ an "energy cell" metaphor in interpreting their priming effect results, they did note that the findings were very much in accord with an associative network-spreading activation model.

Findings in Accord With the Neoassociationistic Framework

For Landman and Manis (1983), some of the demonstrations of a priming effect were so much in keeping with associationistic thinking that they regarded the findings as supportive of this perspective. They singled out the Bargh and Pietromonaco (1982) experiment as especially consistent with "the associationist assumptions about passive processing." In this study, it will be recalled, although the subjects were not consciously aware of the words shown to them on a cathode ray tube screen, "the higher the proportion of hostile words presented during the priming phase, the more negative the [subsequent] impression of the stimulus person [they had been asked to evaluate] and the more extreme the ratings on hostile dimensions." These results, Landman and Manis said, "represent rather strong support for the operation of a passive frequency-based principle of association" (p. 74).

Other findings are also consistent with the neoassociationistic approach. Thus, as further evidence of a frequency-based principle of association, research has shown that categories that presumably have been primed frequently in the person's past tend to be very accessible in a given situation, "seem to be used without one's intention . . . and even outside one's control" (Fiske & Taylor, 1991, p. 265). And then too, Fiske and Taylor also reported that, "Priming effects are strongest . . . when relevant meanings as well as positive or negative valences are primed" (p. 258). This observation certainly suggests that primes that are semantically associated with the target stimulus typically have the greatest influence on reactions to that stimulus.

It is important to recognize the associations between priming experience and response if we are to understand the often subtle influences contributing to aggression in society. A wide variety of situations can be associated with aggression, even in an nonobvious manner, and can, therefore, prime hostile thoughts and action tendencies: scenes of violence (Berkowitz, 1984; Bushman & Geen, 1990), the presence of weapons (Anderson, Anderson, & Deuser, 1992; Turner, Simons, Berkowitz, & Frodi, 1977), tasks that require the use of hostile words (Srull & Wyer, 1980), or that activate memories of either (a) famous people regarded as being hostile (Herr, 1986) or (b) aggressive contact sports (Wann & Branscombe, 1990).

Support for Neoassociationism in Movie Violence Research. Besides demonstrating the wide applicability of the priming effect notion, some of the research into the effects of observed violence yielded findings commensurate with the neoassociationistic interpretation of priming. My investigations of the available target's characteristics are especially informative in this regard. In these experiments, male subjects (a) who had been either provoked or treated in a neutral manner, (b) watched either a brief prize fight scene or another, equally interesting neutral film clip, and then had an opportunity to punish a fellow student who (c) had been introduced to them in a particular way. The results indicated that after viewing the boxing scene the provoked men typically punished the available target most strongly when this person (a) had previously been identified as a college boxer, or (b) had the same name as the loser in the witnessed fight film (see Berkowitz, 1974, pp. 169–170 for a summary).

More recently, Josephson (1987) also reported findings in keeping with the neoassociationist perspective by indicating that similarity can influence the magnitude of the priming effect. In her experiment, the schoolboy subjects generally were most aggressive during a hockey game if they had (a) previously seen a violent TV program, and then, just before the start of the game, (b) encountered a cue (a walkie-talkie radio) that had been featured prominently in the violent program. The second walkie-talkie's physical and functional resemblance to one of the details in the initial priming experience, the violent movie, apparently kept alive and/or intensified the aggression-related tendencies activated by that film.

In all of the studies just mentioned, the violent film's subsequent aggression-activating effect evidently was strengthened by associations between salient details of the priming movie and some stimulus in the following situation. Sometime the subjects had to mentally establish the later situation's connection with the initial priming event (as when they presumably linked the college boxer to the boxing scene), but in other cases the association was made much more passively (as in Josephson's experiment). And we don't have to invoke a fairly elaborate top down processing to account for any of these results.[2]

Negative Affect–Hostility Associations.   But to get back to the matter of priming experience–target associations, the reader should remember one of the central theses in the present CNA model: the theoretically postulated linkage between negative affect and aggression-related ideas, memories, and motor tendencies. Because of this connection, the prime–target association need not always be semantically close; negative affect having no obvious hostile meaning theoretically can also activate aggression-linked ideas, memories, and behavioral inclinations. The target chapter listed some of the research results supporting this proposition. A recent unpublished experiment by Anderson and Deuser (1992) adds to this evidence. In this study, the subjects first played a 10-minute game in a room that was either at a normal temperature, or was warm, or hot, and rated their feelings at that time. Then, right afterward, all of the participants went into another, normal temperature room where they rated their own personalities on several standard hostility inventories.

The people exposed to the unusual heat reported the strongest anger feeling state, confirming the results of earlier investigations. But more interestingly, when all of the subjects described their own personalities later under the normal temperature, the hotter the room to which they previously had been exposed, the more hostile they now described their personalities. It is as if, in remembering how they had felt just before, those who had been angriest attributed their feelings to their own personal characteristics and didn't blame some external cause.[3]

Cognition-Produced Contrast Effects

This last mentioned observation brings us to another feature of the cognitive–neoassociationistic model I'm proposing: Neoassociationism does not attempt to explain all psychological phenomena in associationistic terms and recognizes that cognitive processes often come into operation. Thus, this school of thought is not disturbed by the fact that, under certain conditions, the target stimulus seems to be contrasted with the priming experience instead of being assimilated toward it. Activated cognitive processes undoubtedly are responsible for the target's apparent displacement away from the prior priming experience. I'd like to suggest, however, that there may be at least two different kinds of priming-produced contrast effects so that different cognitive mechanisms are at work in each of them.

The Priming Displacement as Judgmental Context Effect.   One type of contrast occurs when the prime and target stimulus are on the same conceptual dimension but there is a considerable difference between them on this dimension (cf. Fiske & Taylor, 1991, p. 261). In such instances the displacement away from the priming experience seems to be analogous to the context effect that arises in many judgment tasks when the object being judged is greatly different from a previous anchoring experience (Berkowitz, 1960; Hovland & Sherif, 1952; Parducci, 1963). And so, just as we say a lifted weight is lighter than it actually is after we have hoisted a number of heavy objects, we judge Donald's ambiguous behavior as fairly friendly after we have been primed to think of relatively extreme hostility. If this is indeed an apt analogy and the same mechanisms are involved (see Holmes & Berkowitz, 1961, for relevant evidence), Parducci's (1963) analysis of judgments suggests that this particular priming-produced contrast effect is more of a change in the judgmental scale used (e.g., the scale on which degree of hostility is rated) than a substantial transformation or reconstruction of the target stimulus (e.g., Donald's behavior).

Presumed Self-Control of Priming Influence.   A very different process could produce the displacement away from the priming experience when the person is highly aware of this particular experience and its possible effect on her or him. Fiske and Taylor (1991) mentioned one explanation for this phenomenon that is quite similar to the Berkowitz–Troccoli self-regulation hypothesis offered in the target article. Summarizing some of the relevant evidence, particularly findings published by Martin (1986), Fiske and Taylor proposed that, "When people are aware of a blatant prime and its potential link to [the target] stimulus, they may resist its all too obvious influence" (p. 260) so that either contrast or assimilation takes place (p. 261).

This possibility is comparable to my interpretation of what might well happen when moderately aroused people become aware of their not-too-intense feelings (as in the Berkowitz–Troccoli experiments cited in the target chapter). In both cases, we can say, those who are highly conscious of the thoughts and/or feelings that had just been activated in them could at times believe these thoughts/feelings are not appropriate to the present situation. If they do have this belief, they might then "lean over backward," trying to keep these thoughts/feelings from affecting their reaction to the target stimulus.

Let's go on and look at this possibility more closely. If people do at times resist the priming experiences's "all-too-obvious influence," as Fiske and Taylor put it, doesn't this imply that in these instances, first, the prime had automatically, and perhaps passively, activated the presumably inappropriate thoughts or feelings, and second, cognitive processing had to be activated to control these reactions? It seems to me that these ideas are actually implicit in the Fiske–Taylor statement and they are, of course, explicit in the Berkowitz–Troccoli self-regulation hypothesis. Maybe the Fiske–Taylor interpretation of this kind of priming-induced contrast isn't very different at all from my own CNA analysis.

Influence of Mood on Judgments

The two theoretical perspectives probably differ most sharply in their interpretation of why moods influence judgments. I will take the "mood as information" thesis as representative of the cognitivist analysis (although other cognitive formulations are worthy of attention; e.g., Forgas, 1992) because it explicitly says that a fairly high level of intervening mental activity is necessarily responsible for the influence of mood on judgments. After summarizing this view, I then attempt to outline some unresolved problems.

Moods as Sources of Information

The Model's Basic Argument.   The mood-as-information (MAI) interpretation of mood effects is a clear continuation of the Schachter-attribution tradition (also followed by Zillmann's excitation transfer conception) described in the target chapter.[4] According to this MAI model, when people in a given mood state make a judgment of some target stimulus, they are apt to infer their assessment of (or liking for) this stimulus on the basis of their feelings at the time—but only if they can reasonably attribute their present affect to that object. In the early investigation of this possibility published by Schwarz and Clore (1983), as an example, the research participants' weather-induced moods evidently influenced their satisfaction with their lives as a whole only when their attention was not directed to the weather at that time. Take the case of the persons who were feeling good because it was a sunny day. Those who hadn't thought of the weather, and thus were supposedly not conscious of its effect on them, presumably attributed their positive feelings to the stimulus being evaluated (their lives) and then inferred they were happy with their lives. Putting this another way, the participants' mood was taken as information about the value of the stimulus being judged as long as this particular information seemed to be "relevant to the judgment at hand" (Schwarz & Bless, 1991, p. 57).

An experiment by Martin, Harlow, and Strack (1992), also carried out within this framework, is especially pertinent to the present discussion. Extending the MAI thesis to bodily reactions (and, as they note, to the James–Lange theory of emotions), the authors reasoned that people often employ the sensations they obtain from their emotion-related facial expressions as information about their judgments of external events, but will make this inference only to the degree that the bodily sensations cannot be attributed to another plausible cause.

To test this argument the subjects were induced to hold a facial expression simulating either a smile or an angry frown as they read an emotionally ambiguous story. One-third of the men and women in the study did this immediately after 2 minutes of vigorous exercise, another third contracted their faces in the specified manner 90 seconds after they stopped exercising, and the remaining people read the story while holding their facial expressions without having engaged in any exercise.

The expected results were obtained: The subjects who had been induced to smile reported a more favorable reaction to the story than did those who had made an angry face—in both the no-exercise and exercise-then-delay conditions, but not in the exercise-immediate expression group. According to the authors, the participants who read the story immediately after exercising attributed their facial expression-induced sensations to the very salient exercise, and thus didn't use these sensations as information about their judgments of the story. In the remaining cases, however, supposedly because there was no plausible and salient alternative cause of these sensations, the subjects' bodily reactions presumably provided relevant information about their emotional judgments.

Two other details of the researchers' reasoning are worth mentioning. For one, Martin and his colleagues proposed that the facial feedback was used only to infer the valence of the subjects' judgments and didn't provide emotional information more specific than this. And then too, for the investigators their results indicated that the facial expressions had "induced distinct positive or negative reactions" (p. 416).

Some Unresolved Questions.   The MAI thesis is obviously an significant contribution to the psychology of emotions. However, while I accept this formulation's basic insight regarding the importance of the self-perception of feelings (as witness the Berkowitz–Jo research into the construction of the anger experience summarized in the target chapter), it seems to me there are a number of serious questions that Schwarz, Clore, and their associates have still not adequately resolved.

What Evoked the Initial Feelings?   MAI talks about the attributions people make about their aroused feelings—but does not explain at all how the feelings were activated in the first place. Why, in the Schwarz and Clore (1983) study, were the subjects happy on sunny days and relatively unhappy when it was raining? The traditional cognitivist-appraisal interpretation would be that the participants had appraised the weather's significance for their own personal well-being (e.g., they presumably might have thought, even at some unconscious level, that the sunshine was personally beneficial). But if they had made such an appraisal, even unconsciously, wouldn't this mean they basically knew the reason for their pleasant mood (the sunshine)—so that they wouldn't have been able to attribute their happiness to the target stimulus (their lives)?

The MAI theorists would be most consistent, and certainly most parsimonious, if they said the weather had passively and automatically evoked the kind of feeling that had frequently been associated with that type of day in the past.

Much the same question can be raised about the Martin, Harlow, and Strack (1992) study just described: Why had the subjects experienced pleasant or unpleasant feelings at all? Surely they hadn't believed that holding a pen between their teeth would be personally beneficial but that they would be harmed in some way by biting down on the paper towel.

I go even further. As was already noted, Martin and his colleagues implied that their subjects had only responded to the valence of their bodily sensations. That is, they supposedly knew only that they felt good or bad. I wonder, however, if the bodily sensations didn't have an influence that was more specific than this. Couldn't the subjects in the Martin et al. investigation who were clenching their jaws have felt some anger along with their other unpleasant feelings? The Jo and Berkowitz experiment summarized in the target article indicates that people who perform the motor reactions characteristic of the anger/aggression syndrome are apt to experience anger but not other negative feelings such as sadness or anxiety (see Table 1.2). Laird and his colleagues at Clark University (Duclos et al., 1989) also reported that the facial expression and even bodily posture associated with a particular negative emotion can activate the specific and recognizable feeling typical of that particular emotion. Under some conditions, then, the information people obtain from their bodily reactions is more specific than just the pleasantness/unpleasantness of their sensations. How do the traditional cognitivist accounts of emotion explain this?

Is There Really Evidence of the Operation of Attributions?   Whatever the exact reason for the subjects' initial feelings in the MAI experiments, can we be sure that their attributions regarding the cause of these feelings affected their judgments of the target stimulus? I pointed out in the target article that there is no direct evidence at all that attributions had influenced Zillmann's results in his excitation transfer experiments. The same statement can be made about the MAI research. To my knowledge the MAI researchers have not shown that their experimental variations had actually altered the subjects' beliefs regarding the source of their moods and/or that these particular beliefs were directly responsible for the obtained judgments.

It could well be that the experimental manipulations had indeed manipulated the participants' attributions in some cases. This seems likely in the Schwarz and Clore (1983) study aforementioned. But in other cases, such as the Martin et al. (1992) investigation, other possibilities also exist and (for me, at least) are equally plausible. It is quite conceivable, for example, that the subjects who had started reading the story immediately after exercising were very self-attentive; still huffing and puffing from the vigorous activity, their attention could have been focused upon themselves to a considerable extent so that they engaged in the mood-regulation process postulated by Berkowitz and Troccoli. Those who had waited awhile before reading the story, on the other hand, might have calmed down enough so that their attention was no longer on themselves and they weren't as self-regulatory.

All this is not to deny the possible influence of attributions and/or other forms of mental activity on mood effects. I'm suggesting only that there may be more to these effects than the MAI formulation recognizes; and that affect can at times distort evaluations and memory without the intervention of the cognitive processes postulated by the MAI analysis.

Do Only Diffuse Feelings (Moods) Influence Judgments?   In their recent discussion of the influence of feelings on judgments and decision making, Schwarz and Bless (1991) proposed that "specific emotions" (which have "an identifiable cause") are much less likely than "global moods" to influence judgments, supposedly because the moods are more diffuse and can more readily be attributed to the stimulus being evaluated (pp. 57–58). Whether it is true or not that moods are more apt than specific emotions to distort judgments, everyday experience and research findings certainly indicate that even sharply defined emotions can influence evaluations. Haven't all of us, at one time or another, seen someone who was very angry (and who undoubtedly was well aware of his or her anger) make a very unfavorable assessment of a totally innocent person? This kind of *hostility displacement* is more likely to happen, of course, if the to-be-evaluated target is ambiguous, but the point here is that it results from a specific emotion.

Once More: The CNA Interpretation

In contrast to the MAI analysis just summarized (with its core assumption of an intervening and fairly complicated mental activity), the cognitive–neoassociationistic (CNA) model I have offered here suggests that moods and emotions sometimes affect evaluations in a relatively passive and automatic manner without the mediating operation of attributions or other such higher level cognitions. In common with other neoassociationist/network accounts of emotion (e.g., Bower & Cohen, 1982), this formulation holds that a specific feeling can prime the thoughts and memories that had been most strongly associated with this particular affect. If other activated cognitive processes do not block or transform these ideas and recollections, they could then influence the assessment of a stimulus being judged.

All sorts of research findings are in accord with this reasoning, but here I cite only some of the results obtained in an experiment by Forgas and Bower (1987). After the subjects were placed in either a happy or sad mood, they were asked (in a supposedly unrelated study) to evaluate several target persons briefly described to them. As expected, the happy men and women expressed significantly more favorable impressions of the targets than did their sadder counterparts. (Because the mood manipulation was very strong and clear in this study, it is very unlikely that the subjects had attributed their affect to the target descriptions.) More importantly, however, those subjects who were in a good mood made their mood-congruent positive judgments considerably faster than their incongruent negative judgments. And similarly, the sad people took less time to make their mood-consistent negative judgments than their inconsistent positive judgments, although this difference wasn't statistically significant (p. 57). Thoughts congruent with the participants' mood had apparently come to mind, which facilitated the expression of feeling-consistent evaluations.

What About the Effects of Negative Feelings?   In this last-mentioned experiment, as in many other investigations, the expressed judgment was in greater accord with feelings under the positive mood than under the negative mood. Psychologists typically explain this difference by postulating a negative mood-induced regulatory mechanism. This certainly seems to be a plausible reason for the positive–negative mood asymmetry. However, there is a question whether the presumed regulatory/control mechanism is activated by the negative affect in itself, as several writers have proposed, or has to be set in operation by some other aspect of the situation, such as the negative feeling's unexpectedness and/or the person's inward-directed attention, as the present CNA model suggests. As a variation on this theme, Schwarz and Bless (1991) hypothesized that negative feelings in themselves are very likely to produce careful, analytic thinking, whereas the CNA model holds that unpleasant affect can lead to either analytic thinking or, more passively and automatically, to unanalyzed emotional ideas, depending on the situation.

Again, both everyday experience and research findings indicate that negative affect alone does not put affect-regulating/controlling/repairing mechanisms into motion. For one thing, if these mechanisms were activated by unpleasant feelings in themselves, why would there be so many occasions in which people are in a very bad mood and/or say or do bad things as a result of their unhappiness? The experiments cited in the target article showing that many different kinds of aversive experiences often have aggressive consequences, and that aggression-related ideas are apt to come to mind when people are physically uncomfortable, as well as Anderson's more recent demonstration (Anderson, Anderson, & Deuser, 1992) that unpleasant hot and cold temperatures can produce specifically angry feelings and hostile beliefs, all testify to the often-unregulated negative effects of negative affect.

The Situational Activation of Control Mechanisms.   Of course, the CNA analysis (as well as neoassociationism more generally) recognizes that cognitive processes can play a very important role in the formation and operation of emotions. The discussion of cognitive factors in the full development of the anger experience (in connection with the Berkowitz–Jo research) and in the open display of hostility/aggression (in connection with the Berkowitz–Troccoli experiments) illustrates this recognition.

Most pertinent here, in the latter series of studies (e.g., Berkowitz & Troccoli, 1990), I pointed out that people who were feeling bad were decidedly unfriendly to a target person when their attention was diverted away from themselves but not when they were led to focus their attention on their feelings. The distracted subjects in the former condition had apparently voiced, in an unguarded manner, the hostile ideas that had been automatically activated in them. On the other hand, according to the evidence gathered in these investigations, the subjects who were highly aware of their somewhat surprising but not-too-intense feelings seem to have engaged in much more higher level cognitive activity. As a consequence, they considered more of the information and social rules appropriate to that setting and regulated their actions accordingly.

IN CONCLUSION

The lesson I draw from all this (and the conclusion that I hope some of my readers will also come to) is that the neoassociationistic perspective can contribute to our understanding of emotional phenomena. At the very least, I hope I have convinced some of the audience that it is not theoretically or empirically necessary to interpret every emotional reaction by postulating the constructive, relatively elaborate intervening mental activity generally assumed by the traditional social cognition perspective.

Nonetheless, it's also clear that many psychologists are repelled by the mention of associationism, perhaps, partly because of the associations (or would they prefer stereotypes?) that come to their minds fairly automatically when this conception is raised. It may be best, therefore, to avoid the use of this particular label and, instead, substitute the currently more acceptable concepts being developed by a number of contemporary cognitive theorists.

For example, consider my contention that priming experiences can have relatively specific emotional consequences (presumably because of associative linkages). This point seems to be very much in accord with Smith's (1990) call for greater recognition of the specificity in the effects of prior events. Commensurate with the spirit of my own position, Smith maintained that "social cognition may have devoted a disproportionate amount of attention to one class of mediators: schemata and other abstract, generic knowledge structures (i.e., the fairly elaborate cognitive constructions typically assumed by traditional social cognition). . . . Many phenomena appear to depend on other types of mediators, particularly memory traces of specific experiences (p. 2).

Then too, take my argument that some kinds of emotional reactions develop in a relatively passive manner out of the operation of relatively automatic processes. The Bargh and Uleman study of unintended thought certainly seems relevant here. Urging more investigation of what they termed conditional automaticity, Bargh (1989) noted that, "Further research could well determine that effects that seem today to require specific goals or instructions (or elaborate cognitive constructions) may only require awareness of the triggering stimuli." (p. 38). And then, too, consistent with my interpretation of the Berkowitz–Troccoli findings regarding the mediating effects of attention direction on affect-induced emotional reactions, Bargh also suggested that "one can reduce or perhaps eliminate such preconscious influences . . . by an intentional search for and examination of relevant evidence. Such effortful processes require the availability of sufficient attentional capacity" (p. 39).

Maybe, after all, it really doesn't matter what school-of-thought label we attach to the theoretical recognition of all of these particular processes. It is necessary, however, to recognize the many different processes and systems that contribute to emotional phenomena.

ENDNOTES

[1]Some of the writers who claim that social psychology was always cognitive in its orientation seem to believe that social psychology began with the research and theorizing of Kurt Lewin. As I note in an essay to be published later, early social psychology, especially (but not only) that existing before the late 1930s, had a largely associationistic–behavioristic tone.

[2]It is also possible to think of these findings as commensurate with the notion of content specificity discussed by Smith (1990).

[3]This explanation obviously assumes that the subjects engaged in some mental activity in making this inference about themselves. It seems to me, however, that this activity might have been at a relatively low level since it primarily entails only the recollection of their reaction to preceding experience and then an unanalyzed extrapolation from their reaction. (Could this be an example of the operation of the availability heuristic?)

[4]Many contemporary cognitive theories of emotion "assume a wide array of computational and information-processing activities," as Clore, Ortony, and their colleagues have pointed out in their commentary, and in this sense they go beyond the Schachterian emphasis on self-labeling. But many of them also share the assumption, fundamental to the Schachter-attribution tradition, that people's attributions regarding the source of their feelings play a very significant part in determining what are the consequences of this affect. At any rate, this assumption is central to the "mood as information" and "excitation transfer" conceptions.

REFERENCES

Anderson, C. A., Anderson, K. B., & Deuser, W. E. (1992). *Tests of a general theory of impulsive aggression: Effects of extreme temperatures and of viewing weapons on hostility.* Unpublished manuscript.

Anderson, C. A., & Deuser, W. E. (1992). *Effects of hot temperature on arousal and hostility.* Unpublished manuscript.

Bargh, J. A. (1989). Conditional automaticity: Varieties of automatic influence in social perception and cognition. In J. A. Bargh & J. S. Uleman (Eds.), *Unintended thought* (pp. 3–51). New York: Guilford.

Bargh, J. A., & Pietromonaco, P. (1982). Automatic information processing and social perception: The influence of trait information presented outside of conscious awareness on impression formation. *Journal of Personality and Social Psychology, 43,* 437–449.

Berkowitz, L. (1960). Judgmental processes in personality functioning. *Psychological Review, 67,* 130–142.

Berkowitz, L. (1974). Some determinants of impulsive aggression: Role of mediated associations with reinforcements for aggression. *Psychological Review, 81,* 165–176.

Berkowitz, L. (1984). Some effects of thoughts on anti- and prosocial influences of media events: A cognitive–neoassociation analysis. *Psychological Bulletin, 95,* 410–427.

Berkowitz, L., & Heimer, K. (1989). On the construction of the anger experience: Aversive events and negative priming in the formation of feelings. In L. Berkowitz (Ed.), *Advances in experimental social psychology* (Vol. 22, pp. 1–37). Orlando, FL: Academic Press.

Berkowitz, L., & Troccoli, B. T. (1990). Feelings, direction of attention, and expressed evaluations of others. *Cognition and Emotion, 4,* 305–325.

Bower, G. H., & Cohen, P. (1982). Emotional influences in memory and thinking: Data and theory. In M. Clark & S. Fiske (Eds.), *Affect and cognition* (pp. 291–331). Hillsdale, NJ: Lawrence Erlbaum Associates.

Bushman, B. J., & Geen, R. G. (1990). Role of cognitive–emotional mediators and individual differences in the effects of media violence on aggression. *Journal of Personality and Social Psychology, 58,* 156–163.

Duclos, S. E., Laird, J. D., Schneider, E., Sexter, M., Stern, L., & Van Lighten, O. (1989). Emotion-specific effects of facial expressions and postures on emotional experience. *Journal of Personality and Social Psychology, 57,* 100–108.

Fiske, S. T., & Taylor, S. E. (1991). *Social cognition.* New York: McGraw-Hill.

Forgas, J. P. (1992). Affect in social judgments and decisions: A multiprocess model. In M. P. Zanna (Ed.), *Advances in experimental social psychology* (Vol. 25, pp. 227–275). San Diego, CA: Academic Press.

Forgas, J. P., & Bower, G. H. (1987). Mood effects on person-perception judgments. *Journal of Personality and Social Psychology, 53,* 53–60.

Herr, P. M. (1986). Consequences of priming: Judgment and behavior. *Journal of Personality and Social Psychology, 51,* 1106–1115.

Higgins, E. T., & King, G. (1981). Accessibility of social constructs: Information-processing consequences of individual and contextual variability. In N. Cantor & J. Kihlstrom (Eds.), *Personality, cognition, and social interaction.* Hillsdale, NJ: Lawrence Erlbaum Associates.

Holmes, D. S., & Berkowitz, L. (1961). Some contrast effects in social perception. *Journal of Abnormal and Social Psychology, 62,* 150–152.

Hovland, C., & Sherif, M. (1952). Judgmental phenomena and scales of attitude measurement: Item displacement in Thurstone scales. *Journal of Abnormal and Social Psychology, 47,* 822–832.

Isen, A. M., & Hastorf, A. H. (1982). Some perspectives on cognitive social psychology. In A. H.

Hastorf & A. M. Isen (Eds.), *Cognitive social psychology* (pp. 1–31). New York/Amsterdam: Elsevier/North Holland.

Josephson, W. L. (1987). Television violence and children's aggression: Testing the priming, social script, and disinhibition predictions. *Journal of Personality and Social Psychology, 53,* 882–890.

Landman, J., & Manis, M. (1983). Social cognition: Some historical and theoretical perspectives. In L. Berkowitz (Ed.), *Advances in experimental social psychology* (Vol. 16, pp. 49–123). Orlando, FL: Academic Press.

Markus, H., & Zajonc, R. B. (1985). The cognitive perspective in social psychology. In G. Lindzey & E. Aronson (Eds.), *Handbook of social psychology* (3rd. ed.) (Vol. 1, pp. 137–230). New York: Random House.

Martin, L. L. (1986). Set/reset: Use and disuse of concepts in impression formation. *Journal of Personality and Social Psychology, 51,* 493–504.

Martin, L. L., Harlow, T. F., & Strack, F. (1992). The role of bodily sensations in the evaluation of social events. *Personality ad Social Psychology Bulletin, 18,* 412–419.

Miller, N. E. (1941). The frustration–aggression hypothesis. *Psychological Review, 48,* 337–342.

Miller, N. E. (1959). Liberalization of basic S–R concepts: Extension to conflict behavior, motivation, and social learning. In S. Koch (Ed.), *Psychology: A study of a science* (Vol. 2). New York: McGraw-Hill.

Neisser, U. (1967). *Cognitive psychology.* New York: Appleton-Century-Crofts.

Parducci, A. (1963). Range-frequency compromise in judgment. *Psychological Monographs, 77*(2, Whole No. 565).

Ross, L., & Nisbett, R. E. (1991). *The person and the situation: Perspectives of social psychology.* New York: McGraw-Hill.

Schwarz, N., & Bless, H. (1991). Happy and mindless, but sad and smart? The impact of affective states on analytic reasoning. In J. P. Forgas (Ed.), *Emotion and social judgments* (pp. 55–71). Oxford/New York: Pergamon.

Schwarz, N., & Clore, G. L. (1983). Mood, misattribution, and judgments of well-being: Informative and directive functions of affective states. *Journal of Personality and Social Psychology, 45,* 513–523.

Smith, E. R. (1990). Content and process specificity in the effects of prior experiences. In T. K. Srull & R. S. Wyer, Jr. (Eds.), *Advances in Social Cognition* (Vol. 3). Hillsdale, NJ: Lawrence Erlbaum Associates.

Srull, T. K., & Wyer, R. S., Jr. (1980). Category accessibility and social perception: Some implications for the study of person memory and interpersonal judgments. *Journal of Personality and Social Psychology, 38,* 841–856.

Turner, C. W., Simons, L. S., Berkowitz, L., & Frodi, A. (1977). The stimulating and inhibiting effects of weapons on aggressive behavior. *Aggressive Behavior, 3,* 355–378.

Wann, D. L., & Branscombe, N. R. (1990). Person perception when aggressive or nonaggressive sports are primed. *Aggressive Behavior, 16,* 27–32.

Wyer, R. S., Jr., & Srull, T. K. (1986). Human cognition in its social context. *Psychological Review, 93,* 322–359.

Zajonc, R. B. (1980). Feeling and thinking: Preferences need no inferences. *American Psychologist, 35,* 151–175.

Author Index

Subject Index

A

Affect (*see also* Emotion)
  and action, 91-93
  and cognition, 92-93, 137-140
  effects of, 10-11
    on behavior, 33-34
    on information processing, 91-94
    on judgments and decisions, 103,
      149-155, 188-192
  and startle reflex, 121-123
Affect-as-information hypothesis, 103,
  149-155, 189-192
Affect-startle hypothesis, 121-125
Aggression
  animal studies of, 14, 63-64
  determinants of, 13-23, 30-31
  and learning, 7
  motivation for, 18-19
  shortcomings of research on, 2-4
  theories of, 4-9
    cognitive, 4-6
    frustration-aggression, 6-7
Anger (*see also* Emotion)
  definition of, 58-59, 64-65, 69
  determinants of, 171-173
  effects of,
    on cognition, 22-23
    on memory, 20-21
  experience of, 27-28
    construction of, 23-26
    regulation of, 26-28

link to other emotions, 16-17, 75-76,
  96-97
vs. sadness, 16-17, 75-76, 96-97
Anger-aggression syndrome, 9, 19-23,
  51-53, 94
Appraisal of affect, 137-138, 167
  objective vs. subjective, 173-175
  strategies of, 99-104
Associative networks
  in conceptualizations of emotion, 9-
  13, 19-23, 110-115
Attribution of emotion, 4-6, 60-61, 93-
  94, 103-104, 189-191
Automatic vs. controlled processing,
  35-36, 147-148, 168-171

B

Bioinformation theory of emotion, 111-
  119

C

Cognition
  definition of, 140-141
  role of, in emotion, 140-141
Cognitive-neoassociationistic theory of
  emotion, 9-28
  assumptions of, 9-13, 99
  vs. cognitive theory, 57-65
  evidence for, 13-28
  reinterpretation of, 47-49
  statement of, 9-13
Contrast effects, 187-189

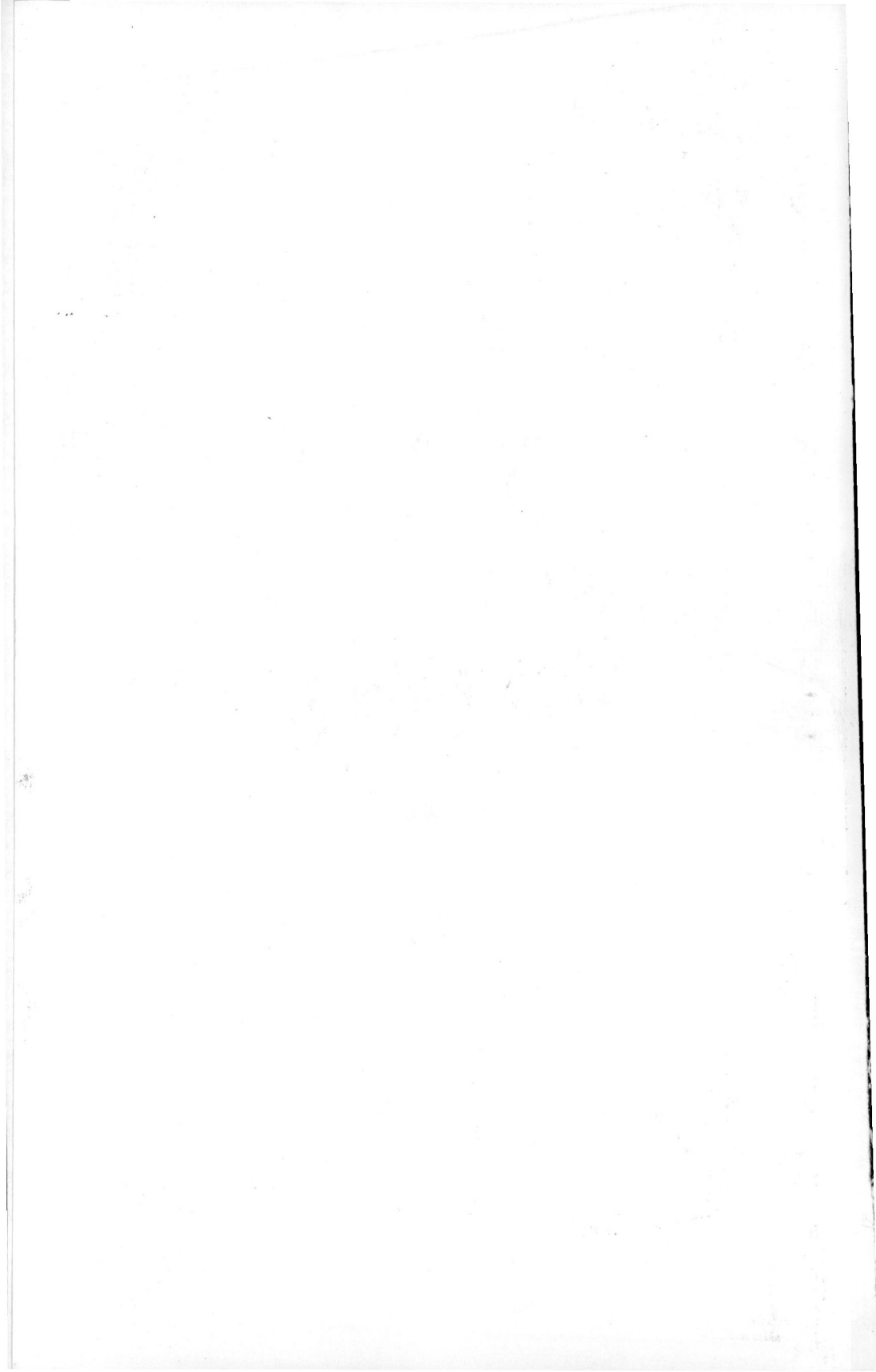